BEER HIKING
BAVARIA

THE MOST REFRESHING WAY TO DISCOVER BAVARIA

BEER HIKING
BAVARIA

THE MOST REFRESHING WAY TO DISCOVER BAVARIA

HELVETIQ

TABLE OF CONTENTS

1

INTRODUCTION

ABOUT THE AUTHOR

Rich Carbonara is an American living in Munich. He teaches English to non-native speakers and likes to joke he came to Germany for the beer but stayed for the girl. He's happily married to a German woman who shares his love for hiking and has grown to love beer too.

His passions have changed over the years but two things have remained pretty constant: a love of hiking and the desire to seek out new beers. He started the former relatively late and the latter considerably earlier, though he imagines in the beginning he sought whatever beer he could get his hands on. The passion for these two things and his growing knowledge of beer hiking in Franconia led him to start the informational site www.beerwanderers.com. This in turn led to doing guided tours of beer hiking in Franconia, and with all the new hikes discovered writing this book, it will likely lead to doing tours all over Bavaria.

ABOUT THE BOOK

Bavaria is about as perfect a place for beer hiking as you're likely to find. It's unique in the sense that as a German state, it is unquestionably the most noted for both beer and hiking. Though by far the biggest German state, it wouldn't rank in the top ten of US states. Bavaria is also filled to the brim with tourist sights so it shouldn't come as any surprise that it's the most visited state in Germany.

While this book's focus may sound narrow, it attempts to integrate most of what Bavaria is noted for: cobblestoned old towns, dense forests, stunning churches, soaring mountains, hilltop castles, pretty lakes, half-timbered houses, brewing monasteries and craggy out-croppings. What it will also do is slow the visitor down. People often race around from one famous must-see to another, often missing much of the subtle nuances that make Bavaria not only a top-notch tourist destination but also a great place to live. I know. I live here! Along with the aforementioned attractions, by walking, the beer hiker will also have a chance to experience rural Bavaria, to see village life up close and to sometimes walk on trails that have likely been utilized in some form or another for hundreds of years.

The hikes vary as greatly as Bavaria itself does. With the popularity of urban hiking, I've thrown a few city walks in but I've tried to steer as clear of overly familiar areas as possible. One thing I've found over the years is how you discover amazing places in the quest for great beer. That can be a town you'd have never visited if it weren't for that brewery you'd heard about or a neighborhood you'd have missed if you'd taken the U-Bahn to it rather than walked. There is a fair share of hikes in or near the mountains since Bavaria is home to the country's greatest range: the Alps. While the Bavarian Alps aren't as high as those in neighboring Switzerland and Austria, many find them just as spectacular as they rise from a lower and often flatter plateau. Forests feature prominently in Bavarian hiking and walks in the rural countryside are among the most popular with locals. I must admit, when I first moved to Bavaria, I only thought of the Alps when it came to hiking, but I've grown to love skirting a forest along a field of barley just before it's time to be harvested. There's something special about seeing beer's ingredients in their growing element that works up a thirst like few other endeavors, especially on a hot summer day.

The hikes are listed by their region: Upper Bavaria, Lower Bavaria, Swabia, the Upper Palatinate, Upper Franconia, Middle Franconia and Lower Franconia. Within the regions they will be grouped by proximity. It's best to have a look at a map if you want to get an idea where each region is. For instance, Upper Bavaria is at the bottom of the state.

The hiking trails will vary in both length and difficulty. Many of the brewery-to-brewery circuits are devised specifically to get to brewe-ries and while lacking perhaps the spectacle of alpine hiking, they are gentle, scenic and full of local color. Whenever possible, I try to utilize circuits rather than one-way trips and I always make every effort to end the hike at a brewery. In a perfect beery world (and that does exist in Bavaria), you will be able to spend the night there, too.

While the main focus of this book is on using hiking trails to get to breweries and hence beer is central, there is no getting around the fact that for Bavarians, beer is almost a food group and that it should be enjoyed with food. So, I won't shy away from giving you a few tips on the (mostly) hearty and somewhat lighter fare on offer.

THE DEFINITION OF BEER HIKING

Beer hiking is defined differently by its various adherents. For many, it means going for a beer after a hike, be it a brewpub or place that has good beer. For others, it is bringing beer along on a hike, to be enjoyed in a special place, away from the hustle and bustle of the world. In Bavaria, it is often walking on trails to reach brewpubs that you'd not be able to reach easily by public transportation. This has evolved into entire beer hiking trails where you pass multiple brew-pubs en route. They can be relatively short or on the longer side, making an overnight stay at one of the brewpubs your best choice. I guess what they all have in common is they let you enjoy a refreshing beer after your time experiencing nature, be it a pleasant easy stroll or a more strenuous endeavor.

TRAIL AND BEER RATINGS

Ratings are by nature subjective and one person's easy hike is another person's difficult one. The hikes weren't always easy to place and it's best to look at the length of the hike and its elevation gain/loss to get the best idea. The same goes with beers. In particular, if you are co-ming from the US and are used to drinking very hoppy IPAs, you might find Bavarian beer not particularly bitter. The nuances are more subtle. Food also plays a part in a beer's perceived flavor as does the order in which you drink them. Drinking an array of beers at a brewpub can show the order effect well. Drinking a malty beer after a hoppy one can have consequences when it comes to your perception, and hence its rating. In general, I had a good idea what beer I was going to use for each hike and always drank that one first to avoid this. At the end of the day, and hike, each person is going to have their own favorites – by all means, drink the beer that sounds good to you. Since some of the beer names can be confusing, the guide provides some basic concept of what that beer is and its basic taste characteristics.

BEER STYLES

To explain the many styles of beer in Bavaria is outside the purview of this book. In general, you will be drinking lagers but they will not be the often bland, generic ones produced by the large conglomerates. They can vary in color from pale yellow to black. A light-colored beer can be stronger and/or more bitter than a dark one, and vice versa. Though you should admire a beer for its color, try not to let it interfere with the rest of your perceptions of it. I love having a friend who tells me they hate dark beer say that the one I told them to try was really good. Some basic German will help you pick by color. Remember Helles is light in color and Dunkles is dark. Pils is a safe-bet light one and Schwarzbier is black. Rauchbier (typical for Bamberg!) is smoky and though they vary in color, I've only seen a couple of truly light-colored ones. Aside from that, you'd be better off looking at what other people are drinking and order by pointing. In fact, if you go into a small brewpub in Franconia and order "ein Bier," you will get what everyone else is drinking, the most popular one. That could be a dark beer or a light one, depending on the region. In much of Franconia, darker beer is still more popular, though often drier and fruitier than their southern Bavarian equivalents. Oh, and always remember that Bock is a strong beer, be it dark or light.

There aren't many ales brewed in Bavaria but Weizen, or Weißbier, is one of the most popular styles. It tends to be lighter in color and you'll generally see "dunkel" used in conjunction if it's not. Dampfbier is a rarity and in ways closer to English ale than it is to Bavarian beer.

So, you can see understanding Bavarian beer is not so easy. Well, not as easy as enjoying it. Prost!

2

HOW IT WORKS

CHOOSE THE BEER OR THE HIKE

HIKE LOCATION

DISTRICT

NAME OF THE BEER

MAP

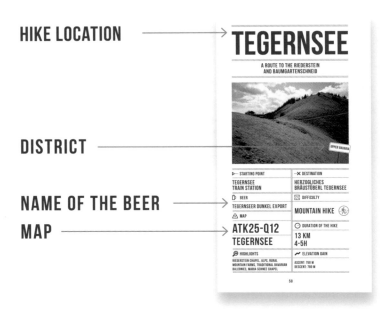

INFORMATION
ABOUT THE BEER

INFORMATION
ABOUT THE HIKE

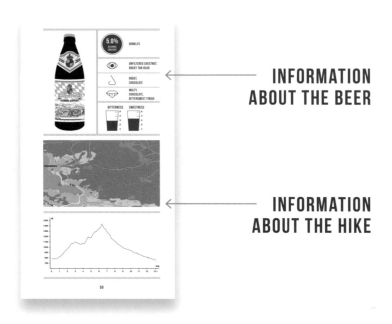

TRAIL DIFFICULTY RATING

Each hike is given a difficulty rating. They are subjective and are for use for this set of hikes only. The ratings are based on good weather conditions, hike length, elevation gain/loss and trail conditions. Even within the rating, bad weather will make any trail harder.

WALKS (EASY TRAILS)

Walks are defined as any trail 10 kilometers or shorter with 150 meters or less of elevation gain/loss. Most of the route is on flat paths and generally walking shoes are sufficient.

HIKES (MODERATE TRAILS)

Hikes are defined as trails longer than 10 kilometers and with more than 150 meters elevation gain/loss. Hikes where the terrain is not even or has roots and or rocks were put in this group even if they missed fulfilling the length or elevation categories. Most beer hiking trails in Franconia are in this category. Hiking boots are recommended.

MOUNTAIN HIKES (DIFFICULT TRAILS)

Mountain hikes are defined as longer than 10 kilometers and with more than 500 meters elevation gain/loss. The terrain is often uneven with roots and or rocks. Hiking boots are highly recommended. The use of your hands may be necessary.

BEFORE DEPARTURE

CHECK YOUR EQUIPMENT

📋 ESSENTIALS

Mountain hikes require more preparation than simple walks. While Bavaria may not have great swaths of wilderness, if you are going to be at high elevations or even on regular longer hikes, you should always carry these essentials:

• Navigation must be taken into consideration. Maps in this book are for planning purposes only. A topographical map and compass are best but only if you know how to use them. GPS devices with extra batteries are another option. Phone GPS Apps are a good backup but shouldn't be relied on as a sole navigation tool.

• Staying properly hydrated when hiking is important. If there are ample huts or brewpubs along the way, you can get away with carrying less as they sell soft drinks as well as beer. Still, you should always carry enough water to get you from one stop to another.

• Snacks are more important for mountain hikes than the two other categories but it's always good to have some snack food like nuts and dried fruit in case of emergencies.

• Don't underestimate the Bavarian sun. It may not feel hot but the sun is powerful regardless. Bring sunscreen and make sure to use it.

• A basic first aid kit is something often overlooked but should be carried, especially on mountain hikes. Hopefully, you'll never have to use it.

• Part of that kit should be a tool like a pocket knife with multiple tools.

• While we never plan on being out after dark, we sometimes overestimate how long the day is so carrying a headlamp is light insurance.

• Too much shoe is better than too little shoe. Many of the rural Franconian hikes can be done in simple walking shoes, but if it's been raining for three weeks prior to your sunny day hike, you may find a lot of puddles and mud on your route. You'll be happy to have water-resistant shoes rather than wet feet.

• Rain gear is light; no matter how good the forecast is, it can change.

• Both sun and warm hats are small, light items to protect you from the elements. Hope for the best, plan for the worst.

 # HIKING SEASON

Higher elevation hikes are the ones most affected by winter closures. Most of the hikes in this book are accessible year-round but you should always consult local authorities regarding trail conditions. While you may be able to hike, you should be well aware that the trail conditions play a big factor on how difficult the hike is. Know before you go.

 # WEATHER

It seems most of the best mountain weather forecasts are on German-only sites. You can change the navigation to English but the forecast will still be in German! It's a good thing that there are graphic depictions. My favorite weather forecast sites are the following:

• **www.bergfex.com**

• **www.wetteronline.de**

Of course, using your favorite weather site in your own language is probably best – and being prepared for anything is even better.

 # OPENING HOURS

While brewpubs in larger towns have more regular opening hours, those in smaller villages can be more flexible. For that reason, you'll notice an opening time, rather than a time period. This gives them the option of closing early if things are slow. Another thing to keep in mind is Betriebsurlaub. This is quite simply when the brewery is closed for vacation. Generally, they take a week or two twice a year but it can vary. There seems to be one in the colder months as well as in the warmer months. It can often coincide with school closures. Quite simply, if their children are out of school, they close the family business to enjoy time with them. I used to find it strange that a business would close during their busiest season, but when you think about it, why shouldn't they enjoy some time in summer too?

If it is one brewpub of a few on a beer hiking circuit, it's not such a big deal, but the disappointment of showing up to see a place that is supposed to be open closed is best avoided by checking ahead. Increasingly, the brewpubs post these closing dates on their website but if not, it's best to call ahead to ensure they will be open.

 # ARRIVAL

While many of the hikes are accessible by public transportation, there are some that are more easily visited by car. In that case, a designated driver is a must – or even better, get a room at the brewery when possible.

@ ONLINE RESOURCES

In addition to the brewery websites listed in this book, you can find further information on the following sites:

- **www.bier.by**

- **www.bierland-oberfranken.de**

- **www.braufranken.de**

- **www.franconiabeerguide.com**

- **www.beerwanderers.com**

THE HIKES

MAP

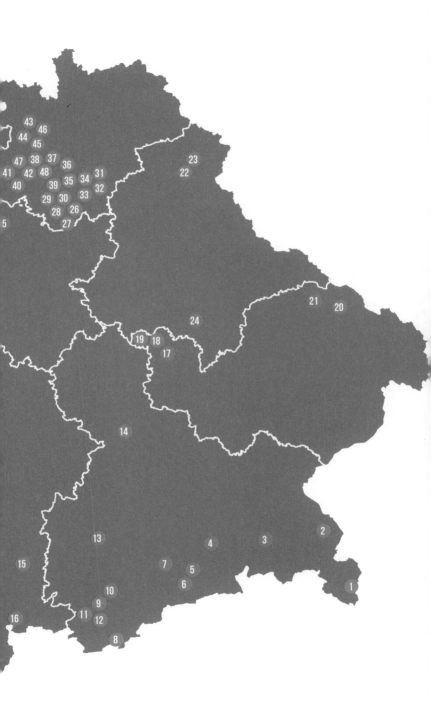

LIST OF HIKES

HIKE	BREWERY	KM	PAGE
Berchtesgaden	Hofbrauhaus Berchtesgaden (Bräustüberl Berchtesgaden)	11	28
Schönram	Landbrauerei Schönram (Bräustüberl Schönram)	13.5	34
Chiemsee	Inselbräu (Inselbräu Bräustüberl)	10	40
Maxlrain (Bad Aibling)	Schlossbrauerei Maxlrain (Bräustüberl Maxlrain)	17	46
Schliersee to Miesbach	Weißbierbrauerei Hopf (Weißbräustüberl)	9.5	52
Tegernsee	Herzoglich Bayerisches Brauhaus Tegernsee (Herzogliches Bräustüberl Tegernsee)	13	58
Reutberg (Schaftlach)	Klosterbrauerei Reutberg (Klosterbräustüberl Reutberg)	15	64
Mittenwald	Brauerei Mittenwald (Brauereigaststätte Postkeller)	9	70
Murnauer Moos	Brauerei Karg (Karg Bräustüberl)	14	76
Murnauer Drachenstich	Griesbräu zu Murnau (Griesbräu zu Murnau Brauhaus)	6.5	82
Oberammergau	Ammergauer Maxbräu	12	88
Oberammergau to Ettal	Ettaler Klosterbrauerei (Klosterhotel & Bräustüberl Ludwig der Bayer)	5.5	94
Andechs (Herrsching am Ammersee)	Klosterbrauerei Andechs (Andechser Bräustüberl)	5 (one-way)	100
Scheyern (Pfaffenhofen a. d. Ilm)	Klosterbrauerei Scheyern (Klosterschenke Sheyern)	13	104
Irsee (Kaufbeuren)	Irsee Klosterbrauerei (Irseer Klosterbräu Braugasthof & Hotel)	7.5 (one-way)	112
Nesselwang	Brauerei-Gasthof Hotel Post (Hotel Post Gaststube & Biergarten)	6	118
Weltenburg (Kelheim)	Klosterbrauerei Weltenburg (Klosterschenke Weltenburg)	5.5 (one-way)	124
Essing	Brauereigasthof Schneider	11.5	130
Riedenburg	Brauerei Riemhofer (Schwan Riedenburg, Gasthaus & Hotel)	2.5	136
Zwiesel	1. Dampfbierbrauerei Zwiesel (Bräustüberl Zwiesel)	7.5	140
Böbrach	Brauerei-Gasthof Eck	6.5	146
Falkenberg to Neuhaus	Kommunbrauhaus Neuhaus (twelve different Zoiglstuben)	14	152
Falkenberg	Kommunbrauhaus Falkenberg (three different Zoiglstuben)	5	158
Regensburg	Brauerei Kneitinger (Brauereigaststätte Kneitinger)	2	164
Uehlfeld	Walter Prechtel Brauerei (Brauereigaststätte Prechtel)	7	170

HIKE	BREWERY	KM	PAGE
Gräfenberg	Lindenbräu	12	178
Weißenohe	Weißenoher Klosterbrauerei (Wirtshaus Klosterbrauerei Weißenohe)	5.5	184
Thuisbrunn to Leutenbach	Brauerei-Gasthof Drummer	9	190
Leutenbach (Walberla)	Brauerei Alt Dietzhof (Brauerei & Gastwirtschaft Alt Dietzhof)	7	196
Leutenbach (Hetzelsdorf)	Brauerei Penning-Zeissler (Brauereigasthof Penning-Zeissler)	9.5	202
Büchenbach	Brauerei-Gasthof Herold	10.5	208
Lindenhardt	Brauerei Gradl (Brauerei-Gasthof Gradl)	13	214
Pottenstein	Brauerei Mager (Gasthof Mager)	5.5	220
Oberailsfeld	Held-Bräu	7.5	226
Breitenlesau	Konrad Krug Brauerei (Brauerei-Gasthof Krug)	13.5	232
Aufseß	Brauerei Reichold (Brauereigasthof Reichold)	14	238
Huppendorf	Brauerei Grasser (Braugaststätte Grasser, Huppendorfer Bier)	16	244
Oberleinleiter	Brauerei Ott (Brauerei-Gasthof Ott)	11	250
Heiligenstadt i. Ofr.	Gasthaus Brauerei Aichinger (Gasthof Drei Kronen Aichinger)	12	256
Bamberg Mahrs	Mahrs Bräu Bamberg (Mahrs Bräu Wirtshaus & Biergarten)	6	262
Bamberg Schlenkerla	Brauerei Schlenkerla (Schlenkerla)	2	268
Schammelsdorf	Brauerei Knoblach (Brauerei-Gaststätte Knoblach)	15.5	274
Lichtenfels to Vierzehnheiligen	Brauerei Trunk (Gastwirtschaft Trunk)	4.5 (one-way)	280
Loffeld	Staffelberg-Bräu (Brauerei-Wirtshaus Bräustübl)	8	286
Stublang	Brauerei Dinkel (Gasthof Dinkel)	5	292
Uetzing	Hausbrauerei Reichert (Metzgerbräu)	8.5	298
Scheßlitz	Brauerei Drei Kronen (Brauerei-Gasthof Drei Kronen)	9 (one-way)	304
Bischberg to Weiher	Brauerei-Gasthof Kundmüller	10	308
Zeil	Brauerei Göller (Brauereigaststätte Göller "Zur Alten Freyung")	15	316
Ebelsbach to Stettfeld	Adler-Bräu (Adler-Bräu Bräustübla)	5	322

UPPER BAVARIA

BERCHTESGADEN

FROM KESSEL TO THE KÖNIGSBACHALM

UPPER BAVARIA

▷⋯ STARTING POINT	⋯✗ DESTINATION
KÖNIGSSEE BOAT DOCK	JENNERBAHN BUS STOP
🍺 BEER	🔲 DIFFICULTY
BERCHTESGADENER DUNKEL	**MOUNTAIN HIKE** 🚶
⛰ MAP	
ATK25-R17	⏱ DURATION OF THE HIKE
KÖNIGSSEE	**11 KM** **3-4H**
🔍 HIGHLIGHTS	〰 ELEVATION GAIN
KÖNIGSSEE, ST. BARTHOLOMÄ CHURCH, KESSEL, ALPS, KÖNIGSBACHALM	ASCENT: 675 M DESCENT: 615 M

5.5%
ALCOHOL
CONTENT

DUNKLES, BREWED
FROM AN OLD FOUND
RECIPE BUT A RELATIVE
NEWCOMER TO THEIR
PORTFOLIO

UNFILTERED CHESTNUT,
ROCKY OFF-WHITE HEAD

DARK CHOCOLATE,
MALT

MALT,
DARK CHOCOLATE,
BITTERSWEET FINISH

BITTERNESS   SWEETNESS

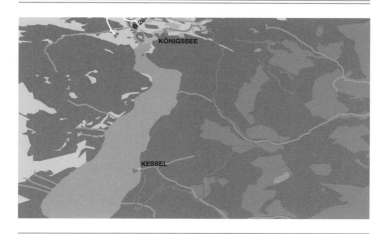

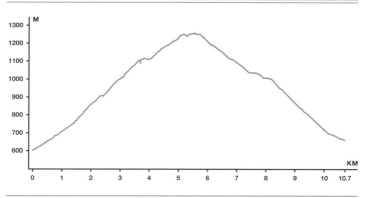

DESCRIPTION OF THE ROUTE

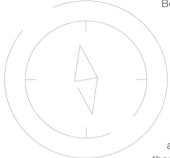

Berchtesgaden National Park is quite possibly Germany's premier park and unquestionably one of the most beautiful areas in not only Germany but perhaps in all of Europe. With the jaw-dropping, mountain-ringed lake aptly named the Königssee (king's lake) as its centerpiece and the equally awe-inspiring Watzmann as its backdrop, the park draws thousands of visitors daily.

While a boat trip on the Königssee is all but mandatory, you can escape some of the crowds by getting up into the magnificent mountains around it. While the hike described is quite popular, it does have the advantage of using the scenic boat trip to access the trail head, and it can be done for a longer portion of the hiking season. Hikes closer to the Watzmann can be closed due to snow, avalanches, and after particularly tough winters, downed trees. The town of Berchtesgaden is not untypical of tourist gateway towns in that it provides ample accommodation and restaurant options, but what it has that sets it apart is an amazing view of the Watzmann, a peak that looms like a sleeping giant from just about every vantage point in the small town.

Königssee is serviced by frequent buses from Berchtesgaden, which is well-connected by train to Munich (via Freilassing) and Salzburg.

Get off the bus at the Königssee, Schönau a. Königssee stop. Take Seestraße to the lake front, where the boats depart. There are signs for the boats along this street lined with restaurants and shops. The hike starts in Kessel so buy a one-way boat ticket to there. The boat trip is about as scenic as it gets and even the short journey to Kessel is pretty spectacular. From the dock in Kessel, you can see the church of St. Bartholomä in the distance. Once you disembark and enjoy the views, look for the obvious trail. The sign says it's a red dot trail which signifies medium difficulty. This is more due to the elevation gain than the trail, which is nicely groomed and well-marked. It also says it's 3 hours to the Königsbachalm, your first destination.

Trails 394 and 393 follow the same route up from the landing. While there are few signs, the route is very clear. The forest is quite lush and has a primitive feel to it. It also provides ample shade, and if it's a hot sunny day, you'll be happy for it as you are going to be going very much up for the first couple of hours. That said, the switchbacks are designed well. There are occasional breaks in the trees so keep your eyes out for gorgeous views of the mountains and lake. You will emerge from the forest at the Gotzentalalm, with a few simple log cabin type buildings and likely a big herd of cows. There is a hiking sign pointing you towards the Königsbachalm, now only about an hour away and on a blue dot trail, so you know most of your climb is finished. Continue along this wider road and open area and you'll soon see another intersection sign. This is where the 493 and 494 split. The Gotzenalm is much further and offers overnight accommodation. You will want to head towards the Königsbachalm. You will go through a small easy-to-pass barrier and look to your right to find the narrower path. You could continue along the road to the mountain hut but this path is much nicer. It climbs a bit and can sometimes be blocked by cows so be careful walking around them. Give a wide berth to mothers with calves and walk slowly. We had to go off the trail slightly to do so, but as soon as you can, get back down to the path. It's only a short section, and soon enough, you'll have a nice open pasture area to enjoy a pleasant stroll with close views of the Alps to your left.

There is a section of forest and you'll come to another intersection, and again, stay on the signed route to the Königsbachalm, now only 30 minutes away. Just after the 5 kilometer mark, there's a little path to your left that leads to a viewpoint. It's not far and worth doing but to be honest, the views from where you just walked through are better. You'll see a fence with a small wooden step designed to keep the cows in and let you pass. Go over it carefully, there is some barbed wire and sometimes the boards are less than securely fastened.

From there, it's an easy open stroll to the Königsbachalm. You can enjoy simple food if you haven't packed a lunch. The Strammer Max (ham and eggs on bread) is good, and beers from a local brewery, Wieninger, are available, too. It's a busy spot as it gets people coming down from the Jenner Pass and others coming up from Königssee on their way to Gotzentalalm or even to Kessel, where you started from. When you're ready, continue down the road you reached the hut on. You'll soon come to a fork and you will take the left side, again well-marked for Königssee. There's a small viewpoint with some benches along the route if you need a break but you're not far from the end at this point. Just before the 9 kilometer mark, you'll walk under the Jennerbahn cable cars. Not long after that, you will come to Richard-Voß-Straße; go left on it. Shortly after, turn left on Jennerbahnstraße. Take this to the Jenner Station to get the bus from there. There are public toilets and, unless you want to do something down by the lake, this is where the bus leaves from, so you'll have a better chance of getting a seat. Take the bus back to Berchtesgaden and head to the Bräustüberl Berchtesgaden for a great meal and a special brew.

BRÄUSTÜBERL BERCHTESGADEN

Hofbrauhaus Berchtesgaden has a long and storied past. Not unlike many old-world Bavarian breweries, it has monastic roots. It was founded in 1645, brewing largely Weißbier, Märzen and Dunkles. It remained as such until secularization in the early 1800s when it came into private hands and eventually passed onto the Hofbrauhaus. The current buildings date back to the early 1900s. Due to financial difficulty in 1970, it was sold first to Thurn and Taxis and later passed onto the Spaten-Löwenbräu group. Thankfully, it is back in private hands as of 2008 and appears to be doing well. They've brought back their Dunkel and Märzen. Perhaps one day, they will make their own Weißbier again.

The Bräustüberl is located next to the brewery but is privately run and quite well at that. A major refurbishment was done in 2002 with an eye towards retaining a traditional air. With a beer hall feel and a cozy courtyard, the establishment draws both locals and tourist in droves. They specialize in dishes made with ox though many of the typical Bavarian pork meals are present, as well. The Bierochse (an ox goulash made with dark beer and served with pretzel dumplings) is excellent as were all the meals we ate while in town. While they mostly stick to standard beer styles, they do brew a high-octane Eisbock, clocking in at 12–16% alcohol.

Beers on tap: Berchtesgadener Hell, Berchtesgadener Dunkel and Berchtesgadener Jubiläumsbier. Bottled Berchtesgadener Gold, Pils and Eisbock. The Weißbier is Franziskaner from Spaten-Löwenbräu – I guess it's a throwback to that era of their history.

PRACTICAL INFORMATION

Bräustüberl Berchtesgaden
Bräuhausstraße 13
83471 Berchtesgaden
+49 8652 976724
www.braeustueberl-berchtesgaden.de

Open daily 10:00 am to 12:00 pm
Hot meals 11:00 am to 2:00 pm and 6:00 pm to 9:30 pm
Snacks 11:00 am to 10:30 pm

SCHÖNRAM

SURSPEICHER WEG 42

UPPER BAVARIA

▷··· STARTING POINT	···✗ DESTINATION
BRÄUSTÜBERL SCHÖNRAM	**BRÄUSTÜBERL SCHÖNRAM**

🍺 BEER	🔲 DIFFICULTY
SCHÖNRAMER IPA	**HIKE** 🚶

⛰ MAP	
AKT25 P16	🕐 DURATION OF THE HIKE
TRAUNSTEIN	**13.5 KM** **3-4H**

🔎 HIGHLIGHTS	〰 ELEVATION GAIN
WEILDORF CHURCH, ST. LAURENTIUS CHURCH, SURPEICHER SUR, ALPS	ASCENT: 238 M DESCENT: 212 M

IPA 57 IBU

DEEP GOLDEN
TO LIGHT AMBER

TROPICAL FRUIT,
FLORAL HOPS

MALT SWEET BASE,
DRY BITTER FINISH

BITTERNESS   SWEETNESS

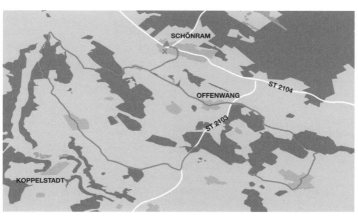

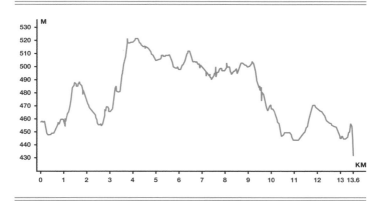

DESCRIPTION OF THE ROUTE

Schönram is a small village approximately 40 kilometers north of Berchtesgaden National Park and 10 kilometers from the Austrian border. With a location like that, the beauty of its setting should come as no surprise. Locals enjoy both walking and biking in the surrounding area, especially on the Surspeicher-Weg that meanders through forests and small hamlets to the large reservoir and dam giving the trail its name. Brauerei Schönram is certainly an equally good reason to visit the area.

Public transportation to Schönram is quite limited, so driving is your best option. This will also give you access to the amazing surrounding area.

You begin the walk in front of the Bräustüberl Schönram. Facing the building, head to your left on Salzburger Straße. Take note of the actual brewery on your left and turn right on Englhamer Straße. You will soon leave the small village and enter open farmland with fantastic views of the mountains if the weather is clear. At the end of this road, you come to a T where you will see the first trail sign for the Surspeicher Weg 42. They are bright yellow and hard to miss. You can go either way, but the signs are much easier to see if you go right. Walk through a very small village farm before rounding a well-marked curve. After walking along the forest, you turn right into it, also marked. This shady section doesn't last long and you will soon be back out in the open heading towards Unterholzen, another tiny village, where you go to your right. Before doing that, look to your left for great views of the mountains with the St. Laurentius Church in the foreground. Along with the now familiar yellow Surspeicher Weg 42 signs are bike signs pointing you towards the Surspeicher. At the well-marked intersection, you make an extreme left. You're not far now from the Surspeicher, a large reservoir the hike is named after and a nice place for a break if you need one.

There is a brief forested section after leaving your respite at the Surspeicher but you will soon be in open farmland again, heading towards Wimmern, the fair-sized village home to the St. Laurentius Church you gazed at earlier. Make your way through the village and follow the Surspeicher Weg 42 signs towards Weildorf. At the end of this road, you go left onto well-marked Laufener Straße (ST 2103). It is quite a busy road and the least pleasant part of your journey. Fear not, just up the road you will duck into the forest on your right, indicated by the familiar yellow sign. Sometimes, the sign will just say Wanderweg 42 and 44 as this is where the two trails overlap, so no need for concern. After a mix of forest and open farmland with all turns obvious or marked, go left on Teisendorfer Straße. Follow this to Weildorf and turn left onto Rathausweg, which will bring you to the small town's namesake church.

After leaving Weildorf, you will be on small paths again. Be sure to look back for nice views of the Weildorf Church with a mountain backdrop before you enter a nice patch of forest. Along with the familiar trail signs, you will see ones for the village of Offenwang. After you cross Laufener Straße (ST 2103), you will be in that village and soon on the last stretch to the T you made the original right on. When you get to it, go right and retrace your entry for a well-deserved beer.

BRÄUSTÜBERL SCHÖNRAM

The Bräustüberl is as well-noted for its food as its beer and that's no small order. It's likely beer has been brewed in town since the early 1500s, but the first recorded mention of a brewery was a good 100 years later. The Köllerer family bought it in 1780 and it's remained in their name ever since. With such a long lineage, it is not surprising that Brauerei Schönram is a very traditional operation. They have a full line-up of Bavarian classics, each well-crafted and of exceptional quality.

Things took an odd turn (especially for rural southern Bavaria brewing) in the late 90s when an American brewer took over at the helm. Weihenstephan-trained Eric Toft obviously couldn't come in and shake things up too much, at least initially, and the Lederhosen-clad brewer has no qualms about brewing the traditional styles. He did, however, slowly introduce styles surely never brewed in this region before. His range now includes an IPA and Imperial Stout, with both garnering accolades among German craft beer aficionados. All that said, his Pils has perhaps gained the most recognition. Also unusual for Bavaria is the ability to order 0.3 liter pours of all their beers on tap. This gives you the chance to sample several different beers during your meal. You will also notice the small section of beer cuisine items on the menu, including a Bierbratl made with beef instead of pork which is truly exceptional.

Beers on tap: Surtaler Schankbier, Schönramer Hell, Schönramer Gold, Schönramer Weißbier, Altbayrisch Dunkel and Schönramer Pils. Seasonal beers and bottled beers are also available, including craft beer entries like an IPA and an Imperial Stout.

PRACTICAL INFORMATION

Bräustüberl Schönram
Salzburger Str. 10
83367 Petting/Schönram
+49 8686 271
www.braeustueberl-schoenram.de

Separate brewery site: www.schoenramer.de

Open Thursday to Tuesday 9:00 am to 9:00 pm
Closed Wednesday

Unfortunately, the brewery doesn't offer rooms. Your best option is a couple of kilometers up the road in Ringham. Both Ringham and Schönram are in the Petting postal code so they're all fairly close.

Winkler Hof in Ringham
Oberdorfstraße 1
83367 Petting
+49 8686 8036
www.winklerhof-ferien.de

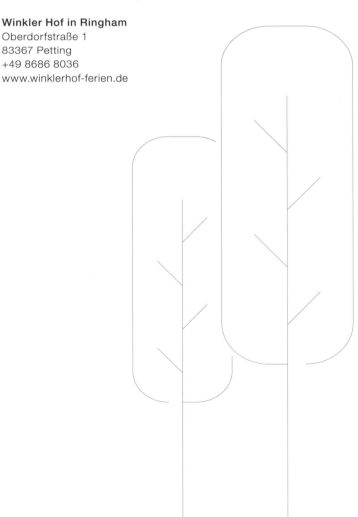

CHIEMSEE

WALKS AROUND THE HERRENINSEL AND FRAUENINSEL

UPPER BAVARIA

▷··· STARTING POINT	···✗ DESTINATION
BOAT DOCK, HERRENINSEL CHIEMSEE	**INSELBRÄU BRÄUSTÜBERL, FRAUENINSEL CHIEMSEE**

🍺 BEER	🀫 DIFFICULTY
INSELBRÄU HELLES ZWICKL NATURTRÜB	**WALK** 🚶

🗺 MAP	⊘ DURATION OF THE HIKE
ATK25-P15 CHIEMSEE	**10 KM 2.5–3H**

🔍 HIGHLIGHTS	∿ ELEVATION GAIN
CHIEMSEE, HERRENINSEL, FRAUENINSEL, ALPS, NEUES SCHLOSS HERRENCHIEMSEE, SEEKAPELLE ZUM HEILIGEN KREUZ, FISHERMEN'S HOMES, FRAUENWÖRTH	ASCENT: 100 M DESCENT: 90 M

ZWICKL, COMES FROM THE NAME OF THE TAP DEVICE USED TO DRAW THE BEER DIRECTLY FROM THE CONDITIONING TANK

UNFILTERED,
LIGHT GOLDEN,
ROCKY HEAD

GRAIN,
SLIGHT HOP

DRY,
FRUITY,
BITTER

BITTERNESS

SWEETNESS

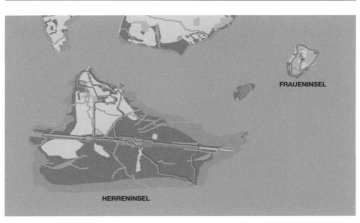

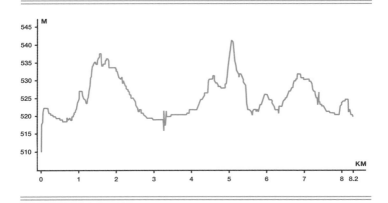

41

DESCRIPTION OF THE ROUTE

Often called the "Bavarian sea," Chiemsee is the largest lake in Bavaria. The state is blessed with many large, beautiful lakes, but this one really is stunning. With a gorgeous mountain backdrop and a few islands thrown in for good measure, it is an understandably popular destination. Boat trips are the top draw and going to this area without doing one is unthinkable. This walk uses the boats to get out to the islands and gets you around to the sights on both of them.

Prien am Chiemsee is serviced by the frequent trains that go between Munich and Salzburg. The trip is just under an hour from either city. The train station is about a 20-minute walk from the boat dock, but there is a tourist steam train that can be combined with the boat trip ticket. Buy your ticket for both there or for the boat separately down at the dock.

After your glorious boat trip out to the Herreninsel, walk through a wooden structure that has a real northern German seaside look to it. On the other side, there will be an open area with a gift shop to your right and tickets, beverages, and snacks straight on. Go to the left of these buildings. There are some steps going up to a restaurant and museum area but you are going to go right onto an unpaved road. There's a green trail sign saying Rundweg. In smaller lettering is Seekapelle, the first destination of your walk. There are a lot of trails on this large island. To walk on all of them would take quite a few hours. This walk will take in almost all of the most popular ones and some of the less utilized ones too. This first stretch is popular but certainly not everyone goes up this way. Follow the wide gravel road into a nice forested section that soon opens up. At the end of the road is the small lakeside Seekapelle zum Heiligen Kreuz (The Holy Cross Lake Chapel). You can go beyond it a short bit for a nice view. The area is popular for swimming in the warmer months.

From the chapel, most people head up Kreuzkapellenweg, a wide road lined with trees. Your route continues on the unpaved road that bends just ahead and leads towards the forest. Follow the trail and you'll be happy to be in the shade if it's a hot summer day. At around the 1 kilometer mark, look for a trail to your left. Take that past a fairly obstructed pond to your left back towards the Kreuzkapellenweg. When you get there, go right on the paved road. There are often horses in the field here. When you get to the stables on your right, you will go left towards the Schlosshotel, which is marked. Follow this path until you come to a stone church. Veer right to go around the hotel and then left towards the Biergarten. Go right at the Biergarten to walk on a wide gravel path lined with trees. A former Augustinian

monastery, now a museum, will be on your right. At the end of the
path, most people will go straight to head towards the castle. If you'd
like a shorter walk, this is a good place to diverge from this description. To stay on our course, go right to walk around the left side of the
museum. This will bring you to a quiet area and just up the way, on
your right, is a shady picnic table.

At the intersection, go left to walk down the Birnenallee. You'll see the
green Rundweg sign again. This is a wide gravel road lined with pear
trees. It's quite scenic with mountains in the distance beyond them.
Follow this to the intersection for the castle. Again, if you want a
shorter walk, you can go left here to go straight to the castle. Our
route takes you in the opposite direction down the canal. Walk beyond
and around the large pond on your right. Take the straight, unpaved
path along the left side of the canal to its end. Though pretty, not
many people venture this way. There are nice views at the end and
you'll notice a row of wide rocks going across the canal. This makes it
possible to walk back on the other side. If you don't care to do this,
just walk back on the side you just took. Once back at the pond, walk
down the path towards the castle. There is a sign with some information in both German and English. The path leads to a large open area
filled with intricately interesting fountains in the foreground of the
castle.

Explore both them and the castle at your leisure. You can also return
to the boat dock directly from here but there is one more section of
our hike to do. During late spring or early summer, this part can be
buggy – the day I did it, there were a lot of mosquitoes. If you're there
during the cooler months or you aren't bothered by bugs, go to the far
end of the fountain area, close to the castle on the right-hand side.
There is a wide gravel road to your right. Follow it, and when it soon
forks, take the left side. Follow it across an open area before plunging
into the forest. Take it all the way to a T at just under the 5 kilometer
mark where you'll see the green Rundweg sign. Go left here onto a
wide gravel road. Follow this, and when the road bends hard to the
left, there will be a side trail to a small beach to your right. There is a

picnic table near the lake. It looks like an ideal, secluded place to swim. Back at the curve, follow the trail as you make your way back across the island. You'll pass two T's but continue straight to follow the green Rundweg sign. When you come to the pair of tree-lined paths back to the castle, walk to the further one before going left. As you do, you'll have a great view of the castle in the distance to your left. Walk down the long path, with trees on both sides as far as the eye can see.

At the end of the path, go right followed by a quick left to walk around the castle. You'll be back at the fountain area if you didn't get enough the first time. Walk along the right side of the area to its end. Stay on the right-hand pedestrian path and after going through some hedges, go right. You shouldn't have any problems finding this as everyone will be going this way. It's the quickest route back to the boat dock. If people are walking unusually fast, there must be a boat coming soon. It's about a kilometer from the fountain area. The path goes through a forested section before opening up, where it veers left. Follow the signs for the boat dock. When you come to a fork, take the right side, towards the boat dock. Once there, if you've timed things well, you can jump on a boat to the Fraueninsel. There are two sides of the dock: one for back to the mainland, the other towards the Fraueninsel.

When you arrive at Fraueninsel, go straight until you come to a group of signs. You might notice Inselbräu is straight on but to continue on our route, you'll go right here. When the path forks, take the right side to get closer to the lake. Follow this through a very cute part of the walk, with fishermen's houses and artists' cottages. They are on the left side but on the right side are their small parcels of lakeside paradise. Don't venture onto them, they are private property. You will see the occasional stand selling smoked fish and even smoked fish sandwiches. They are made with a local white fish called Renke and are tasty. The path wraps around the island and on the other side is the more commercial area with larger restaurants. This is where Inselbräu is but it's not time to stop just yet. Continue past the brewpub towards the church tower with its onion dome.

At the far end of the island is a public swimming area. Go left there to make your way fully around the small island. Once back where you started, go left towards the nunnery. When you come to a T, you can go left to check out the Benedictine nunnery or go right towards the church. The first left takes you to the church, which is well worth checking out – the metal door is fantastic. You can do this after the brewery too. Continue on the path from the nunnery. You'll pass a playground on your left and Inselbräu is just ahead on the same side. This is the back entrance, on the Biergarten side. Before you go in, admire the 1000-year-old linden tree on your right. It's a beauty.

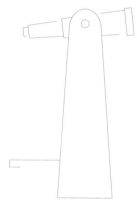

INSELBRÄU BRÄUSTÜBERL

The island's history is full of fishermen and an ancient Benedictine order, so obviously there was brewing in the picture as well. The Klosterbiers served on the island are contract brewed as they stopped brewing 300 years ago. Thankfully, an islander decided to revive brewing on the Fraueninsel and opened his organic brewery here in 2006. Pride is taken in using only the freshest ingredients from organic farmers. The interior of the Bräustüberl has a rustic flair with wood-beamed ceilings. The front terrace has lake views which are perfect for sunsets. The Biergarten out back is shady with views of the linden tree. In addition to Bavarian dishes, there are a few featuring the local whitefish, both smoked and fried.

All of their beers are unfiltered and are drier and fruitier than is typical of the region. I found both very refreshing and they went well with the fish.

Beers on tap: Helles Zwickl naturtrüb, Weißbier naturtrüb. Seasonal Märzen.

PRACTICAL INFORMATION

Inselbräu Bräustüberl
Frauenchiemsee 28
83256 Frauenchiemsee
+49 8054 902088
www.inselbraeu-frauenchiemsee.de

Open daily from 11:00 am
Closed Tuesday in colder months
Winter opening can be weather-dependent so please contact the brewery before heading out.

MAXLRAIN
(BAD AIBLING)

AI2 AND AI5

UPPER BAVARIA

▷··· STARTING POINT	···✕ DESTINATION
BAD AIBLING TRAIN STATION	**BAD AIBLING TRAIN STATION**
🍺 BEER	🔀 DIFFICULTY
MAXLRAINER SCHWARZBIER	**HIKE** 🥾
⛰ MAP	
ATK25-P13	⏱ DURATION OF THE HIKE
ROSENHEIM	**17 KM** **4-5H**
🔍 HIGHLIGHTS	〰 ELEVATION GAIN
MAXLRAINER CASTLE, MOUNTAIN SCENERY, LÜFTLMALEREI OR HAND-PAINTED TRADITIONAL HOUSES	ASCENT: 180 M DESCENT: 180 M

5.0%
ALCOHOL CONTENT

SCHWARZBIER
MADE OF DARK ROASTED
MALT, HALLERTAU HOPS,
TRIPLE MASH PROCESS

 CHESTNUT BROWN,
CREAMY TAN HEAD

 ROASTED MALT,
SLIGHT CHOCOLATE

ROAST BITTERNESS,
DARK CHOCOLATE,
DRY BITTERSWEET FINISH

BITTERNESS   SWEETNESS

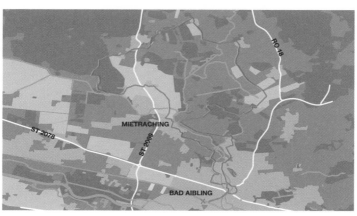

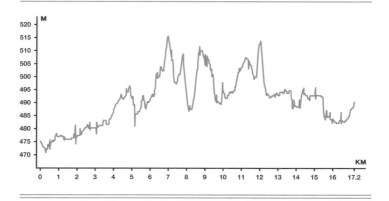

DESCRIPTION OF THE ROUTE

Maxlrainer Castle dates back to the 9th century but it burned down in 1577. It was rebuilt soon after and partially remodeled in the 18th century. The last of the Maxlrainers date back to similar times, but the castle has nonetheless remained in private hands and cannot be visited. It's still a sight to behold: a stately octagonal building with four towers topped with onion domes.

This hike combines two local trails, the Ai2 and Ai5, both marked by green signs. The "Ai" is short for Bad Aibling, the town that maintains them as well as serves as their best access point. It's set in the foothills of the Alps, and on clear days the mountains are clearly visible.

Trains to Bad Aibling are frequent and take about an hour from Munich. Please note: you will need to change trains in either Rosenheim or Holzkirchen.

Coming out of the Bad Aibling train station, you'll make your way down the Bahnhofstraße passing a couple of intersections before it veers slightly to the left. Keep going and you will pass the larger Münchenerstraße before making your way onto the much quieter and narrower Schmiedgasse. This street hugs the Glonn River and is quite scenic. Schmiedgasse soon comes to a small wooden bridge, well-marked with a green Ai2 sign. Turn right and cross it. Continue on Glonngasse for a short bit and go left on Schützenstraße, also marked with a green Ai2 sign. Cross another small bridge over the Glonn River, go to your left, and almost immediately take another right onto Heckenweg. Follow Heckenweg and take note of a football field to your right. Just after that, go right onto Rennbahnstraße which will run into Röntgenstraße. Don't go left here, stay on your route as it is the continuation of Röntgenstraße. At the very first street, go right. This path curves to the left and over another small bridge. Once over the bridge, go immediately to your left. This path follows the river on your left.

This quiet street soon opens up onto the much busier Thürnhamer Straße. Go to your left and cross the street carefully when you get a chance. You will soon be making a right onto the trail, easily seen from either side of the road. This is the Ai2 towards Mietraching. Follow the trail across the open field and go naturally left on Niederfeldweg. On a clear day, you should have mountain views to your left. When you get to the small village of Mietraching, go right on Dorfstraße.. Not far up, go left on Dorfstraße and follow it as it curves through the village. Make a right on Heimatsberger Straße and take note of the hand-painted traditional house featuring the Lüftlmalerei, a noted type of artwork in southern Bavaria. Heimatsberger Straße soon forks at a fire station. Take the left side. Stop following signs for the Ai2, that would take you back to Bad Aibling. You will do that part of the Ai2 on your return.

It's time to start following the Ai5 signs. They will lead you to Wilpasing and Maxlrain. The street soon becomes Horst-Siedlung. Take the right fork which soon wraps to the left. At Zum Unterfeld, take a right. Not long after that, you're on the Weg in die Moosbachwiese. This is a scenic stretch and you'll soon cross the Moosbach over yet another small bridge. The route takes you through the very small village of Wilpasing. This is about the only tricky part. Once on the other side of the village you'll see bike signs for Maxlrain ahead, indicating to go right. You will also see the Maxlrain brewery in the distance. You'd surely get there via that route but the hiking trail is quite nice if a bit longer. Look to your left towards the main road. You'll see another bike sign as well as an Ai5 sign attached to a Yield sign. Go to the road and make a right, being careful of the traffic. This is Ebersberger Straße and you're only on it for a few steps. Cross as soon as it's clear as you will turn left onto Adfurter immediately. Follow Adlfurter as it winds first to the left and then the right before coming to another small village. Going straight would follow the Moosbach, scenic but in the wrong direction.

Turn right and follow this road as it skirts a pretty forest. As it curves to the left, take note of the mountains to your left and the twin onion-domed church in the village, also to your left but a bit ahead. You'll not get to those domes today – an Ai5 sign soon tells you to go right into the forest you've been skirting. If it's a hot sunny day, enjoy the shade as you make your way to Weihenlindener Straße. Turn right onto the main road, marked with an Ai5 sign as well as a street sign heralding Maxlrain being a mere one kilometer away. The first part of the trail is in the forest but it soon opens up into an open field before running into the small hamlet of Maxlrain. If the light's good and you're not too hungry, you can explore the castle grounds a bit or at least walk beyond the Bräustüberl Maxlrain and snap a quick photo of it. If your mind is more on beer, you'll pass the castle as you leave anyway.

BRÄUSTUBERL MAXLRAIN

Though the Schlossbrauerei Maxlrain was first mentioned in 1636, the current operation dates back to around 1900. It's a nice old building scenically situated near the castle. Conveniently, the current owner and resident of the castle also runs the brewery. They pride them-selves on only using the finest local ingredients including Hallertau hops, malts grown for them by local farmers and crystal clear fresh water from the Mangfalltal. They brew a large range of beers including some fine seasonal beers like their Doppelbock Jubilator.

The Bräustüberl is a large vaulted ceiling affair, oozing old world charm with friendly servers clad in traditional Bavarian attire. In the warmer months, there is a nice Biergarten with a view of not only the mountains but also their small hop field in the foreground. The menu is full of Bavarian classics at fair prices.

Beers on tap: Maxlrainer Schwarzbier, Maxlrainer Zwickl (an unfiltered Helles) and Maxlrainer Weißbier, as well as the seasonal Maxlrainer Jubilator (Ash Wednesday to April), Maxlrainer Kirtabier (September to October) and Maxlrainer Festbier (during the Christmas Advent). They also offer a large selection of their other beers in bottles.

I'm a big fan of both their Schwarzbier and Jubilator. While they are not hard to find in bottles in Munich, finding them on tap and enjoying them in such an atmospheric place is another story. Coupled with a fine walk to get there, it's a combination not easily passed up. Speaking of walking, you will have to return the same day as there is sadly no hotel on the premises or anywhere in Maxlrain, unless you know the current residents of the castle.

No worries as the walk back is even prettier than your entry route. Exiting the Bräustüberl, you continue along the street you arrived on, Weihenlindener Straße, towards Aiblinger Straße. You can take an immediate left here and walk in front of the brewery and continue along towards the castle. You will also pass the Schlosswirtschaft, the higher-end eating option in the village. This will bring you to the front of the castle. A better photo option is to cross Aiblinger Straße and walk across the open field on an unnamed path. Look to your left for grand views of the castle and to your right for equally stunning views of the mountains. As the path rounds towards the castle at the end of the field, you get a really nice perspective of the brewery as well. As you leave the path, go to the left on Maxlrainer Freiung. You can continue to get views of the front of the castle through the locked gate or head to the right along the right side of the walled garden area to an opening on the side. You can have a peek in and then continue along the moss-covered wall on Maxlrainer Freiung.

At the end of this road, you'll make another right along a wider asphalt street that further on is lined on both sides by trees. When you're out of the trees, you have fantastic mountain views to your right. Then you come to the tiny village of Fischbach, where you make a right. It's well-marked with a green sign saying Holzhausen is 1.2 kilometers away on the Ai5. The road veers to the left and crosses the Glonn River before leading you to the village. You'll make yet another right on entering the village and exit it soon after. You're in open farmland now with fantastic views first to your right and then straight on as the road veers towards the mountains in the distance.

Down the road apiece, there's an Ai5 sign sending you right, and not long after that you will round a small dairy farm. In an equally short distance, you duck briefly into a patch of forest which winds a bit before emerging into Wallweg. This soon becomes Heimatsberger Straße, a name that should sound familiar from much earlier in the walk. If you continued straight, you'd be back at the fire station but instead, you will make a left on Josef-Hochwind-Weg. A green sign saying Bad Aibling is 2.9 kilometers away also lets you know you're back on the Ai2. This road becomes Auweg as it hugs the Glonn River. As it veers away from the river, the road turns right and becomes Mühlmoosstraße as you enter the northern end of Bad Aibling. Continue to Am Birkenhölzl where you turn right, followed by a relatively quick left on Stürzerstraße. Follow this for a short time and turn right where the Ai2 sign leads you. At the end of that street, go right on the fairly busy Thürhamer Straße. After crossing the Mühlbach on a wide bridge made for cars, carefully cross Thürhamer Straße and proceed down the narrow path that follows the Mühlbach. This is a pretty residential stretch that emerges onto Sperlallee as it departs from the river's course. This becomes Gerberstraße as it curves to the left. You're not on this for long when you come to a bridge. Turn left and cross the Glonn River yet again. Quickly go right on Hofmühl-straße and make another quick right on Kirchzeile. This wraps around as you enter the heart of the Old Town center, becoming the Marienplatz as the town hall comes into view. This becomes Münchener Straße before you cross the Glonn River one more time. Once over the bridge, turn left on Bahnhofstraße and follow it back to the train station.

PRACTICAL INFORMATION

Bräustüberl Maxlrain
Stachöderweg 2
83104 Tuntenhausen
+49 8061 92422
www.maxlrainer-braeustueberl.de

Open daily from 11:00 am to 11:00 pm

SCHLIERSEE TO MIESBACH

FROM A GORGEOUS MOUNTAIN LAKE TO A GORGEOUS WEIßBIER

UPPER BAVARIA

▷⋯ STARTING POINT	⋯✖ DESTINATION
SCHLIERSEE TRAIN STATION	**WEIßBRÄUSTÜBERL, MIESBACH**
🍺 BEER	🔡 DIFFICULTY
HOPF HELLE WEIßE	**HIKE** 🚶
⛰ MAP	
ATK25-Q12	🕐 DURATION OF THE HIKE
TEGERNSEE	**9.5 KM** **2–3H**
🔎 HIGHLIGHTS	〜 ELEVATION GAIN
SCHLIERSEE, ALTSTADT MIESBACH, BÄUERLICHE LANDSCHAFT, TRADITIONELLE HÄUSER	ASCENT: 220 M DESCENT: 315 M

WEIßBIER

UNFILTERED HONEY-
COMB, MASSIVE HEAD

MIX OF FRUIT AND YEAST,
SOME BANANA

FRUITY, DRY, VERY
SLIGHT BANANA/CLOVE,
REFRESHING

BITTERNESS   SWEETNESS

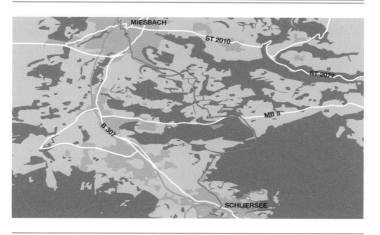

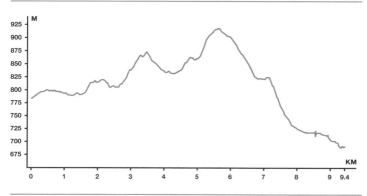

DESCRIPTION OF THE ROUTE

Schliersee is one of the prettiest of the group of mountain lakes southern Bavaria is blessed with. Aside from its obvious beauty, it is also one of the most popular for swimming due to its relative warmth compared to deeper lakes in the area. The water is incredibly clear and the mountains make for a dramatic backdrop even if sitting on the lake's edge is all you care to do. The town itself is set up well for tourists and there are ample hiking trails emanating from it. The hike described goes from the Schliersee train platform to Miesbach but can be done in reverse if you'd like to end up with a dip in the lake in Schliersee. The brewery is, however, at the end of this route. With a train day ticket, you can easily go between the two so the best of both worlds isn't out of the question.

Schliersee is serviced by frequent trains from Munich. The trip takes less than an hour. Miesbach is on the same line and it takes about 45 minutes to return to Munich.

Exiting the Schliersee platform you will come out on Werner-Bochmann-Straße and you will see numerous hiking trail signs. The one to Miesbach über Stadlberg has a blue dot. The hike is to the left, but if you won't be returning to Schliersee, you really should go right to have a look at this stunning lake. It's less than a 5-minute walk. To begin the hike, go left on Werner-Bochmann-Straße and cross Bahnhofstraße to continue on Werner-Bochmann-Straße. This crosses a large intersection at Miesbacher Straße. On the other side, continue straight on Karl-Haider-Straße. There's a cute bakery with Lüftlmalerei (frescoes on the facade) as the street bends to the left. Continue through a nice neighborhood until about the 1 kilometer mark, where you will come to a fork.

The left side goes to Hausham, so keep right on Karl-Haider-Straße. The road bends to the right as you go through a smaller village called

Kalkgraben – you will have views of Hausham to your left. Keep going straight and cross over Schatzelweg. There is a fenced-in area with horses on your left and a hiking sign saying Miesbach is 2 hours and 15 minutes away on Trail 571. You'll still be on asphalt here but it's a country road with fine views in all directions. Continue on to a farm, where you'll make a well-marked right to stay on the 571 to Miesbach, an unpaved road. This bends to the left as you enter a forest. When it forks, stay to the right side as it veers right. Continue straight through the forest until the fork at the 3 kilometer mark, then take the left side. It starts to bend to the left and soon emerges into an open area. There's a sign saying Miesbach is 1 hour and 45 minutes away, and sweeping views to your right.

Follow the wide gravel road to a large asphalt street and go left onto it. Carefully follow the street, keeping an eye out to the right for the trail. There's a bus stop sign, another sign for Hof, and the route goes uphill, so it will be easy to spot. Cross the street and follow the smaller paved road. The hiking sign says you're only 1 hour and 15 minutes from Miesbach now. As the trail rises, you will have great views to the left of the foothills of the Alps. Walk through Hof, nothing more than a small farm, and follow the road as it goes right. Just past Hof, you will come to a fork and continue straight as the road starts to climb steeply. As it veers left and levels out, take a look back at the nicest views of the walk. Continue on this road as it goes to the right, with a nice row of trees on your right-hand side and an open area on your left. In the warmer months, there are often cows out there. You'll come to another farm and you're now on Stadlbergstraße. Stay on this to Gschwendtnerweg where you will take a left, with a yellow hiking sign saying Miesbach is 1 hour away. Continue on to Floiger, a small farm. Look for a very small dirt footpath to your right. There is a small wooden gate-like device used to keep livestock in their area that you will need to climb over. There's also a yellow hiking sign saying Miesbach is 30 minutes on Trail 571. Once on the other side, you will walk across the small open area on the worn grass. There's a small yellow sign on the other side if the path is not obvious. Once over the next wooden device, you'll continue on the narrow but clear path through a very lush stretch of forest.

When you come to a road that is going into a big left curve, you can either follow the road around it or cut across the short green area straight on. It seems most people do the latter. Once across that, go left to join the road, now called Floigerweg. Follow this paved road through a nice neighborhood towards Miesbach. Just past the 8 kilometer mark, the road veers right and becomes Kleinthalstraße. Follow this to Stadlbergstraße, carefully cross it and continue on the pedestrian path through a small parking area to avoid the large road to its left. Exiting this lot, there's a pedestrian underpass to help you cross the very busy Bayrischzeller Straße. On the other side, continue on Schlierseer Straße. Stay on this street until you come to the Waitzinger Keller and take a left on Susanna-Waitzinger-Straße. Follow this as it winds right, goes downhill and becomes Habererplatz. Cross the large parking area, staying on its left side. Straight on is the Moserhaus-Passage, a route by some stores that will bring you into the center of Miesbach. Once through it, go left. You'll walk by Haus Wendelstein on your left, look for Lebzelterberg, a cute little path that quickly becomes Frauenhoferstraße. Turn right at the first intersection onto Heimbucherwinkl. Follow this to Kirchgasse. Keep left and continue straight on to the Marienplatz. It has a small park in its center and the Weißbräustüberl is just ahead on your right. The Miesbach train station is a short stroll from it when you're ready to head back to Munich.

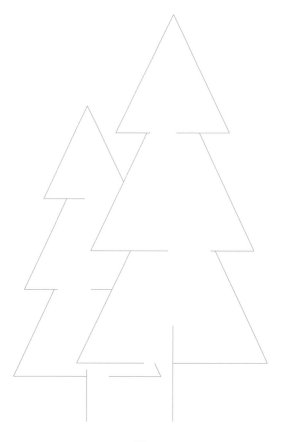

WEIßBRÄUSTÜBERL

Weißbierbrauerei Hopf is located just north of the Miesbach train station. They don't have a tasting room, but you can see it from the train on the left-hand side as you return to Munich. Their brewery tap is a fine traditional Bavarian affair, awash in light colored wood and a classic green tile oven. The outside seating overlooks the small park on the Marienplatz, a great place to celebrate your hike with one of the brewery's signature Weißbiers. Their menu features typical Bavarian cuisine but also a large selection of burgers and, a bit surprisingly for these parts, a small number of vegetarian dishes. Servers are decked out in traditional Bavarian attire and the town is known for its handmade quality clothing.

In 1923, the Hopf family took over the original Weißbierbrauerei that had been founded in 1892. They only make wheat beers, a typical style of Bavaria. Though the Reinheitsgebot (Bavarian Purity Law) of 1516 stipulated beer could only be made of water, malt and hops, wheat was later given the okay as it was a style of beer that had a long brewing history, especially in Bavaria. Sadly, the style's popularity waned in the 1960s and nearly disappeared in the 1970s before making a tremendous comeback in the 1980s. Hopf played a key role in the 1980s in helping to develop the technology that made it possible to keg the style. It was formerly considered too lively for further maturation due to the yeast left in the bottles. Some say bottled Weißbier is better due to this maturation process and even though the beer is on tap at the Weißbierstüberl, it is also available there in bottles for those who prefer it that way. Why not try both and find out for yourself?

Beers on tap: Hopf Helle Weiße. Bottled: Hopf Helle Weiße, Hopf Dunkle Weiße, Hopf Die Leichtere (a low-octane wheat beer with 3.4% alcohol) and Hopf Die Alkoholfreie (a no alcohol alternative). Seasonals are also bottled: Hopf Spezial Weiße, Hopf Weißer Bock, Hopf Muospacher Bockfotzn, Hopf Sauberne Schixs and Hopf Bluat vo da Gams.

PRACTICAL INFORMATION

Weißbräustüberl
Marienplatz 6
83714 Miesbach
+49 8025 9979883
www.weissbraustuberl.de

Open daily from 10:00 am

Brewery site with beer descriptions (in German):
www.hopfweisse.de

TEGERNSEE

A ROUTE TO THE RIEDERSTEIN
AND BAUMGARTENSCHNEID

UPPER BAVARIA

▷⋯ STARTING POINT

**TEGERNSEE
TRAIN STATION**

🍺 BEER

TEGERNSEER DUNKEL EXPORT

⛰ MAP

ATK25-Q12
TEGERNSEE

🔍 HIGHLIGHTS

RIEDERSTEIN CHAPEL, ALPS, RURAL
MOUNTAIN FARMS, TRADITIONAL BAVARIAN
BALCONIES, MARIA SCHNEE CHAPEL

⋯✕ DESTINATION

**HERZOGLICHES
BRÄUSTÜBERL TEGERNSEE**

🎛 DIFFICULTY

MOUNTAIN HIKE 🥾

🕐 DURATION OF THE HIKE

**13 KM
4–5H**

〰 ELEVATION GAIN

ASCENT: 750 M
DESCENT: 780 M

DUNKLES

UNFILTERED CHESTNUT,
ROCKY TAN HEAD

ROAST,
CHOCOLATE

MALTY,
CHOCOLATE,
BITTERSWEET FINISH

BITTERNESS   SWEETNESS

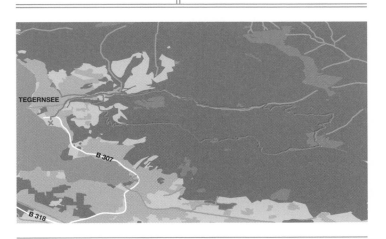

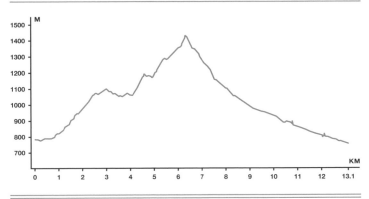

DESCRIPTION OF THE ROUTE

Tegernsee is one of the beautiful lakes south of Munich that make the Bavarian capital such a nice place to live. Set in the foothills of the Alps, the scenic lake is ringed by green hills, making even a simple stroll along its shore a delight. Adding to its charm is traditional Bavarian architecture with lovely carved wooden balconies adorned with flowers in warmer months. The former monastic and royal brewery on its shores is no secret to anyone living in southern Bavaria – throngs of people descend on it year-round. Nice weather weekends are particularly busy, so if you can time your visit for during the week, you'll have a bit more elbow room. That said, weekends are a fun time to observe one of the great pastimes of locals and tourists alike, enjoying the natural beauty of this gorgeous setting, whether it be hiking or just lounging lake-side. With a good variety of hikes, Tegernsee makes a great place to spend a few days.

Tegernsee is serviced by frequent trains from Munich and the trip takes about an hour.

Coming out of the Tegernsee train station, you'll need to go right on Bahnhofstraße to do just about anything in town. For this trail, follow it to Max-Josef-Straße and turn left. There are yellow trail signs right at the turn with numerous routes on them. This one describes the red route to the Baumgartenschneid Mountain. In this area, the color helps distinguish the difficulty and red is harder than blue. The first part to the Riederstein is blue and offers great views, so if you want to just turn back at that point, it's an easier option. Either way, follow this street as it starts to go uphill and soon follows the Alpbach, a pretty brook. When it comes to an intersection, look for the little Maria Schnee Chapel on your right. This is a major trail junction and you'll return here later on your way back. There's no real wrong way to go, but I like to get the steeper parts of a hike over early and have a gentler return. There's a hiking sign saying the Baumgartenschneid is 2.5 hours away. You'll have a few stops like the Galaun (a small restaurant) and the Riederstein, with a few benches, on the way up to take breaks at if needed. Walk by the chapel and follow the fairly steep and much narrower path up. You'll soon pop out on Schützen-straße and go right to walk by an ice rink on your left. The road wraps around to your right and climbs steeply. When you come to the intersection, go left on Auerweg rather than continuing on Sonn-leitenweg. This part really goes up but you'll be rewarded with great views of the large lake below to your right.

When Auerweg starts to bend to your left, look for a small trail on your right. It's quite narrow and sometimes a bit overgrown but there's a hiking sign there. If you continued on Auerweg, the Galaun would be an hour. Going this way, it's 50 minutes – so you know it's a steeper route. It's also less busy and a beautiful trail. It's a dense forest, so if you've been walking up the road in the sun, you'll be happy to be in the shade. It starts to zigzag as it goes up, and a bit after the 2 kilometer mark, you will come to a clearing with a crucifix and a bench. This is the Pfliegeleck. It's a nice spot to take a break, drink some water and enjoy the view of the lake and town down below. Next, walk up the gravel road behind you. It's an open stretch and you'll likely see some signs of logging activities. When there are breaks in the trees, you'll have some nice views of nearby peaks. You'll see signs for Galaun, your closest goal. There's a nice forested stretch just before you come to the opening where it's located. There's a small rustic restaurant in the clearing with nice views into the valley. If you look above it, you see the little chapel on the top of the Rieder-stein. It looks incredibly steep and oddly far away but it really isn't either. That said, get ready for some steps. If you think you're just doing the Riederstein, this is a good place to have a refreshment on your way down. If not and you're thirsty now, take advantage now as you won't see it again.

Continue past the Galaun area and look to your left for the opening for the trail to the Riederstein. You can't miss it – the sign says it's 30 minutes away. It's an uphill slog but a fair one, mostly over wooden steps. To make things more interesting, there are possibly the nicest Stations of the Cross I've ever seen. They are well-spaced out with fourteen in total, bringing you all the way to the top. At the first one, there is a junction sign for an easier route up. It's slightly longer and a bit less steep. You can use that to return on if you want to cut the hike short but the steeper route is well worth the effort. Follow along and after the fourth station, you will see a shrine built into an enormous rock on your right. You can take a side trail over to have a closer look but return to the main trail to keep climbing. At the thirteenth station, there is another junction sign. The Riederstein is another five minutes to your left, and to your right is the easier route back to the Galaun or the red route to the Baumgartenschneid. Make the climb up the Riederstein to find the incredibly cute little chapel. There are often traditionally attired Bavarians enjoying a snack on the wooden bench there, sometimes playing the accordion. It's right out of a storybook and not staged – these are real people just enjoying themselves. Walk around the small chapel to find a hidden bench with great views of not only the lake but the Alps rising in the distance.

When you're finished enjoying the Riederstein, return to the junction and decide if you want to head back the way you came or continue to the Baumgartenschneid. It's not a lot harder but it is another climb and the route is not quite as well-marked. There is generally a steady stream of hikers to follow, especially on weekends. If you're doing the hike early in the season and the winter has been harsh, there can be some trees blocking the trails and, unfortunately, sometimes those trees are the ones with the red dots on them, so have a map and an idea of where you are going. It's not uncommon for alternate routes to become more established than the true ones but if you keep your eyes open, you should find your way. Much of the route is forested, and it's only an hour away. The start has ample markings on the trees, often as slashes rather than dots. There's a bit of up and down and one fairly steep section before coming to a partial clearing. You'll see some typical Bavarian pasture areas and soon enough, you'll see the Baumgartenschneid looming in the distance, straight ahead. It's more of a rounded hill, but it's still a bit of a haul if it's hot out as it's totally exposed. It has a few switchbacks towards the end that seem particularly grueling but just after the 6 kilometer mark, you'll be standing at the top. It's a different perspective of the lake and a more open one of the Alps. If you look hard enough, you'll spot the Riederstein which looks very small and much lower. It's funny how your relative position to something makes it look so different. There's a small bench made of a log – if you're lucky enough to get a spot on it – and a bit further up on the true top, another ubiquitous crucifix. When you're ready to go, the route down is a little beyond it. There's a couple of signs but all starting in the same direction. Tegernsee is two hours from here. The initial drop is a steep and gravelly route, so be careful with your footing. If you've been carrying walking sticks, this is a good time to pull them out. As you descend, you will see a mountain hut and perhaps some cows in the pasture surrounding it. If you don't see them, listen for cowbells ringing – a sure sign they aren't far away. Walk towards the rather nice hut as the trail continues just past it. You'll be happy to see another sign saying Tegernsee is fifteen minutes closer. You haven't covered so much distance but that steep bit takes some time to traverse.

The route back is largely through forest. A little after the 7 kilometer mark, you will come to another junction. To the right is the trail to Schliersee, another popular Bavarian lake. You will want to go left towards Tegernsee über Alpbachtal. Once you are on this part of the trail, you'll be back on the easy to follow blue dot route. It's generally better maintained due to its accessibility and popularity. You'll come to a few junctions so keep following the route to Tegernsee über Alpbachtal to finish the described trail. There are other ways back to town but I find this one very pleasant and if you're tired, it's probably the easiest on the legs, too. You'll eventually link up with the Prinzenweg, which mirrors the Alpbach – that brook you started out on. As you emerge from the forest and make your return to civilization, there are lots of nice homes along the way, sometimes with flower-clad wooden balconies.

When you come to the intersection with Max-Josef-Straße, you'll want to take the left fork, Waldschmidtstraße. This will bring you more directly to the Bräustüberl — surely what's been on your mind for a good hour or so. At about the 12 kilometer mark, look for a small fork and take the left again, Mühlgasse. If you miss it, it's not a big deal as the main road will take you to the brewpub, too, but this little path is a more scenic way. It's a narrow, fenced path and on your left, you might spot some sheep lounging in the sun. Straight on, you'll see the top of two towers. That's the former monastery. That should get you to pick up the pace. You're almost there!

HERZOGLICHES BRÄUSTÜBERL TEGERNSEE

The former Benedictine monastery dates back to the 8th century and the brewery has claims of having been founded around 1050, but it's been a very long time since monks have been at the helm here. The royals took it over in the 1800s during secularization and it's still a blue-blood operation. Thankfully, the stunning church is still used as such, but the rest of the monastic buildings house the much expanded brewery as well as two restaurants. The more rustic Bräustüberl has vaulted ceilings and lots of wood. Although it seems to be perpetually busy, there always seems to be a seat to spare. The outside seating area is super popular on sunny days, but the interior is a cool place to be on a hot day due to the thick walls and high ceilings. They have a fairly simple, traditional menu and are well-noted for their Haxen (pork knuckle), Bierbrattl (pork belly with a crispy crust) and one of the best Obazdas you'll find anywhere. The latter is a tasty cheese spread that goes well with beer and pretzels. By far, their most popular beer is their Helles and certainly on a hot day after a hike, it has more than its share of devotees. For my money, the unfiltered Dunkel Export can't be beat, especially coupled with their pork dishes.

Beers on tap: Tegernseer Hell, Tegernseer Spezial and Tegernseer Dunkel Export.

PRACTICAL INFORMATION

Herzogliches Bräustüberl Tegernsee
Schloßplatz 1
83684 Tegernsee
+49 8022 4141
www.braustuberl.de

Open daily 9:00 am to 11:00 pm

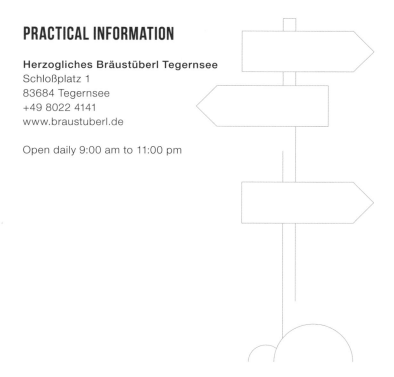

REUTBERG
(SCHAFTLACH)

A SCENIC STROLL TO A DARK BEER HEAVEN

UPPER BAVARIA

▷··· STARTING POINT	···✗ DESTINATION
SCHAFTLACH TRAIN STATION	**SCHAFTLACH TRAIN STATION**
🍺 BEER	🔁 DIFFICULTY
REUTBERGER EXPORT DUNKEL	**HIKE** 🚶
⛰ MAP	
ATK25-Q11 BAD TÖLZ	🕐 DURATION OF THE HIKE
	15 KM 3–3.5H
🔍 HIGHLIGHTS	〰 ELEVATION GAIN
REUTBERG MONASTERY, MOUNTAIN SCENERY, PONDS	ASCENT: 169 M DESCENT: 170 M

4.8%
ALCOHOL CONTENT

DUNKLES
MADE WITH
DARK MALTS

CHESTNUT,
ROCKY TAN HEAD

MALT,
SOME CHOCOLATE

RICH MALT, CHOCOLATE,
UNDERLYING HOPS, DRY
BITTERSWEET FINISH

BITTERNESS   SWEETNESS

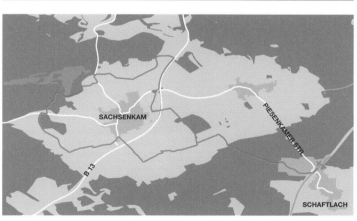

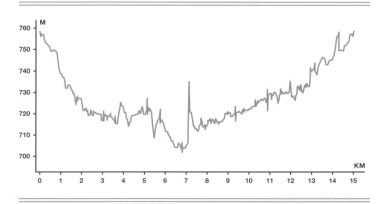

DESCRIPTION OF THE ROUTE

Founded in 1618, Kloster Reutberg is a Franciscan convent scenically situated in the foothills of the Alps, 40 kilometers south of Munich. Though closed by secularization in the early 1800s, it was brought back to life by King Ludwig I, who played a big part in revitalizing monasteries around Bavaria. The buildings are not in pristine condition but this adds to their charm and the setting is hard to beat. Cyclists and walkers descend on the area, especially on good weather weekends.

There is limited bus service directly to Kloster Reutberg from Holzkirchen during the week but none on weekends. Holzkirchen is well-connected to Munich by train and S-Bahn. The closest train station to Kloster Reutberg is Schaftlach, which is serviced by frequent trains from Munich. With such limited transport, a car is the easiest way to get there, but the walk described below from the closest station is quite nice and takes in the hiking circuit near the monastery.

Coming out of the Schaftlach train station, go right on Bahnhofstraße. This soon becomes Piesenkamer Straße as it turns right and crosses the tracks. Once over the tracks, you will see hiking signs pointing you in various directions. Go left to reach the trail to Kloster Reutberg most easily. This is conveniently called Reutbergstraße. Follow this as it winds right, through a residential area. You will pass a couple of streets. When you come to a fork, both sides are confusingly named Reutbergstraße. Take the left one, which almost immediately plunges you into the forest. You will emerge from it at just under the 2 kilometer mark. This is Schaftlacher Straße. You will take the first left – but not the rather large driveway leading to a private property you walk by first. At the end of this small farm road, you will merge with the Rundweg. You could go either way, but going left will get the longer part of the circuit completed before the monastery and brewery. You will be walking towards the mountains at this point, with fantastic views on clear days. You will pass a few small roads but continue more or less straight until you come to a farm. First go left and then a quick right on Rauchenbergstraße. At the T, go right and walk towards the highway. You will walk under the overpass once there. There is a sign for the Rundweg to reassure you. Waakirchner Straße will be on the other side. You are now walking towards the village of Sachsen-kam but you'll turn hard left onto Tölzer Straße to avoid it and make your way to Kloster Reutberg on a more scenic, if slightly longer route.

A bit after the 5 kilometer mark, turn right onto another farm road, with a Rundweg sign showing the way. You'll be in open farmland and soon skirt a forest on your right before coming to a small parking lot and a larger street. Carefully cross it and go right and then another quick left to remain on the trail. This is Am Neuweiher. There are also signs for the Fußweg zum Kirchsee (footpath to Kirchsee). Follow this to a fork, stay to the right to avoid the farm and walk along the wetland area on your right. At the end of this protected area, go right to remain on the trail. It soon veers left towards the monastery, which you will begin to see in the distance. After passing another small wetland area (Mühl-weiher), you go left away from it and towards your destination, now well in view. The road goes right and brings you directly to the Biergarten, one many say has one of the best views in Bavaria.

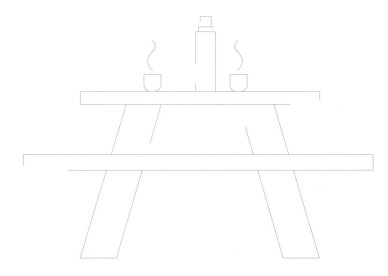

KLOSTERBRÄUSTÜBERL REUTBERG

Though the convent was founded in 1618, the brewery didn't get going until 1677. After a brief closure, it's been running as a cooperative since 1924. A red brick brewing chimney is still out back and since it's on the way to the church, well worth a peek, as is the pretty church interior. The Bräustüberl is a dark wood traditional affair, serving up excellent Bavarian dishes. The roast pork with dumplings is exceptional and goes well with their marvelous Dunkel Export. It's a cozy place on a cold winter day, especially if the Josefi-Bock is available. If the weather is fine, there's no better place than out in the Biergarten with its sweeping views of the crowd-drawing landscape.

Beers on tap: Reutberger Export Hell, Reutberger Kloster Hell, Reutberger Export Dunkel and Reutberger Kloster Weiße. Josefi-Bock during Lent. Aegigius Trunk in late summer. Bottled Märzen, Pils, Daisenberger Dunkle Weiße, Heller Bock and Weißbier-Bock.

About the only thing Kloster Reutberg lacks is rooms, so if there are no more buses or you just want to walk off that roast pork and dumplings, get back out on the road you came in on and go in the opposite direction. When you get to Reutbergstraße, go left. You'll come to an overflow parking area (site of their Strong Beer Festival during Lent!) and you'll take a right after it. Follow this as it goes right and then left before coming to a fork. At the fork, take the left side. This wraps around the open area and comes back next to the main road, but not on it. Though this is not the most direct route back, there

are some nice mountain views straight on as you mirror the road.
At the end of this section, you will come to a big intersection with an
overpass to your left, but you'll follow Rundweg signs sending you
right along the larger street and then left fairly quickly. Follow this
small unnamed road to the larger Piesenkamer Straße and go left.
You'll go under an overpass and then make a right on Hirschberg-
straße. At the end of this, take a left to reach Schaftlacher Straße. Go
right and follow this until the road forks at around the 13 kilometer
mark. Take the left side into the forest you walked in on. Walk back to
Reutbergstraße and go right. This will take you back to the station.

PRACTICAL INFORMATION

Klosterbräustüberl Reutberg
Am Reutberg 2
83679 Sachsenkam
+49 8021 8686
www.klosterbraeustueberl.de

Open daily 10:00 am to 11:00 pm

MITTENWALD

AN EASY HIKE WITH ALPINE VIEWS AND TWO MOUNTAIN LAKES

UPPER BAVARIA

▷··· **STARTING POINT**

KRANZBERG CHAIRLIFT, MITTENWALD

🍺 **BEER**

MITTENWALDER NATURTRÜBES KELLERBIER

⛰ **MAP**

ATK25-S10
MITTENWALD

🔍 **HIGHLIGHTS**

KARWENDEL, FERCHENSEE, LAUTERSEE, QUEEN MARY CHAPEL, WOODEN MOUNTAIN HUTS, CHURCH OF ST. PETER AND PAUL

···✕ **DESTINATION**

BRAUEREIGASTSTÄTTE POSTKELLER, MITTENWALD

🎲 **DIFFICULTY**

MOUNTAIN HIKE 🚶

🕐 **DURATION OF THE HIKE**

9 KM
2.5–3H

〰 **ELEVATION GAIN**

ASCENT: 270 M
DESCENT: 530 M

KELLERBIER SERVED
DIRECT FROM THEIR
CELLAR, ONLY AVAILABLE
HERE

STRAW,
ROCKY HEAD

GRAIN,
FAINT HOPS

DRY,
FRUITY,
GRAIN

BITTERNESS

SWEETNESS

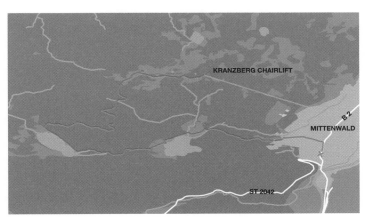

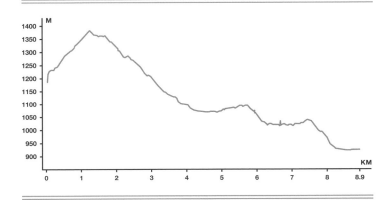

DESCRIPTION OF THE ROUTE

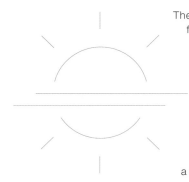

The Bavarian Alps may not be as famous or as high as their neighbors but they are every bit as spectacular. Mittenwald is a storybook alpine town with houses adorned with colorful murals and their traditional wooden balconies decked out in colorful flowers. With ample and varied accommodation and eating options, Mittenwald makes a great base to explore an area rich in scenic delights.

Though the town is unquestionably cute, it is the setting that makes it special. The Karwendel is one of the iconic images of the Bavarian Alps – a jagged group of mountains more stunning than the nearby highest peak in Germany, Zugspitze. With a couple of beautiful mountain lakes within walking distance and numerous trails emanating from the town center, one could easily spend a few days enjoying Mittenwald.

Mittenwald is serviced by frequent trains from Munich. The trip takes about 2 hours and stops in Garmisch-Partenkirchen en route.

Hiking up into the Karwendel is an amazing experience with one small caveat: once in it, you can no longer see it. This hike takes you up high on the hills across from the Karendel, where the views of it are breathtaking. Make your way to the Kranzberg chairlift station. It's just on the edge of town, and whether coming from the train station or your accommodation in Mittenwald, you can enjoy the quaint old town center on your way. Be sure to check out the Church of St. Paul and Peter and the quirky statue of a giant violin, both surely on your route if coming from the station. The popular chairlift station is well-marked so it won't be hard to find, but the last part of the walk is steep with great views of the old town and the Karwendel as its dramatic backdrop. Once at the station, get a one-way ticket and hop on. This is a chairlift, not a cable car, so if you have problems with heights, have a look before buying your ticket. If you don't care to use the chairlift, there is a well-marked trail up to the Kranzberg from here. It's a relentless slog and exposed to the sun, so unless you have vertigo or just want a good workout, I suggest the chairlift. I've done both and you even get better views from the chairlift.

After your chairlift journey, you'll see many hiking trail signs when you exit the station. Look for the one to Hoher Kranzberg. It's Trail 830 and is a blue dot trail, meaning it's fairly easy. That said, almost all of the 270 meters of elevation gain you're going to do is on this stretch, which takes approximately 40 minutes. There's not a lot of shade, so if it's a hot day, try to do the hike early. Head up the trail towards St. Anton's, a nice restaurant with great views. At the path to it, go right to stay on the trail to the Hoher Kranzberg. It's a wide gravel road – so it will be easy walking aside from the incline. It's a very distinct route, so continue towards the Hoher Kranzberg, taking the Fußweg when it's available but otherwise sticking to the road. You'll pass some traditional wooden huts along the way. Just before the 1 kilometer mark, you'll come to an intersection. Straight on is Ferchensee and Lautersee, the two lakes which comprise your eventual destination, but first head up the trail to the Hoher Kranzberg. It's only steep for five minutes. The views on the way and up above are spectacular and there will be wooden loungers for you to take a break on. When you're ready, head back down to the junction.

Continue on Trail 813 towards Ferchensee. This begins as a wide gravel road and is again easy to follow. Savor the views to your left as soon enough, you'll be dropping down. You'll pass one small junction but stay on the route to Ferchensee, straight on. You will soon dip into the forest on a narrower path for the trip down. When you emerge from it, you'll be at another gravel road – go left here and look for the trail junction to your left in the curve of the road. Take the left towards Ferchensee and Lautersee, back into the forest. You will come to a smaller junction where you have the option to go directly to Lautersee and Mittenwald but you want to continue straight on the 813 to Ferchensee. You drop down, mostly in the forest, but whatever open areas you pass offer great views.

Just after the 4 kilometer mark, you will come to another wide gravel road. Go left here, towards Lautersee and Mittenwald. You'll walk by Ferchensee – a gorgeous lake with stunning peaks as its backdrop. There are a couple of options for having a meal or a drink if you're up for it. If not, continue along the lake and you'll come to another small junction. Follow 872 to both Lautersee and Mittenwald. At the end of the lake is a path that goes right to go around it but you will veer left to remain on the route to Lautersee. You'll soon be on Trail 872 to Mittenwald/Lautersee and 828 to Lautersee. When you come to a major road, you'll cross it to continue on the other side on Trail 828 towards Lautersee. Just up the trail, go right, and when you come to a fork, take the right side to remain on 828. This leads to a series of steps that bring you down to the second lake. Lautersee is as beautiful as Ferchensee, with even more eating and drinking options. The first restaurant even has the Mittenwalder beers on tap, if you can't wait!

Follow the path along the lake and you'll see a small chapel just past the end of it. At that junction, you can go right to walk around the chapel towards Mittenwald on a variety of trails. Towards the end of this open area, you'll see a sign towards Mittenwald on Trail 828. You could ignore this sign and continue along the unofficial but fairly obvious path straight on. If not, follow the sign to an intersection. You'll see another sign for those two trails back to Mittenwald (828), but if you want a quicker route to the brewery, go right. The sign is backwards on the pole. If you look on the other side, you'll see Mittenwald ü. Felseneck. Take that and you'll see the path I mentioned earlier, joining it. Continue on and the trail becomes a wider gravel path as it goes through the forest. There will be a small junction, but keep going straight. It says you're about 10 minutes from Mittenwald. Just up the path, you will cross a paved road and continue on the other side on a narrow, but still very clear path. This skirts a small fenced property before some steps that drop you down into town on Lauterseeweg. At that street, go left and continue to the intersection. Keep right, cross the street (Elmauer Weg) and look for Wetterstein-straße. Go down the small set of steps and follow this residential street for a few blocks to Ludwig-Murr-Straße. Cross this intersection and continue straight on the other side, now Adolf-Baader-Straße. Take this to Innsbrucker Straße and go right onto it. Brauereigaststätte Postkeller is just ahead on your left.

BRAUEREIGASTSTÄTTE POSTKELLER

Brauereigaststätte Postkeller is one of three pubs tied to the brewery and, as it's right next to it, it's the closest to the source. To my knowledge, it's the only one serving the Kellerbier right from the storage tanks. Those technicalities aside, it has great views, and after a recent renovation, is quite modern, though it retains a traditional flair. In addition to typical Bavarian dishes, they have some innovative twists and their menu is translated into English and Italian.

The brewery was founded in 1830 and the fifth generation of the Neuners family is now steering it into the modern era. For example, they've streamlined their logo and seem to offer more of their beers on tap. Still, they remain a traditional company and take great pride in using local malt and the finest Hallertau hops. Of course, beer is mostly water and theirs come from a spring near the Lautersee – the lake you just walked by.

Beers on tap: Mittenwalder Karwendel Hell, Mittenwalder Naturtrübes Kellerbier, Mittenwalder Berg Gold, Mittenwalder Jager Dunkel, Mittenwalder Pils, Werdenfelser Weiße. Seasonal: Mittenwalder Edel-Märzen, Weihnachtsbock (Christmas), and Josefibock (Lent) are also on tap. Bottled: Werdenfelser Hefe Dunkel and Werdenfelser Hefe Leicht.

You can find more information on the types of beer on the brewery's website: www.brauerei-mittenwald.de

PRACTICAL INFORMATION

Brauereigaststätte Postkeller
Innsbrucker Straße 13
82481 Mittenwald
+49 8823 9379480
www.brauereigaststaette-postkeller.de

Open Thursday from 5:00 pm
Friday to Tuesday from 10:00 am
Closed Wednesday

One of the other Mittenwalder restaurants, which has the advantage of having overnight accommodation:

Gasthof Stern
Fritz-Prölß-Platz 2
82481 Mittenwald
+49 8823 8358
www.stern-mittenwald.de

Closed Monday

MURNAUER MOOS

HOME TO THE BLUE RIDERS AND KARG BREWERY

UPPER BAVARIA

▷··· STARTING POINT	···✕ DESTINATION
MÜNTER-HAUS, MURNAU	**MÜNTER-HAUS, MURNAU**

🍺 BEER	🁢 DIFFICULTY
KARG HELLES HEFE-WEISSBIER	

⌖ MAP	# HIKE

ATK25-Q10	🕐 DURATION OF THE HIKE
MURNAU A.STAFFELSEE	**14 KM** **3-4H**

🔍 HIGHLIGHTS	〰 ELEVATION GAIN
MÜNTER-HAUS, MOORS LANDSCAPE, ALPS, SMALL CHAPEL	ASCENT: 205 M DESCENT: 208 M

WEIßBIER

UNFILTERED HONEYCOMB,
DENSE ROCKY HEAD

BANANA,
CLOVE

FRUITY,
DRY FOR THE STYLE,
BANANA

BITTERNESS

SWEETNESS

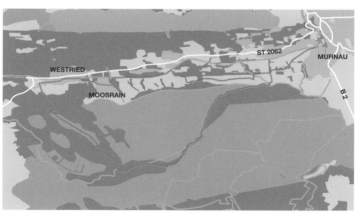

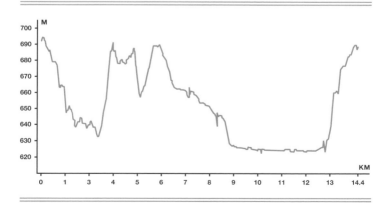

DESCRIPTION OF THE ROUTE

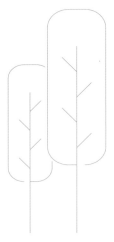

Murnau is a charming town southwest of Munich, set scenically on the rather large lake called the Staffelsee. Though in a relatively flat valley, its location makes it seem even closer to the mountains, and on clear days, it's easy to feel like you're right among them with little effort. It is perhaps most noted as the home of Der Blaue Reiter (The Blue Rider), a renowned if short-lived art group led by Wassily Kandinsky prior to WWI. He and Gabrielle Münter lived together in what is now the popular attraction, the Münter-Haus. The Murnauer Moos is one of the largest moors in central Europe and offers quite a different landscape from its surrounding mountains. This often stark contrast is breathtaking and popular with both walkers and cyclists.

Murnau is serviced by frequent trains from Munich and the trip takes about an hour.

Whether day-tripping from Munich or wisely spending an evening or two in Murnau, you'll need to make your way to the Münter-Haus. There are plenty of signs to get you there from just about anywhere in the old town center or the train station. Even if you don't care to go inside, it's a pleasant sight and right on the way to the Murnauer Moos, where your hike takes place. From the Münter-Haus, you will continue along Kottmüllerallee heading away from town (to your right, if you are standing with your back to the house). You'll see signs for the Murnauer-Moos-Rundweg 5. As it bends to the left, it becomes a long, glorious narrow path lined with trees on both sides. When you emerge from the tunnel, the trail veers to the right and you have open areas to your left and if it's a clear day, fine views of the Alps. Not far along the path, the route goes left to head downhill. This is a picturesque spot, especially late in the day. At the first plateau, you have two choices. If you continue straight and downward, you come to the Ramsach-kircherl, a cute little chapel conveniently next to a nice little Biergarten. It's perhaps wise to go right towards the Drachenstich instead. You won't make it all the way there today but along this route is a small metal telescope of sorts. If you look through it, you'll see the tops of three churches, the closest of which is the one you'll walk by on the way back. It's known as the Asam-Punkt as all three churches were built by the famed Asam brothers. The two trails start to separate, so follow the signs for the Murnauer-Moos-Rundweg. When you come to a larger road, you'll go right. Continue along this road, bypassing the left turn that would bring you down to the scenic river area. You'll return that way later. It's an open stretch of rural scenery but you have the mountains to your left the whole way.

At the end of this road, you'll have only one choice, follow the signs for the Moos-Rundweg-Wanderpass and go right. As you may have guessed, you're headed up. Thankfully, when you hit a small series of wooden steps, there are some shady trees. At the top and out in the clear, you'll see a small log cabin-type shelter. You can walk to it and continue past it but the trail takes you right, followed by a hard left. This is a bit roundabout but unless you plan on taking a break at the shelter, it's a nice route and offers very nice views of the log cabin structure with mountains as its backdrop. You'll be walking along the train tracks for a short time, and soon you will cross them after making a right, followed by quick left. You walk along the other side of the tracks before crossing back over. As you veer to the left and leave the tracks behind, you enter a small patch of forest before emerging in the village of Moosrain. You'll turn right here at the well-marked sign still following Moos-Rundweg 5. It's also Moosrainer Straße so you are on asphalt for a spell. This runs along the tracks as it veers left.

Pleasantly, you soon come to a fork and go left away from the tracks (for the last time) on Graf-Alban-Straße, and then through a nice little neighborhood where all the houses have fine views. At the five-way intersection, go left on Im langen Filz, again following the now-familiar Moos-Rundweg 5 signs. You'll soon enter a nice dense forest and then an open moors area, heralded by protected area designation signs. It's a boardwalk path, much as you might see in Scandinavia, and protects not only your boots from getting wet but also the fragile terrain you're traversing. Please stay on the path. It's a pretty stretch, made all the more spectacular by the mountains looming in the distance as you walk towards them.

As you emerge from this magical area, you're back out in open fields. When you see a small wooden bridge, take the opportunity to cross the Lindenbach – a brook you'll walk along for the first part of your journey back. It veers away and meanders a bit but the route is obvious, so you can enjoy the majesty that abounds. When you return to the flowing water, it's now the Ramsach, which you'll mirror back to the small chapel you saw from the Asam-Punkt. You'll cross back over on a small bridge and go left on Ramsachstraße. You can peek in the chapel and if you can't wait to get back to town for a beer, the Gaststätte Ähndl has about as fine a view as you'll find in these parts. If the weather is fine and you can find a spot in their small Biergarten, beers from the local Karg brewery are available here too. Whether you stop or not, you'll continue by the chapel as it veers left back up the road you saw earlier. Walk up it to reach the intersection, continue uphill until it goes right, enjoying the scenery in perhaps even better light if it's the late afternoon. Retrace your steps through the Kottmül- lerallee back to the Münter-Haus. From there, head back to town and make sure to walk down the Untermarkt so you can drop in at Karg for a much-deserved Weißbier.

KARG BRÄUSTÜBERL

Brauerei Karg's traditional tap is conveniently located on the main street of the old town center. The Karg family took the brewery over in 1912, a mere twenty years after its founding as Weißbierbrauerei Hirschvogel. With the fifth generation very much at the helm, it will undoubtedly remain a family enterprise. Southern Bavaria is noted for this somewhat odd style of beer. It's odd in the sense that it's made with wheat, an ingredient not listed in the Bavarian Purity Law of 1516 but since it's top-fermented (also not common in Bavaria), it seems to not be under such strict constraints. Odd also in that it has yeast in the bottle so is bottle-conditioned and served cloudy. This is where the "Hefe" comes in – the German word for yeast. Some of the very best are brewed in this region and Karg is at the top of the list, brewing nothing but Weißbier – or Weizen as it's more known in points north of Munich. The restaurant has fine Bavarian fare and if you haven't tried the regional delicacy Weißwurst-Frühstück (literally white sausage breakfast), this is about as good a place to do it as any. It's generally only served until 11:00 am so you'll either have to have it before your hike, get a very early start hiking or best yet, spend the night at Griesbräu just up the street and have it the following day.

Beers on tap: Karg Helles Hefe-Weißbier. Bottled Dunkles Hefe-Weißbier, Leichtes (low alcohol) Hefe-Weißbier and some seasonals like their Weizenbock in the cooler months.

PRACTICAL INFORMATION

Karg Bräustüberl
Untermarkt 27
82418 Murnau am Staffelsee
+49 8841/8272
www.karg-weissbier.de

Open Wednesday to Sunday
10:00 am to 2:00 pm and 6:00 pm to 11:00 pm
Closed Monday and Tuesday

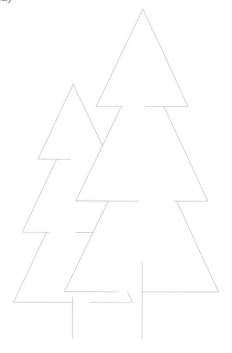

MURNAUER DRACHENSTICH

FROM THE PLACE OF SPEARING DRAGONS TO THE PLACE OF DRINKING DRAGON'S BLOOD

UPPER BAVARIA

▷··· STARTING POINT	···✕ DESTINATION
GRIESBRÄU ZU MURNAU	**GRIESBRÄU ZU MURNAU**
🍺 BEER	🎲 DIFFICULTY
GRIESBRÄU HELLES	**HIKE** 🚶
⛰ MAP	
ATK25-Q10	⏱ DURATION OF THE HIKE
	6.5 KM
MURNAU A.STAFFELSEE	**2–2.5H**
🔍 HIGHLIGHTS	〰 ELEVATION GAIN
DRACHENSTICH, STAFFELSEE, ASAM-PUNKT, MOUNTAIN SCENERY, MARIA HILF CHURCH	ASCENT: 150 M DESCENT: 160 M

 UNFILTERED HELLES

 UNFILTERED LIGHT AMBER

 CITRUS HOPS,
GRAIN

FRUITY,
GRAIN, DRY,
BITTER FINISH

BITTERNESS   SWEETNESS

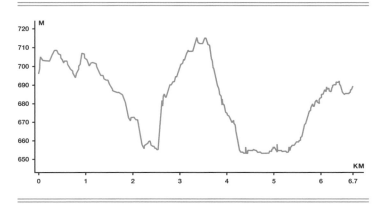

DESCRIPTION OF THE ROUTE

Murnau is an artsy town with a strong lineage – it is the home of the Blaue Reiter (Blue Riders) art group. If you've already done the Murnauer Moor hike (see page 76) and have wisely decided to spend the night in town, this walk will take you to not only the large lake Murnau is blessed with but also to an area where it may be that dragons were slain. All that and if it's summer, you'll have a chance to drink dragon's blood.

Murnau is serviced by frequent trains from Munich and the trip takes about an hour.

Coming out of Griesbräu on the main street, go right onto Obermarkt. This is a popular street to sit in a cafe and "people watch" and you will be one of those people being watched as you make your way towards the church straight head. If you don't feel like popping in, you can admire its tower with the mountains as its backdrop. Go right on Postgasse and follow it to Bahnhofstraße and carefully cross this busy intersection. Continue on Kohlgruber Straße on the other side. This becomes a pedestrian path, then at the T, go left. A street sign points you to both the Staffelsee and Münter-Haus. You're going to the latter first. There is also a sign for the Drachenstich-Rundweg. That's your route. Go left and follow this path through a small park at the Rundweg (circuit) junction. You will return to this point later but now you will continue straight. After crossing a small wooden bridge, go down some stairs and veer to the right, following the Rundweg signs. Go through the park to the train tracks. Carefully cross them and continue in the park on the other side. This is a pretty stretch with some fine old trees. The trail curves left and briefly follows the tracks along a lane lined with trees on both sides. You'll come to a crucifix and across from it will be a small information board. This was a popular spot for the Blauer Reiter art group. It has a great perspective from which to view the church across the way. Continue on and soon the Münter-Haus will be on your left.

The first part of this route follows the Murnauer Moos walk. This is an access trail that many other trails use, and thankfully, it's so pleasant, no one minds walking it more than once. Go right on Kottmüllerallee, following signs for the Drachenstich-Rundweg. The paved road soon becomes a narrower path and when it gets to the back of some homes, go up the middle path which will be well-marked. When you come to a junction, go straight to remain on Kottmüllerallee rather than going left to Lourdesgrotte. This is a gorgeous section of trail with large trees lining it on both sides. As you might imagine, locals use it for evening and morning strolls so don't be surprised to find it busy. You'll come to a viewpoint with a small shelter. From here, you get great views of the mountains and the moors of Murnau. Follow the trail as it veers right and levels out. When it turns left, you will drop down to another trail junction. Confusingly, the Drachenstich goes straight and to the right. To follow this route, go right, maintaining your elevation, rather than dropping down. You'll come to a sculpture of a hand holding a telescope. Look through it to see the tops of three churches built by the Asam brothers. This is appropriately named Asam-Punkt (Asam point). When you come to a junction, veer right and continue along the route to the Drachenstich. It's little more than a cleared area in the forest with a small information board only in German. From the name of the spot (Drachenstich means "to stab a dragon"), I'd imagined dragons were reportedly slain here but after reading the sign, it turns out it was where a play called the *Drachenstich* was performed. I have to admit I was a bit disappointed. Still, I looked at the empty area and imagined a dragon lying there. It didn't help. I was still disappointed. I guess without a dragon, it's hard not to be.

You will come to a long staircase and ascend it. It's quite a little climb. Up top, you will go through a nice forest, crossing a couple of small bridges. Go left to walk parallel to the railroad tracks until a Drachenstich sign says to go right. Carefully cross the tracks just after the 3 kilometer mark. On the other side, another sign directs you to the right and you will follow the unpaved road to the paved Kohlgruber Straße. Carefully cross it and go right, walking on the pedestrian/bike path mirroring it. Make your first left towards a clinic but stay on the left-hand side of the road. Turn left when you see a sign saying Zum Staffelsee. The Drachenstich sign below it says the lake is less than a kilometer away. Follow this through the forest to the lake and take a well-marked right there. Walk along the lake shore, enjoying the fine views. If it's a hot day, locals will be swimming or canoeing. It's an understandably popular spot. The unpaved road becomes the paved Seewaldweg as it nears the end of the lake. There's a kiosk if you want to enjoy a drink lakeside.

The signs here are a bit confusing but the most direct route is to continue straight. Seewaldweg becomes Seestraße and there will be a footpath that runs along the left side of the road. When it forks, take the left side, followed soon by a right. This brings you back to Seestraße, which you should cross carefully to go through the underpass straight ahead. Drachenstich signs point you towards the town center. On the other side, you'll see another underpass. Go through that one, too. There's some colorful graffiti here, including one of a dragon. On the other side, follow the Drachenstich signs that lead you over an elevated walkway to your right. This is at about the 6 kilometer mark and is right next to the tracks. On the other side, you'll be at the circuit junction you went straight on near the beginning of the walk. Go left at the small city park this time. Follow it back to pedestrian path leading to the town center. Go right there and follow Kohlgruber Straße to the intersection and straight on to Postgasse. Go left on Obermarkt. Griesbräu is not far up the street on your left.

GRIESBRÄU ZU MURNAU

Griesbräu zu Murnau is a place with a feel-good story attached. There were records of a brewery being on this site as early as 1676 and Griesbräu was founded in 1836, only to cease brewing less than a 100 years later. The story took a happy turn in 2000 when the Gilg family reopened the brewery after an 83-year hiatus. The historically recognized buildings were restored and the town regained not only a brewery but a piece of its heritage. Today, it stands as a great mix of old tradition and new innovation, brewing not only the typical Bavarian styles but also some craft beer offerings. The interior has the new-age requisite copper kettles but the atmospheric old room still breathes the past. To get food, you go up to a cafeteria-style area, where you order what you'd like and bring it back to your table yourself. Drinks are ordered at your table and brought to you by traditionally-dressed servers.

They have a host of events, including beer seminars, and are into educating people about brewing and new styles of beer. They have many seasonal beers and I was happy to see older Bavarians enjoying their IPA, a style relatively new to the region. I went in May and had both the regular Maibock and a craft beer version and was very impressed by both – quite different and interesting to compare. And if you do the hike in June, what could be a better way to celebrate than having their Drachenblut (Dragon's Blood)?

Beers on tap: Griesbräu Helles, Griesbräu Weiße, Griesbräu Ur-Dunkel. Traditional seasonals: Griesbräu Murnator (Lent), Griesbräu Maibock (May), Braunbier Bruno (August), Griesbräu Märzen (September), Griesbräu Weizen Dunkel (October), Weihnachts-Weizenbock (Advent season). Craft beer seasonals: Griesbräu IPA (January), Pfeifal (January), MaiOr (a craft beer Maibock, May), Drachenblut (June), Sommerfrische (August), Barley Wine (end of August), Ein Stout zu Nikolaus (November/December), HoWeiBo (Advent).

PRACTICAL INFORMATION

Griesbräu zu Murnau
Obermarkt 37
82418 Murnau a. Staffelsee
+49 8841 1422
www.griesbraeu.de

Open daily
10:00 am to 11:00 pm

Rooms are available and can be booked on their website, which is also available in English.

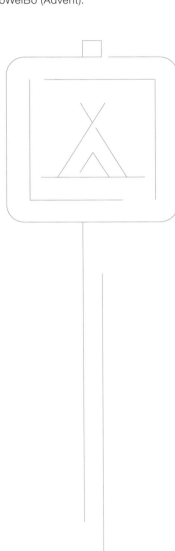

OBERAMMERGAU

CLIMBING THE BREWERY'S LOGO

UPPER BAVARIA

▷⋯ STARTING POINT	⋯✕ DESTINATION
AMMERGAUER MAXBRÄU, OBERAMMERGAU	**AMMERGAUER MAXBRÄU, OBERAMMERGAU**
BEER	DIFFICULTY
AMMERGAUER MAXBRÄU NATURTRÜBES KELLERBIER	**MOUNTAIN HIKE**
MAP	
ATK25-R09	⏱ DURATION OF THE HIKE
	12 KM
GARMISCH-PARTENKIRCHEN	**4–5H**
HIGHLIGHTS	〜 ELEVATION GAIN
KOFEL, LÜFTLMALEREI, ALPINE SCENERY, ST. PETER AND PAUL CHURCH, AMMER RIVER	ASCENT: 640 M DESCENT: 620 M

4.9%
ALCOHOL CONTENT

TOP-FERMENTED KELLERBIER MADE WITH VIENNA, PILSNER, AND SPELT MALT AND HERSBRUCKER SPÄT AROMA HOPS

UNFILTERED DARK HONEYCOMB

CITRUS HOPS, HINT OF PEACH

DRY, FRUITY, COMPLEX MALT, CITRUS HOPS, BITTER FINISH

BITTERNESS

5
4
3
2
1

SWEETNESS

5
4
3
2
1

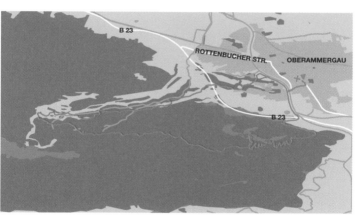

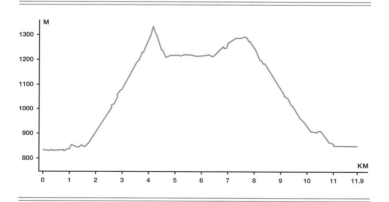

DESCRIPTION OF THE ROUTE

 Oberammergau is a popular tourist destination due in part to its being one of the most noted places were the Passion Play is performed. This religious pageant dates back to the 1600s in the small mountain village and is a once-a-decade event that attracts people from around the world. Another draw is the abundance of traditional mountain buildings adorned with Lüftlmalerei, an art form most prevalent in Upper Bavaria and Austria whereby architectural elements like windows and doors are depicted in paintings. Village and rural life are also popular subjects. Oberammergau native Franz Seraph Zwinck is perhaps the most well-known of the artists in the style. Adding to the allure of these often quaint buildings is their spectacular mountain setting. Some of the most prevalent images of Bavaria are the very ones you will see live if you venture to this pretty little hamlet.

Oberammergau is serviced by frequent trains from Murnau and Oberau, both of which are on the busy line between Munich and Garmisch-Partenkirchen.

Disembarking from the train, the first thing you are likely to notice is a beautiful looming peak that looks so close you could touch it. Well, pretty soon, that is just what you are going to be doing. If you are the type who always wants to be on top of the mountains you see, this is the hike for you. Make your way to Ammergauer Maxbräu to start this hike – though it might be best to hold off on the beer until after you complete it.

Leaving the brewpub, go left on Ettaler Straße. Look back at the charming St. Paul and Peter Church. You'll soon be looking down on it from the Kofel, that stunning peak you've been unable to escape as you walked through town to the brewery. Take a soft right, followed by another quick right on König-Ludwig-Straße. Follow this to the Ammer River and cross it. Here you can enjoy the views to your left of the Kofel from the bridge as they are some of the nicest in town. Turn left on Malensteinweg once over the bridge and walk along the river path, just off the main road. It's a pleasant stroll. You'll pass a cool-looking hostel and some tennis courts along the way. Walk under an overpass and go to your right towards a parking lot. There is a hiking sign for the Kofel; its height is 1342 meters and it will take you another hour and a half to reach it. Follow this road with the parking lot on your right and a cemetery on your left until you come to another sign sending you left. This is about the 1 kilometer mark and the trail will start to rise gently. You will be in the forest with a partial view of the cemetery as your wrap around it. You'll pass the Mariengrotte, a small shrine built into the side of a large rock. When you come to a small intersection, go right. To the left is a second parking area for the hike – necessary due to the hike's popularity. You'll soon be in an open meadow with a direct view of the Kofel. It has a different shape from this vantage point and looks intimidatingly steep. It's easier than it looks but make no mistake about it, it's steep. Walk across the open area towards it and enter the forest. Get ready for some switchbacks – there's plenty coming up. Thankfully, this is all in the forest so there's ample shade. You'll see painted red dots on various stones and trees – that's your route, but the switchbacks are generally obvious. It seems whenever there's even a slight doubt about where to go, a red dot pops up. Make sure to look back at the valley and mountains in the distance when there are openings in the canopy. This is a good place for some water and to catch your breath.

When you come to an intersection, there will be a small wooden shelter and some hiking trail signs. The one for the Kofel says 20 minutes and also "Geübte," meaning it's for the experienced hiker. It begins on rockier terrain and eventually comes to even steeper rocks. There are cables and handholds affixed to these sections. Take your time and be careful, always letting others who are quicker and perhaps more experienced, pass. There are some nice views before you reach the top so take time to enjoy them. If you haven't done anything like this and feel overwhelmed, you can turn back at any time. Always remember, you will have to come back the way you came. When you get to the top, enjoy a wonderful 360 degree panorama of peaks and Oberammergau below. Yup, that's the church you just left way down below. If you look hard, you can see the brewery, too. Don't get too excited, you have some work to do before having that beer.

After enjoying a much-deserved break on top and hopefully a snack to replenish your energy, it's time to head down. Take your time going down, always placing your feet carefully. Once back at the intersection, pat yourself on the back and follow the route towards the Kolbensattelhütte. It's about an hour away and compared to what you've just done, fairly flat. It's mostly a forest route. You will occasionally pass a ravine or area where the trail is washed out so be careful crossing those. A little after the 6 kilometer mark, you'll come to a small intersection. Our route goes to the Kolbensattelhütte but if you're tired or there's bad weather, you could take the shorter route back to Oberammergau via the Kolbenalm. The longer walk to the hut only climbs a bit initially and is mostly flat. The hut is more of a large log cabin-type restaurant but if you're hungry or thirsty, it will do the trick and offers amazing views of the Kofel from yet another perspective. From there, it's all downhill back to Oberammergau. It's exposed to the sun and you'll be glad you're not walking up this way. Those doing just that will surely envy you, so try not to look too smug. You'll pass the Kolbenalm en route and could easily continue on Kofelauweg until it runs into König-Ludwig-Straße, but this route describes a slightly longer way back.

After descending from the Kolbenalm, you'll be in a lovely meadow with great views of the Kofel to your right. Look for a sign (often obstructed by trees) for the Kreuzigungsgruppe (crucifixion group). It also says Oberammergau is 25 minutes compared to the straight route which is 20 minutes. The shorter route is even shorter if you're going directly to the brewery, but this detour is worthwhile if you can wait. It heads blissfully into a nice, shady patch before coming to a large stone crucifix, a generous present from King Ludwig II, who was so moved by his viewing of the Passion Play that he felt compelled to make this donation.

From the Kreuzigungsgruppe, head down the stairs, through another patch of forest and you'll soon be on König-Ludwig-Straße. Again, you could continue straight on to town on this street and more directly to Maxbräu but you can also go left onto a small path. It's a more scenic way back to the train station and also a nice way back to the brewery. There are signs for the Bahnhof (train station) and Ortskern (town center). It goes through some more forest with a cute forest kinder-garten along the route. You will pop out in a lovely residential area before making your way back to the Ammer River. When you get to the river, go right and walk along the path as it mirrors the river. Follow it back to König-Ludwig-Straße and take a left there, crossing the same bridge you used at the beginning of the hike. Continue on to Ettaler Straße and then left to Maxbräu. Time for a tasty Kellerbier!

AMMERGAUER MAXBRÄU & HOTEL MAXIMILIAN

Ammergauer Maxbräu is part of an upmarket spa hotel set among many Lüftlmalerei buildings with a majestic view of the Kofel. In fact, the logo for the brewery is this perspective of the iconic peak. What could be more appropriate than sipping a brew while looking at the mountain you've just climbed? It's a new age brewpub, dating back to only 2007, but they are innovative while remaining in a traditional framework. They have an eclectic menu with touches of fusion as well as more typical Bavarian standards. In addition to the modern brewpub with shiny copper kettles on display, there is a fine-dining restaurant called Benedikt's, also connected to the hotel. Though there's only one regular house brew, it uses three types of malt as well as aroma hops and, atypically, it is top-fermented. In addition to it, there is a rotating specialty beer. In summer, it's a Weißbier.

Beers on tap: Ammergauer Maxbräu Naturtrübes Kellerbier plus one seasonal.

PRACTICAL INFORMATION

Ammergauer Maxbräu & Hotel Maximilian
Ettaler Straße 5
82487 Oberammergau
+49 8822 948740
www.maximilian-oberammergau.de

Open Wednesday to Sunday 11:00 am
Closed Monday & Tuesday

Rooms can be booked on their website which is also available in English.

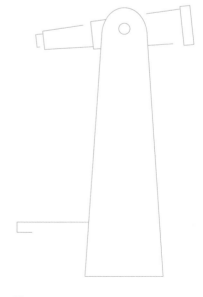

OBERAMMERGAU TO ETTAL

A SCENIC WALK BETWEEN TWO BREWERIES

UPPER BAVARIA

▷··· STARTING POINT	···✕ DESTINATION
AMMERGAUER MAXBRÄU, OBERAMMERGAU	**KLOSTER ETTAL, ETTAL**
🍺 BEER	🎲 DIFFICULTY
ETTALER DUNKEL	**WALK** 🚶
⛰ MAP	
ATK25-R09	🕐 DURATION OF THE HIKE
	5.5 KM **1.5–2H**
GARMISCH-PARTENKIRCHEN	
🔍 HIGHLIGHTS	〰 ELEVATION GAIN
ETTAL MONASTERY, KOFEL, LÜFTLMALEREI, ETTAL DAIRY	ASCENT: 155 M DESCENT: 120 M

 DUNKLES

 CHESTNUT,
OFF-WHITE
ROCKY HEAD

 ROAST MALT,
HINT OF DARK CHOCO-
LATE

 ROAST, MALT, DARK
CHOCOLATE,
BITTERSWEET FINISH

BITTERNESS   SWEETNESS

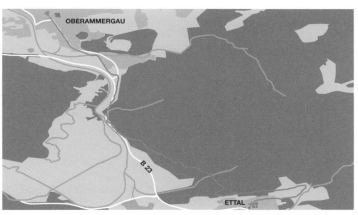

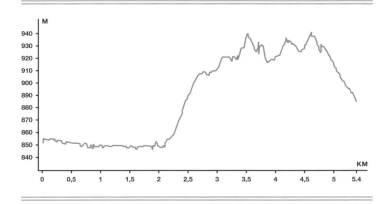

DESCRIPTION OF THE ROUTE

Kloster Ettal (Ettal Monastery) may not be quite as big an attraction as the Neuschwanstein Castle or Germany's highest mountain, the Zugspitze, but its relative proximity to those two tourist mainstays ensures plenty of visitors. To be fair, its stunning setting and architecture would be sufficient to lure its share of passing travelers even if it weren't for its strategic position. The Benedictine monastery dates back to 1330 though the Baroque expansion and eventual masterpiece is a product of the 1700s. The church interior is a marvel and awestruck tourists are a common sight. As is the case with most Bavarian monasteries, there is brewing in its history and thankfully, it's not only still going on but is actually being carried out by the monks themselves.

 Though most visitors arrive by bus or car, there is no more dramatic way to arrive than on foot, via the route described. If you are in Oberammergau, it makes a great excursion but it can be done as a day trip from Munich, as well. Oberammergau is serviced by frequent trains from Murnau and Oberau, both of which are on the popular line between Munich and Garmisch-Partenkirchen.

Make your way to the town center and Ammergauer Maxbräu to begin your hike. If staying there, you can sleep in or get a spa treatment before or after this route. Exiting Maxbräu, go left on Ettaler Straße and follow it all the way out of town. Though you'll be on the street, you'll pass many beautiful examples of the Lüftlmalerei the town is noted for. As the road veers to your left, you'll see a smaller foot path going straight, past a mini-golf course. It's the Fußweg nach Ettal (footpath to Ettal). You'll walk behind a small neighborhood with simple homes that have great views. Take a look to your right and you'll be treated to views of the town's iconic peak, the Kofel. The path veers left as it reaches Ettaler Straße. Cross Ettaler Straße carefully and on the other side, look for the path going right. There will be signs for "Ettal über Vogelherdweg". The route is parallel to the busy street but there are fantastic views of the Kofel nearly the whole way. At times, obstructions on the trail or rocky sections will force you closer to the street, but this section is less than a kilometer so persevere. Often you are in a car and wish you could get out and take a photo of a mountain but can't find a place to pull over. Well, now you are in position to take those photos! Soon after passing a small shrine built into a large rock, you will head into the forest for good, leaving the cars and street behind. As you gain some elevation, look back for a different perspective of the Kofel.

The trail flattens out and becomes wider when you see signs heralding Ettal being a mere 40 minutes away, but of course, there is more than one way to reach it, so don't get your hopes up just yet. When you come to a signed fork, take the right side that says Ettal is 25 minutes away, rather than the longer and obviously uphill route. At the next fork, take the left side towards Ettal, not Ettaler Mühle. The path rises up and you will cross a couple of small bridges. There are also educational write-ups on the types of trees in the forest as well as a Goethe quote at one point. These are all in German but the tree information has photos to help you identify the types of trees none-theless. The trail descends to a T and you will want to go left even though it's the longer route to Ettal: the Höhenweg. The one to the right may be shorter to the village but not to the monastery. More importantly, you'd miss the best part of the entire trail. At around the 4 kilometer mark, you will arrive to stunning views of the monastery to your right. Looking slightly down at the magnificent complex with the mountains as a backdrop is surely what makes the entrance to Ettal so special. Once past the monastery, you veer slightly away from it and uphill a bit, too. It seems like a cruel joke if you're tired or hot but once you come to the next intersection, you go right to find a Kneip-panlage on your right-hand side. This is the perfect relief you may need right now. Filled with cold water from a flowing spring, it's a man-made pool with a small railing. You can walk around the pool, lifting your feet out of the water as you go. It's a bit painful the first time around, but after you come out of the pool, your legs (and feet!) will feel a lot better. There's a bench to relax on — the views from this particular one are about as good as I've found. After you warm up, go around again if you like. Bring sandals as you won't want to put your boots back on!

From there, head down through the farmland surrounding the monastery. You can't really go wrong but keep your eyes out to your right for a sign for "Ortskern über Kloster" for the most direct path. You'll be entering the monastic complex before you know it. There's lots to see and do. Obviously, the basilica is the main attraction, but you can also tour the brewery and distillery if you time things right. There's a shop selling the various wares from the monks and a dairy where you can buy their cheese. We met a monk walking into the complex and he said the butter is out of this world. Ok, he didn't say that, but he said it's really amazing. With so much to do, you might want to have some lunch and of course, you will be ready for a beer by now! There's no cavernous beer hall on hand like at some other monastic breweries, but just across the road is the Ludwig der Bayer Bräustüberl, conveniently attached to the Klosterhotel Ludwig der Bayer.

Photo by Doreen Carbonara

KLOSTERHOTEL & BRÄUSTÜBERL LUDWIG DER BAYER

With its scenic setting, an onsite spa and a host of hiking possibilities in its vicinity, the Klosterhotel Ludwig der Bayer is a great place to spend a few days. There are various dining rooms but it's tough to top the rustic traditional Bräustüberl, or if the weather is fine, their atmospheric Biergarten which offers views of the monastery. With a menu full of typical Bavarian fare and beer flowing from the Ettal Klosterbrauerei, it's the perfect place to end your hike. With 400 years of uninterrupted brewing, the Ettaler Klosterbrauerei was founded in 1609 and brews a small but very traditional selection including a Dunkler Doppelbock called Curator and a Heller Bock.

Beers on tap: Ettaler Kloster Dunkel, Ettaler Edel Hell, Benediktiner Weißbier. Bottled Ettaler Kloster Curator.

PRACTICAL INFORMATION

Klosterhotel & Bräustüberl Ludwig der Bayer
Kaiser-Ludwig-Platz 10-12
82488 Ettal
+49 8822-9150
www.ludwig-der-bayer.de

Open daily 9:00 am to 9:30 pm

Rooms can be booked on their website which is also available in English.

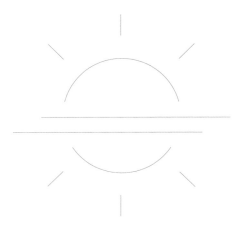

ANDECHS
(HERRSCHING AM AMMERSEE)

FASTING IS FUN AS LONG AS THERE'S LIQUID BREAD

UPPER BAVARIA

▷··· STARTING POINT	···✗ DESTINATION
HERRSCHING S-BAHN STATION	**ANDECHS BRÄUSTÜBERL**
🍺 BEER	🀫 DIFFICULTY
ANDECHSER DOPPELBOCK DUNKEL	**HIKE** 🚶
⛰ MAP	
ATK25-010 **STARNBERG**	⏱ DURATION OF THE HIKE
	5 KM **1H (ONE-WAY)**
🔎 HIGHLIGHTS	〰 ELEVATION GAIN
ANDECHS MONASTERY, MOUNTAIN SCENERY	ASCENT: 200 M DESCENT: 6 M

 DOPPELBOCK

 DEEP MAHOGANY,
MASSIVE TAN HEAD

 ROAST MALT,
CARAMEL

 FULL, RICH MALT, ROAST,
DARK CHOCOLATE,
UNDERLYING HOPS

BITTERNESS   SWEETNESS

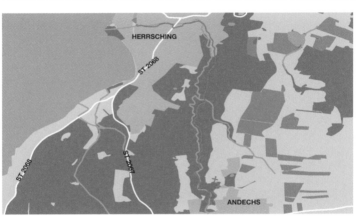

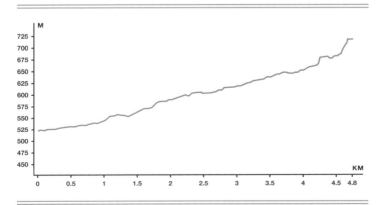

DESCRIPTION OF THE ROUTE

Kloster Andechs (Andechs Monastery) has been drawing pilgrims for close to a thousand years. As of late, however, they are more likely to be on a beer pilgrimage! This place is no secret to those living in the Munich area, so on nice weather weekends it can get quite crowded. If you can, plan an early weekday visit and you'll be sure to enjoy it more.

The S-Bahn runs from Munich to Herrsching am Ammersee every 20 minutes. There is a bus that goes from the station to Kloster Andechs and back. Obviously you would miss the beautiful hike by taking it but it can come in handy if you are too tired to walk back to the station.

Coming out of the train station, you'll see the Tourist Information Office. Please note that it's closed on weekends (another good reason to go during the week). Facing the Tourist Office, walk right and then turn left on Fischergasse which becomes Kienbachstraße. Turn right onto the busy Mühlfelder Straße and then a quick left onto Abert-straße. Follow Abertstraße for a short while as it meanders left and then go right on Andechsstraße. As you cross Steindlgasse/Schön-bichlstraße, take note of the pretty Church of St. Martin with the golden statue Mariensäule. You will start to see signs for Jakobsweg (Way of St. James), depicted by a golden scallop on a dark blue background. This is the Pilgerweg (pilgrim's way) to Andechs. Continue on the same street, to the left of the statue, and bear right when it splits on Andechsstraße. The road quickly splits again, but this time, take the left fork: Kientalstraße. It's more or less straight from here, with intermittent Jakobsweg signs prodding you on. At this point it would be unusual not to see another pilgrim, going in either direction. You will pass through a very nice neighborhood, likely wishing you lived there, and that's before you even get to the monastery to sample their fine beer!

Before you know it, you will be in a nice forest on a path that runs along the Kienbach River, which you will cross a few times on small bridges. You'll start to gain some elevation and as you near your destination, you'll have a few options to reach the monastery. Personally, I like going all the way to the opening of the forest and then turning left at the large set of wooden stairs. This has the advantage of bringing you beyond the church and you can get some nice photos from this vantage point. At the top of the stairs, go to your left and enjoy the views. The other route is also nice, if a bit more crowded, but it brings you directly to the church's doorstep with a more dramatic entrance. You also have the option of stopping off at a large crucifix with an incredible view of the countryside, and on clear days, the Alps in the distance.

Even if it weren't for the great beer brewed here, it would still be worth peeking into the large church that dominates the complex for its rich Baroque interior. The only decision is whether to do it before or after having that beer you've just earned!

ANDECHSER BRÄUSTÜBERL

While you can certainly find Andechser beer in many spots around southern Bavaria, there's surely no more atmospheric place to enjoy one than at the sprawling Bräustüberl. The often boisterous interior imbibing area of the brewery, with its amazing vaulted ceiling, is one place where drinking a liter mug of the potent Doppelbock doesn't seem decadent. This beer was first brewed by the monks to get them through Lent when they were fasting and was hence dubbed "liquid bread." If you noticed a strong smell of pork when you got up the hill, you'll see the rightly popular and delicious pork knuckle on display – a perfect accompaniment to the hearty dark brew. For those looking for something lighter, try the Obazda, a tasty cheese spread that goes well with their large home-baked pretzels.

You can return via a number of routes but most have less shade than the route you walked up. Or, if you have the time and means, why not spend the night and enjoy the surroundings at a more relaxed pace after the day trippers have gone back down the hill?

PRACTICAL INFORMATION

Andechser Bräustüberl
Bergstraße 2
82346 Andechs
+49 8152 376-261
www.andechs.de

Open daily 10:00 am to 8:00 pm

A place to spend the evening:

Bernhardhof Andechs
Andechser Str. 32
82346 Andechs
+49 170 4411222
www.bernhardhof.de

SCHEYERN
(PFAFFENHOFEN A. D. ILM)

WALKING IN THE FOOTSTEPS OF THE PILGRIMS TO THE HOLY BEER

UPPER BAVARIA

▷··· STARTING POINT	···✕ DESTINATION
PFAFFENHOFEN (ILM) TRAIN STATION	**KLOSTER SCHEYERN, SCHEYERN**

🍺 BEER	🔢 DIFFICULTY
SCHEYERN KLOSTERBIER-DUNKEL	

⛰ MAP	**HIKE** 🥾
ATK25 L11	⏱ DURATION OF THE HIKE
PFAFFENHOFEN A.D.I	**13 KM / 3-4H (ONE-WAY, WITH A BUS TO GET BACK)**

🔍 HIGHLIGHTS	〜 ELEVATION GAIN
SCHEYERN ABBEY, KLOSTER SCHEYERN BASILIKA, KLOSTERBRAUEREI SCHEYERN (THE THIRD OLDEST BREWERY IN GERMANY)	ASCENT: 210 M DESCENT: 160 M

5.5% ALCOHOL CONTENT

DUNKLES MADE WITH LOCAL DARK MALTS AND THEIR OWN ARTESIAN WATER SOURCE

CHESTNUT, ROCKY TAN HEAD

SLIGHT CHOCOLATE

RICH MALT, CHOCOLATE, UNDERLYING HOPS, BITTERSWEET FINISH

BITTERNESS

SWEETNESS

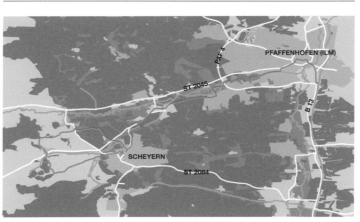

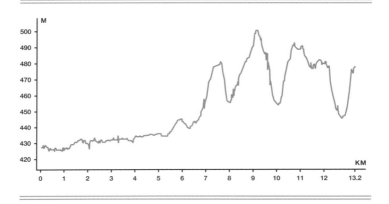

DESCRIPTION OF THE ROUTE

The area where Kloster Scheyern now stands is where the famed Wittelsbach family has its roots. They gifted their castle to the Benedictine monks of Petersberg when they moved in 1119, the accepted founding date of the monastery. As with most Bavarian monasteries, it endured much destruction during the Thirty Years' War followed by the secularization of the early 1800s. Unsurprisingly, King Ludwig I restored the monastery as he had numerous others and it has been a Benedictine abbey since 1843. The grounds were renovated in the Romanesque style some years later and are well-kept to this day. Its real claim to fame, however, is being the home to the Scheyrer Cross, an ancient relic of great religious importance that's drawn pilgrims to Scheyern since 1180. The hike described starts with a section of Jakobsweg (Way of St. James), so you'll be walking in the pilgrims' footsteps – whether to see the Holy Cross or drink the monastic brews. The second and more scenic part is a circuit that gets you out into the rural countryside with views of the monastery from nice vantage points. It also gets you close to some of the hops fields the region is noted for. There are a few other trails in the area, so a night spent in Scheyern would be a nice way to see more of this pretty region.

Pfaffenhofen (Ilm) is serviced by frequent trains from Munich and the trip takes around half an hour. If you'd like to bypass the walk out to the monastery, there is regular but limited bus service from Pfaffenhofen (Ilm) to Kloster Scheyern during the week but not on weekends. Buses back are equally limited so plan your trip to start early, especially if doing the full walk and not spending the night in Scheyern. So, if planning on using the bus, even if only for the return trip, you need to do it during the week. Going by car is another option and it's an easy drive from Munich.

Coming out of the station in Pfaffenhofen (Ilm), look for signs to the center. Go right on either Bahnhofstraße or Münchener Straße. Either way, you'll be on the latter as it winds left into town. You'll come to a circle framed by Schulstraße and Stadtgraben. You'll walk through it to remain on Münchener Straße. This soon brings you to the Hauptplatz, a large pretty square. The Old Town Hall is here but across the way as you enter is the Hotel Müllerbräu, perhaps the most colorful building on the square. Go left and walk through the long square and you'll start to see signs for the Jakobsweg – a blue background with a yellow scallop shell on it. At the end of the square, you'll see the pretty pink Spital Church of the Holy Ghost with its distinctive dome on your right. Go left here, on the conveniently named Scheyerer Straße. Follow this to a circle and continue straight on it. There are Jakobsweg signs to guide you plus bike signs for the Hopfentour, a bike route through the hops region. Keep an eye to the left for Niederscheyerer Straße before the 2 kilometer mark. Go left there. You've been on asphalt so far but now look for an unpaved path on your right, well-marked. Take that right. You'll walk through a green area with a playing field on your right before crossing Adolf-Rebl-Straße. Now you'll be in a pleasant city park and your route follows the Gerolsbach, a small brook. Continue on it, crossing Schrobenhausener Straße just after the 3 kilometer mark. You may see some sheep on your right-hand side just after the crossing and before a fork, where you'll take the well-marked right side. When you come to the T at Zur Mühle, go left. This leads you back to Niederscheyerer Straße, where you'll take a right. Follow this out of the town of Niederscheyern and towards a smaller village. Walk through it and go left on Scheyerer Straße. As you walk along it, you'll start to see some hops fields on your right. At about the 6 kilometer mark, go left onto a smaller road. Bike signs say Kloster Scheyern is 1.1 kilometers away. This crosses a brook and you'll wind right around a pond. At the end of the pond, go left onto the path that mirrors Scheyerer Straße. Take this to the Kloster, visible to your right. Walk through the archway and into the courtyard to behold the abbey. The basilica is across it, to your right. It's well worth having a look at it and the Scheyrer Cross before or after your beer.

Continue across the courtyard to another archway and on the other side you'll see the actual brewery. To your left is the Klosterschenke Scheyern, where a fine beer and meal await you, but you'll have to make your own decision as to when. If you plan on doing a day trip and are hungry, it might be best to have lunch now and then do the Panoramaweg afterwards. The buses back to Pfaffenhofen (Ilm) are limited, but during the week, it's possible to catch one in the afternoon after the 6 kilometer circuit hike and a beer with lunch. Know your bus times before heading out. If you're planning on spending the night, drop off your gear and enjoy the place at your leisure.

When you're ready for the Panoramaweg, walk across the busy street from the Klosterschenke, looking for hiking signs with a green dot saying Panoramaweg and the street called Schöneck. Follow it to a fork, take the right side. It's a flat forested path that brings you down to a large pond. Walk along the right side of it, following the green dot signs. There's the historic Klostergut Prielhof, where art exhibitions and markets are regularly held, and just past that the Kloster Scheyern farm area with some goats. This is about 8 kilometers from the Pfaffenhofen (Ilm) station. Continue straight on the country road and look for a small turnoff on your right. It's got the green dot and a street sign saying Station Kometen (part of the "Planetenweg Scheyern", a planetary path). Follow this uphill and take a marked right at just under the 9 kilometer mark. You'll have good views of Kloster Scheyern to your right from here. There are some hops fields straight on to the right, also. You go into a forested section briefly as you drop back down to the street. Once you pop out, you'll veer left and come to a large, busier road. Carefully cross it and go right, followed by a relatively quick left. Follow this a short time and take your first right to walk through a very small village as it bends left. At about the 10 kilometer mark, you'll be back out in the open countryside with fine views of the monastery on your right. You'll take a well-marked right and start your journey back. After you cross another larger road, the path goes back uphill. Then, just before the 12 kilometer mark, go right, towards the monastery. This is a farm track but soon becomes the asphalt Hohlweg. As you follow this to the main road, there is a gorgeous hops field to your immediate left. If it's early August, you won't be able to miss it. If it's early in the season or after the harvest, it will just look like some empty poles. At the intersection, carefully cross the street and continue on Hohlweg, past a pond on your right. This goes uphill past some houses and then a cemetery with a small chapel on your left, just before you reach the Scheyerer Straße. Take a right there and you'll be back at Kloster Scheyern in no time.

KLOSTERSCHENKE SCHEYERN

The Klosterschenke is a sprawling series of rooms fitted out for various functions. The Bräustüberl common area is tastefully traditional with vaulted ceilings befittingly adorned with hops. It's a great place for a hot roast meal perfectly suited to their renowned dark beer. If the weather is fine, the Biergarten is as perfect a place to finish a hike as you'll find. Meals are typical Bavarian fare with high-end touches at countryside prices. There's even a healthy option thrown in for good measure. Servers are decked out in Lederhosen and Dirndls – not for show but to reflect the mission statement of the establishment. Another plus is good value rooms on site.

The Klosterbrauerei Scheyern was founded in 1119 when the monks arrived, making it the third oldest brewery in Germany. It unfortunately took a long break, having Hasen-Bräu in Augsburg brew their wares until 2006. The beers you see in stores are still contract brewed by them, but after refurbishing the dilapidated old brewery, they now brew all the beer that is served on the premises, as well as the bottled beer from their own shop. I've had both and there is a difference between them, and while I'll not say which is better, I will say there is no better place to enjoy them than right here. After the hike, I think you'll agree!

Beers on tap: Klosterbier-Hell, Klosterbier-Hell naturtrüb (unfiltered, more a Kellerbier), Klosterbier-Dunkel and Kloster-Weißbier. Seasonal dark and light Bocks. Bottled: Dunkel, Weißbier and Pils.

PRACTICAL INFORMATION

Klosterschenke Scheyern & Schyrenhof Hotel
Schyrenplatz 1
85298 Scheyern
+49 8441 27890
klosterschenke-scheyern.de

Open daily 10:00 am to 11:00 pm

Rooms can be booked on their website.
While the whole site isn't available in English,
the booking part is.

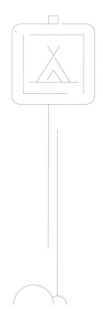

SCHWABIA

IRSEE
(KAUFBEUREN)

WHERE THE THIRSTY PILGRIM IS JUSTLY REWARDED

SCHWABIA

▷··· STARTING POINT	···✕ DESTINATION
KAUFBEUREN TRAIN STATION	**KLOSTER IRSEE**

🍺 BEER	DIFFICULTY
IRSEER KLOSTER-URTRUNK	**HIKE** 🚶

⛰ MAP	
ATK25-P07	⏱ DURATION OF THE HIKE
KAUFBEUREN	**7.5 KM** **2–2.5H (ONE-WAY)**

🔍 HIGHLIGHTS	〰 ELEVATION GAIN
IRSEE MONASTERY, CHURCH OF PETER & PAUL, KAUFBEUREN OLD TOWN HALL, ALPS	ASCENT: 215 M DESCENT: 175 M

5.4%
ALCOHOL CONTENT

KELLERBIER,
HALLERTAU HOPS,
STORED 80 DAYS

LIGHT AMBER,
UNFILTERED

LIGHT HOP,
VANILLA,
FRUIT

FRUITY,
LONG, DRY,
BITTER FINISH

BITTERNESS   SWEETNESS

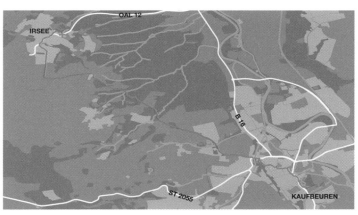

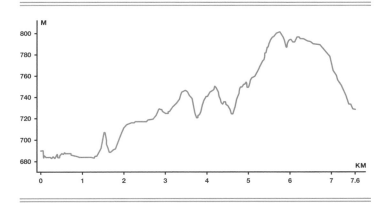

DESCRIPTION OF THE ROUTE

 Kloster Irsee is a former Benedictine monastery set scenically in the foothills of the Allgäuer Alpen. Though not as well-known as the Alps clustered around the Zugspitze, Germany's highest peak, they are nonetheless a sight to behold as you make your pilgrimage to the former home of brewing monks. Fear not, a very capable group of secular brewers are still making their beer according to the age-old recipes, evidently it's a bit of a secret as no information about such is available on the website.

Speaking of pilgrimages, you will be predominately on the Crescentia-Pilgerweg (pilgrim's way) on your trek to quench your thirst. This is an 86 kilometer route that passes Ottobeuren and Markt Rettenbach – but don't worry, you won't be walking that far today. The yellowish signs feature the bust of a nun and are easy to follow.

Trains from Munich to Kaufbeuren are frequent and take about an hour.

Coming out of the Kaufbeuren train station, you will see a small city park across the street. Cross the street and either walk through the left side of the park or go left on the Bahnhofstraße and make a quick right onto Ganghoferstraße. You'll wind up on this busy street no matter your initial choice. Follow Ganghoferstraße as it bears to the left before coming to a memorial to local soldiers in the form of a statue of a man with a sword. Here, you'll turn left on Schraderstraße. You will then take another very quick right on Ringweg, a narrower street in the heart of the Old Town. After about 150 meters, you'll come to the Old Town Hall with its pretty pink facade. Go left onto Kaiser-Max-Straße and continue towards a large church and a fountain of Neptune. At this point, bear to the right but take the left fork into the Salzmarkt. These turns are marked with bike path signs to Irsee.

The street winds a bit but stay on Salzmarkt which turns into Schmiedgasse. Follow this for 140 meters until you come to a fountain commemorating the town's annual dance festival. The former brewery, Gasthof Rose, is here on the corner too. Turn left into the Obstmarkt and take note of the Crescentia Kloster. Go right onto Unter dem Berg and then a quick left to Blasiusberg. This is where you will start to see the Pilgerweg signs. Climb the steep cobblestone path up to the St. Blasius Church for nice views over Kaufbeuren. Walk around the church to the right and drop down from the hill to Schießstattweg and turn right. This part of the trip is well-marked with Pilgerweg signs. Turn left on Kemptenerstraße. A roundabout comes up quite quickly, go around it and continue on Kemnaterstraße to the next roundabout. Go through this one too and take notice of the small lake on the left.

Stay on the left side of the road. The street gets a bit steeper here and there is a pleasant walking/cycling path to follow, all well-marked. There is a horse farm to the left, and on a clear day you will get nice views of the Alps from here.

Just before the town of Ölmühlhang, the Pilgerweg signs will direct you to cross Kemnaterstraße. There is a small monument to Heilige Crescentia, a local nun who lived in the Crescentia Monastery and was declared a saint in 2001. Crescentia-Pilgerweg is the full name of the trail. You're now on a nice, small path through a mostly pine forest, crossing streams over wooden bridges and popping out into open meadows intermittently. About half-way through, you will pass a small picnic table – good for if you need a break. Soon after, you will come to the small village of Bickenried with a somewhat odd modern crucifix and a more comforting statue of St. Francis of Assisi, the saint who spoke to birds. After the village, you'll walk across a large open area with views of the Alps to your left. Enjoy the stroll until you come to a sign heralding Irsee Ort (center) being to your right in 15 minutes. Once in the small town, it's a nice walk down Hochstraße through a pretty neighborhood. This main street veers to the left before splitting into Oberes Dorf. Take the left fork and pass by St. Stephan's Church and cemetery on your right, after which you will come to Marktstraße. Turn right and continue on to the Klosterring with great views of the Church of Peter and Paul, worth popping into for its pretty Baroque interior, ornate organ and unique pulpit.

Signs abound for the complex's various sights, but by now, the sight you're bound to be looking for is the Irseer Klosterbräu. It's time for a well-earned Bavarian meal washed down with their renowned Irseer Kloster-Urtrunk.

IRSEER KLOSTERBRÄU BRAUGASTHOF & RESTAURANT

Kloster Irsee has a long and storied past dating back to the Middle Ages but was secularized in the early 1800s. Its use as a mental institution in the 19th and early 20th century is arguably its darkest period. The complex is now a conference center but the past is easily invoked when walking around the grounds. There's also a brewery museum on the premises. The Klosterbräu Restaurant has old-world charm and is a popular destination for non-hikers too, who come for hearty Bavarian fare and the brewery's renowned beer. Open fermentation tanks are still utilized, whereby the beer is not only open to the elements but also under less pressure, thus slowing down the fermentation process. Most brewers feel this allows for a fuller fermentation and more characterful beer. Their beers are stored for a minimum of 80 days, with their Starkbier matured for 180. This is quite long, not to mention costly, and undoubtedly adds to the beer's well-rounded flavors. Noted British beer writer Graham Lees of CAMRA (Campaign for Real Ale) proclaimed their Kloster-Urtrunk one of only a handful of four-star beers in his *Good Beer Guide to Munich and Bavaria*, which was the reason for my first visit in 1997. I've had the beer quite a few times over the years in bottled form and always imagined I'd inflated the beer's status in my mind. Upon returning and having it on tap once again, I can safely say, it is one very fine brew and definitely hoppier than the non-tap version.

The Klosterbräu Hotel is a great place to spend the night and there are numerous hiking trails in the area to explore. If you want to head back the same day, check bus schedules prior to the trip as there is limited service between Irsee and Kaufbeuren. It's a short distance, so a taxi is also an option. Of course, you could return the way you came, on the Pilgerweg. That walk back might be more enjoyable after a night in the comfy onsite hotel. Oh, did I mention they have a sauna with a vaulted ceiling?

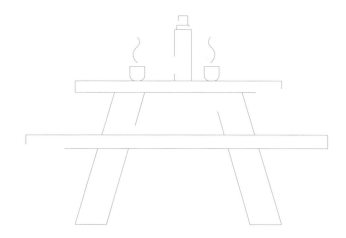

PRACTICAL INFORMATION

Irseer Klosterbräu Braugasthof & Restaurant
Klosterring 1–3
Irsee 87660
+ 49 8341-43 22 00
ikb@irsee.com
www.irsee.com

Open daily 10:00 am to 11:00 pm

Rooms can be booked on the website
which is also available in English.

NESSELWANG

A WALK UP TO MARIA TROST

SCHWABIA

▷··· STARTING POINT	···✕ DESTINATION
BRAUEREI-GASTHOF HOTEL POST, NESSELWANG	**BRAUEREI-GASTHOF HOTEL POST, NESSELWANG**
🍺 BEER	🔢 DIFFICULTY
NESSELWANGER WEIZEN	**HIKE** 🚶
⛰ MAP	
ATK25-Q07	🕐 DURATION OF THE HIKE
MARKTOBERDORF	**6 KM 2-3H**
🔍 HIGHLIGHTS	〰 ELEVATION GAIN
MARIA TROST CHURCH, ALPS, ST. ANDREAS CHURCH, THE OLD TOWN HALL OF NESSELWANG	ASCENT: 358 M DESCENT: 368 M

 WEIßBIER

 UNFILTERED AMBER

 BANANA,
CLOVE,
YEAST

 FRUITY, BANANA, CLOVE,
YEAST, SOUR, BITTER-
SWEET FINISH

BITTERNESS   SWEETNESS

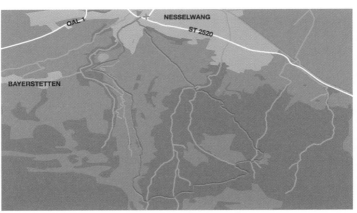

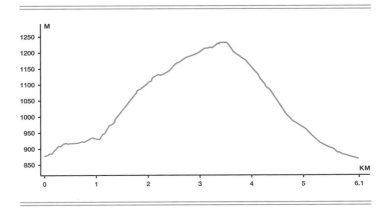

DESCRIPTION OF THE ROUTE

Nesselwang is a cute little market town set in the foothills of the Allgäu Alps, some of the most majestic mountains in all of Bavaria. It's not all that far from popular tourist attractions like the Neuschwanstein Castle, so it could serve as a base to explore those areas, especially if you have a car and want to enjoy the brewery at a more leisurely pace. Maria Trost Church is a popular outing from town. Located at 1,123 meters, it can only be reached on foot.

Nesselwang is serviced by frequent trains to Kempten (Allgäu), which is well-connected to Munich and Ulm.

Coming out of the Brauerei-Gasthof Hotel Post, look across the street at the St. Andreas Church. It's worth a quick visit to check out its lovely Baroque interior, or keep it in mind for when you return from your hike. Go left on Hauptstraße and almost immediately turn left again on An der Riese. There's another quick left on Maria-Trost-Allee. You'll start to see trail signs and Maria Trost's hiking time of 45 minutes. Follow this street and take note of the red brick brewing chimney to your left before heading out of town and up. You'll follow the well-marked signs to the right at a small chapel as you continue on Maria-Trost-Allee. It's a nice, open area and you gain elevation gently. The route is lined with trees on both sides. Look back occasionally for nice views of Nesselwang and the St. Andreas Church. Straight on are the hills you're about to head up on. It's a pleasant stroll and you'll pass a hotel on your right before reaching the forest at about 1 kilometer. Maria Trost is only 30 minutes away at this point, so the trail will start to climb more steeply and the shade of the trees will be most welcome. At about 2 kilometers, you are out in the open and the church is a nice sight to behold. It's worth a peek inside before continuing on.

Once out of the church, walk past it and veer to your right on the wide path. Follow the red-striped signs for Nesselwang and the Alpspitzbahn parking area. It's a mix of forest and open areas. I did it in early spring and there was quite a bit of snow the whole way. When you emerge out into a more open area and see the cables for the Alpspitzbahn, you're going to head right, back towards Nesselwang and the Alpspitzbahn. Don't go left to the Alpspitze unless you're planning on a longer hike than the one described here. When you get to the Alpspitzbahn station, take the right fork to continue downhill towards town. If the station is open and running, you can take it to the top of the Alpspitze if you like. The Alpspitzweg goes nearly all the way back to town, meandering a bit but mostly sticking close to the ski lifts that run along it. When you get to the bottom, you'll go left on An der Riese and follow it back to the brewery for one of the region's tastiest Weißbiers.

BRAUEREI-GASTHOF HOTEL POST

Founded in 1650 and in the Meyer family since 1883, the Brauerei-Gasthof Hotel Post is very much a hotel and restaurant as well as a brewery. Though they brew a large selection of traditional beers, they have started delving into the craft beer. The latest generation features a female brewer/beer sommelier who pairs their various beers with the restaurant's traditional meals. The cozy interior features a wooden ceiling and a green tile oven. The outside seating area is set between the pub and the brewery itself. In this region noted for Weißbier, this is a refreshingly tangy one, perfect for an after-hike refreshment.

Beers on tap: Nesselwanger Hell, Nesselwanger Gold, Nesselwanger Dunkel, Nesselwanger Weizen and Nesselwanger Bock. Craft beer offerings are generally in bottles and include Hopfen Royal and Braukatz Red Ale.

PRACTICAL INFORMATION

Brauerei-Gasthof Hotel Post
Hauptstraße 25
87484 Nesselwang
+49 8361-30910
www.hotel-post-nesselwang.de

Open daily 11:00 am to 10:00 pm

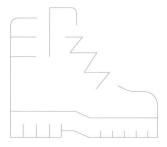

LOWER BAVARIA

WELTENBURG (KELHEIM)

VIEW THE THE OLDEST MONASTIC BREWERY IN THE WORLD FROM THE CLIFFS AND THE WATER

 LOWER BAVARIA

▷··· STARTING POINT	···✕ DESTINATION
WÖHRDPLATZ, KELHEIM	**KLOSTER WELTENBURG**
🍺 BEER	DIFFICULTY
WELTENBURGER KLOSTER ASAM-BOCK	**HIKE** 🚶
⛰ MAP	
ATK25-J12 KELHEIM	🕐 DURATION OF THE HIKE
	5.5 KM / 1.5–2H (ONE-WAY, RETURN BY BOAT)
🔍 HIGHLIGHTS	〰 ELEVATION GAIN
KLOSTER WELTENBURG, CHURCH OF ST. GEORGE, DANUBE CLIFF SCENERY, BEFREIUNGSHALLE, FRANZISKANER CHURCH	ASCENT: 120 M DESCENT: 102 M

6.9%
ALCOHOL
CONTENT

DOPPELBOCK MADE WITH
DARK AND CARAMEL
MALT, AND PERLE HOPS

DARK BROWN,
MAHOGANY HIGHLIGHTS,
DENSE TAN HEAD

DRIED FRUIT,
HINT OF LICORICE

RICH MALT, DRIED FRUIT,
LONG DRY BITTERSWEET
FINISH

BITTERNESS

SWEETNESS

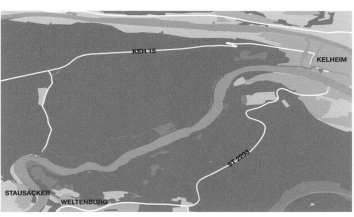

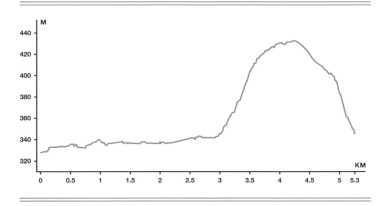

DESCRIPTION OF THE ROUTE

Kloster Weltenburg has a storied past with many ups and downs. Dating back to around 600 AD, it is the oldest of Bavaria's monasteries, and with its breathtakingly scenic location, it understandably draws many visitors, from religious pilgrims to photo-snapping tourists. Arriving by boat, bus, bike and on foot are approximately half a million visitors every year. The monks vacated the monastery at the beginning of the 10th century due to invading nomadic groups. They returned 30 years later only to be plundered during the Reformation in the 1500s. The modern-day version of the monastery was built by the renowned Asam brothers in the 1700s and was extensively renovated after a major flood in 2005. The stunning Baroque Church of St. George is its main draw, featuring a statue of the sainted slayer of dragons behind the main altar, backlit for awe-inspiring effect. Let's not forget nature. The landscape surrounding the monastery is every bit as arresting as the treasures within the monastery, with soaring cliffs, verdant hills and the powerfully flowing Danube right at its door.

Kelheim is serviced by frequent buses from Saal (Donau) station, which has good direct connections to Regensburg and Ingolstadt. Coming from further afield involves a few changes and driving might be a better option.

While arriving at Kloster Weltenburg by boat is admittedly as spectacular a way of doing it as any, the hike there is also gorgeous. If you take the boat back, you will get to see it from the water, too. If you arrive in Kelheim by bus, you should get off at Wöhrdplatz. This is also the stop for the boats that ply the Danube to the monastery. Walk across the parking lot to any of the staircases you'll see from the bus stop. The walkway starts from up there and you will already have great views of the Danube and this bustling area. Once up the stairs, go to your right towards a red-roofed church. This is the Franziskanerkirche (Franciscan Church). High up on the hill is the yellow Befreiungshalle (Hall of Liberation), overlooking Kelheim like a sentry. You'll cross over a small bridge and start to see yellow signs for the Altmühltal-Panoramaweg.

This route is 200 kilometers and goes all the way to Gunzenhausen but that's not your destination today. According to the signs, Kloster Weltenburg is only 6 kilometers away. You're also following the Jakobsweg (a blue sign with a yellow scallop shell) and the Red Triangle route. It is very well marked. Continue along the road until it forks and take the right side up into the very green forest. The trail veers from the water occasionally, possibly due to the water levels. In fact, the last time we did the hike, some of the trail was quite muddy and other parts had some low water on it. It had been raining a lot and the route is right on the powerful Danube. Plan your footwear accordingly. That said, it's a gorgeous, easy trail, offering glimpses of the Danube through the trees and popping out into the open at times to reveal more of the cliffs lining it. At about 2 kilometers, you'll pass a former monastery, now a lovely Biergarten called Klösterl. Stop now if you like, you won't be coming back this way today.

Just before the 3 kilometer mark, follow the signs and turn right; the trail starts to climb gently. You'll soon go left and walk along a beautiful, easy-to-follow route. Whatever turns you have to make are well marked. Between 4 and 5 kilometers, there are some unmarked turnoffs to your left as you make you way to the monastery, some are better than others. My suggestion is to look for other hikers and if there are a few, it's probably worth it. Surely, the ones closer to your destination are well worth taking a peek. From the cliff tops, you can look down at the monastery, sitting on the Danube. At the 5 kilometer mark, you will start to hike down to the Danube. Once down on the road, you'll see signs for the boats. These are not the big ships you've probably seen along the hike ferrying large groups between Kelheim and Kloster Weltenburg. These are small motor boats that bring hikers from this side of the Danube over to the monastery. Hop in and you'll be there in a few minutes. It's interesting to watch the captains navigate the strong currents on the approach. The monastery looks wonderful from the boat. Once on the other side, you're on a stony beach and you can make your way up to all the sights. You should allot a bit of time to explore, but if you're hungry or thirsty and you see an open spot in the Biergarten, I'd suggest grabbing it. This place gets pretty crowded on nice days.

KLOSTERSCHENKE WELTENBURG

Claiming the title of "oldest monastic brewery in the world," the Klosterbrauerei Weltenburg dates back to 1050 and only took a break during a brief period of secularization in the 1800s. Weihenstephan, dating back to 1040, but currently not a monastic brewery disputed their claim, but what's 10 years when you're looking at close to a 1000 years of history? At any rate, it's been brewing for a long time and while it was greatly modernized in 1973 by the Bischofs brewery in Regensburg, their beers remain world-class. Their Barock Dunkel has won numerous awards, and their Asam-Bock is considered a world classic of its style. Bischofs actually brews the Weltenburger beers for commercial distribution. The beers served (and even sold in bottles) at the monastery are designated Weltenburger Kloster beer and are still brewed on site by the monks. I'm not sure if it's the power of suggestion or if they are indeed different, but they sure taste better to me when I'm there!

The Klosterschenke has an old-world feel with lots of dark wood and vaulted ceilings, but if the weather is fine, the leafy Biergarten is where you want to be. If it's a nice weekend afternoon, it will be packed so if you can arrange it, try to go during the week and earlier in the day. No worries, you always seem to find a place, but you'll likely have to squeeze onto a table with others, typical Bavarian style. They serve traditional Bavarian food, with nice roasts and even the tasty cheese made by the monks. Most people drink the award-winning Barock Dunkel but the Asam-Bock on tap can't be missed if you like that style. Be forewarned, it's 6.9% – if you drink a few of them, you'll surely be taking the boat back to Kelheim.

Beers on tap: Weltenburger Kloster Barock Dunkel, Weltenburger Kloster Anno 1050 , Weltenburger Asam-Bock and Weltenburger Kloster Hefe-Weizen.

You could return to Kelheim via the same route you hiked in on, and there are a few trails on this side of the Danube too, but whether you drink the Asam-Bock or not, the ship is the best way to make the journey. The views from the boat are magnificent and really shouldn't be missed.

PRACTICAL INFORMATION

Klosterschenke Weltenburg
Asamstraße 32
93309 Kelheim
+49 9441-67-57-0
www.klosterschenke-weltenburg.de
www.weltenburger.de

Open daily 9:30 am to 7:00 pm (from mid-March to early November)
Closed Monday and Tuesday and open 11:00 am to 5:00 pm, in other months
Closed in January

Best to check their website for current information as dates may vary from year to year.

They also offer rooms, which you can book on their website, if you want to stay longer.

ESSING

HIKING ON THE CLIFFS THE VILLAGE IS SET IN

LOWER BAVARIA

▷··· STARTING POINT	···✗ DESTINATION
BRAUEREIGASTHOF SCHNEIDER, ESSING	**BRAUEREIGASTHOF SCHNEIDER, ESSING**
🍺 BEER	🎲 DIFFICULTY
SCHNEIDER LAGER DUNKEL	**HIKE**
⛰ MAP	
ATK25-J12	🕐 DURATION OF THE HIKE
KELHEIM	**11.5 KM 2.5–3.5H**
🔍 HIGHLIGHTS	〰 ELEVATION GAIN
CLIFF SCENERY, RANDECK CASTLE, DANUBE CANAL, ONE OF THE LONGEST WOODEN BRIDGES IN EUROPE, ST. BARTHOLOMÄ CHAPEL	ASCENT: 334 M DESCENT: 334 M

4.8%
ALCOHOL CONTENT

DUNKLES MADE WITH BOTH DARK BARLEY MALT AND ROASTED MALT

MAHOGANY, OFF-WHITE HEAD

ROAST, CHOCOLATE

RICH MALT, ROAST, CHOCOLATE, BITTERSWEET FINISH

BITTERNESS

SWEETNESS

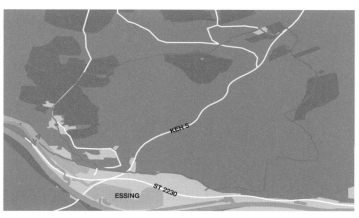

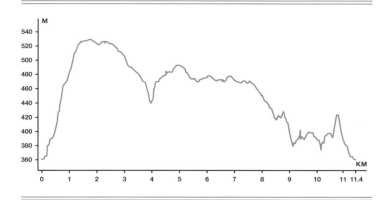

DESCRIPTION OF THE ROUTE

Essing is a picturesque little village set dramatically at the base of a wall of cliffs in the Altmühltal, the pretty valley home to both the Danube Canal and the smaller Ludwig's Canal. The mixture of flowing water, jagged rock formations and numerous caves draws both casual and outdoor-activity-based tourists in great numbers. Boat trips are justifiably popular, but the area is also well-known for both hiking and cycling, much of it in a nature reserve. Though small, this is one of the most beautiful villages in the region, with a much photographed wooden bridge leading to the town's entrance gate.

Essing is serviced by frequent buses from Saal (Donau) station, which has good direct connections to Regensburg and Ingolstadt. Coming from further afield involves a few changes and driving might be a better option.

Starting at the Brauereigasthof Schneider on Altmühlgasse, go right as you exit the brewery. It soon merges with Unterermarkt, the main street in town. At the point where the streets merge, take note of the pretty Parish Church of the Holy Spirit on your right. As you pass the church parking lot, the road will fork, take the Burgweg to the left. There are signs for various hiking trails, and they often overlap on the small network of trails. You will be following Rundweg 2 today, the first portion of which is towards Burg Randeck. The street goes up steeply at first, and if you look back, you'll have a nice view of the church. Not far up the road, be on the lookout for a well-marked dirt track to your left. This path rises gently behind a nice row of homes before ducking into the forest. It goes to the left a bit before coming to a junction with a picnic table. There are signs for the Schulerloch, a cave, pointing to your right and Randeck, the castle to your left. You're headed to the castle but since it's a circuit you'll return via the other side.

The forest path climbs steeply and soon you have some spurs to your left that lead to fantastic views from the cliff tops down to Ludwig's Canal, to the "Tatzelwurm" (one of the longest wooden bridges in Europe), an abundant array of green hills, and the friendly little church you passed not long ago. This is all within the first kilometer – so you'll know that you've ascended the trail pretty fast. When you tire of the views, continue on the trail towards Randeck. There are some teasing views of the castle but most are obstructed by trees. After you pass a restaurant called the Ritterschänke, you can stop in at the castle if you like. If not, the trail continues on asphalt for a bit, starting out in Randeck and heading out of the small village. At this point, the road forks but you should continue straight on the main road. The left fork goes to another castle in Prunn, but that's a hike for another day.

You'll be out in open farmland now and soon you'll start to see the small St. Bartholomä Chapel in the distance to your right. Before you know it, there's a well-marked turn to your right for the chapel. The route you're on passes by the chapel, but it's worth the small turnoff to investigate it more closely if you are so inclined. Even if you don't go all the way to it, there's a scenic little pond with the chapel as its backdrop. If the light is right, it's quite photogenic. The trail veers left and skirts the forest before popping back into it. You'll also start to see signs for the Naturfreundehaus (Friends of Nature house). You'll pass another open area, which is a farm, to your right. You will skirt the forest around this area and then turn left onto a farm road. Continue up this road and carefully cross the larger street at its end. After you cross, you will go back into the forest on a narrow path up to the Naturfreundehaus. Make sure to check out their lovely little Biergarten and celebrate the fact that you are almost half way with a cold beer!

When you're ready, continue along the road the Biergarten is located on until it comes to a larger street. Go right and carefully follow this road as it makes a big bend to the left. The Rundweg 2 signs seem to be missing here, but you're now heading towards the Schulerloch – a popular destination. The route is marked with green rectangle signs. When the big curve ends so does the road – go straight and carefully cross the road in front of you and then continue straight on the other side. Once in the forest, do not take the small dirt path to your left. That goes towards Kelheim. The road you're following has green rectangles and goes through patches of both forest and open fields. It's quite pleasant, and after you go through a small village, you pass one more open section before heading back into the forest. At that point, the Rundweg 2 signs return and you'll be going towards the Schulerloch/Tropfsteinhöhle. There are a few turns but all are well marked. As you near the cave area, you'll start to see more people. There's a small museum with a restaurant along the trail. Once you pass this area it will start to get more crowded as many people just walk up to the cave. That said, it's a great section of trail with views over the valley to your left and some smaller caves on your right. It's short-lived, however, and soon drops down to the valley and skirts along the edge of the forest with open fields to your left. There are plenty of signs pointing to Essing. You're close but not quite there.

Along the way you'll cross a few small roads. Once this path ends, you'll come to a larger street. Carefully cross it and look to your left for a small opening in the forest. Go through it and at the end of this small shady section you'll come to the bend of a larger busy street. Cross it and follow the bend as it goes left. Look to your right for an opening. There will be a set of wooden stairs to climb along with some uphill walking. You have to get back up to the original junction between Randeck and Schulerloch. Once there, you can drop back down into town on the path you came up on, passing the nice neighborhood and now very familiar yellow church. Head right back to Brauereigasthof Schneider for a cold one. You deserve it!

BRAUEREIGASTHOF SCHNEIDER

This traditional brewpub with a modern flair was founded in 1640 and has been run by the Schneider family for the last three generations. Brothers Matthias and Johannes act as brewer and chef respectively. Their father Joseph is the managing director. The interior is cozy, but if the weather is fine, sitting outside under a leafy tree on the small river can't be beat. The family takes great pride in the quality and presentation of the food. They buy local products and even butcher whole animals on site to avoid waste. Fish are bought and kept in a freshwater basin until preparation. Matthias is an avid hunter, so game meats are often on the menu. Everything that comes out looks fabulous and tastes just as good. Of course, the beer is the reason you're here and it is up to par with the food, and that's saying a lot! Thankfully, they also have rooms as you'll need more than one visit to fully appreciate all they (and the area) have to offer.

This was another hard place to pick a favorite beer, but I'd specifically come here after reading a great review of their dark lager by Campaign for Real Ale writer Graham Lees so I stuck with that choice. That said, their Lager Hell is surprisingly hoppy and their Josefibock, if available, shouldn't be missed either – especially coupled with one of their marvelous desserts.

Beers on tap: Schneider Lager Hell, Schneider Lager Dunkel, Schneider Hefeweizen with occasional seasonals. Bottled Rotbier (top-fermented), Märzen and Josefibock (during Lent).

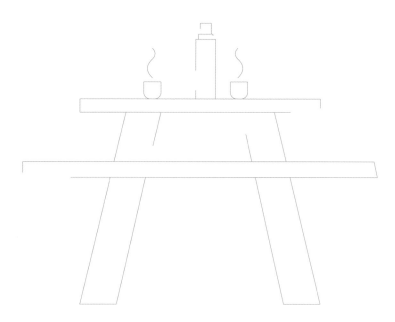

PRACTICAL INFORMATION

Schneider Hotel & Brauereigasthof
Altmühlgasse 10
93343 Essing
+49 9447 9180-0
www.brauereigasthof-schneider.de

Open daily 8:00 am to 11:00 pm
Full hot meals are available
from 11:30 am to 1:45 pm and 6:00 pm to 9:00 pm.
Cold dishes and smaller hot dishes are available in the afternoon.

Rooms can be booked on their website
which is also available in English.

RIEDENBURG

THREE CASTLES AND A SWAN

▷⋯ STARTING POINT	⋯✕ DESTINATION
BRAUEREIGASTHOF SCHWAN	**BRAUEREIGASTHOF SCHWAN**
🍺 BEER	▦ DIFFICULTY
RIEMHOFER SCHWANEN-WEIßE	**HIKE**
⛰ MAP	
ATK25-J12	⏱ DURATION OF THE HIKE
KELHEIM	**2.5 KM** **1–1.5H**
🔍 HIGHLIGHTS	⁓ ELEVATION GAIN
ROSENBURG CASTLE, RABENSTEIN CASTLE RUIN, TACHENSTEIN, RIEDENBURG OLD TOWN SQUARE, DISTANT VIEWS OF PRUNN CASTLE	ASCENT: 162 M DESCENT: 166 M

WEIßBIER

LIGHTLY FILTERED
GOLDEN

FRUITY,
YEAST,
BANANA

FRUIT,
SLIGHT PEACH,
YEAST

BITTERNESS   SWEETNESS

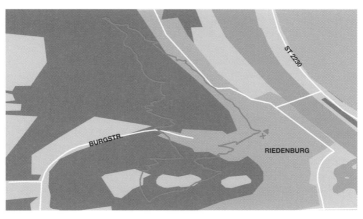

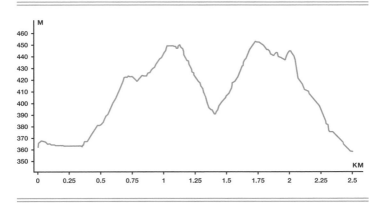

DESCRIPTION OF THE ROUTE

Riedenburg is one of the main tourist towns in the Altmühltal, a lush landscape of rolling hills and rocky outcroppings. Located on the more than 200 kilometers Altmühl river, its main claim to fame is that it has not only a hilltop castle but also two castle ruins. With a range of places to both stay and eat, it makes a good base to explore the surrounding area. There are numerous trails emanating from it and two breweries to quench your thirst. The Drei-Burgen-Steig is a very short and steep trail that takes in all three castles and offers nice views over the town and river valley.

Riedenburg is serviced by frequent buses from Saal (Donau) station, which has connections to Regensburg and Ingolstadt. Coming from further afield involves a few changes and driving might be a better option.

Exiting the Brauereigasthof Schwan, you go right along the Markt-platz, followed by a quick right on Austraße. Follow this street as it leaves the old town center. There are numerous Drei-Burgen-Steig trail signs to follow through a residential area. As you head up the road and the houses thin out, take note of the Riemhofer brewery straight on – they brew the beer you will be drinking after the hike. You're not headed there now so keep an eye out on your left for signs for your turn. Turn left towards Tachenstein and remain on the Drei-Burgen-Steig trail. You'll go up some stairs and then rise on a narrow path behind some homes. There are nice views of the valley as you do. You will soon enter an atmospheric, lush forest that continues to go up as you make your way to the Tachenstein. You'll be there before you know it. There's not a lot remaining, but the castle keep that is there is quite enchanting – due as much to the setting as the structure. It's a great hike for kids and kids at heart or lovers of medieval history. There's also a viewpoint offering a spectacular vista of the river flowing through the valley, and in the distance, the castle in nearby Prunn.

When you tire of daydreaming of knights, return to the trail and follow signs for Rosenburg and Rabenstein, both on the Drei-Burgen-Steig trail. The trail drops down. Once you come to the clearing, carefully cross the Burgstraße – the street used to drive to the castle. Once on the other side of the street, follow the Drei-Burgen-Steig signs sending you back into the forest. The trail rises again as you make your way to the Rosenburg castle. Once at the castle, you can visit it and its falconry but there is an entrance fee. If you're not interested, continue on around the castle, following the same trail signs and soon, ones for Rabenstein. There's another viewpoint that, while not quite as good as the one at Tachenstein, is worth checking out. The trail descends yet again and you start to see signs for Riedenburg. Make your way to Burgstraße and the Marktplatz. The Schwan and its beer is waiting for you there.

SCHWAN RIEDENBURG, GASTHAUS & HOTEL

The Schwan has a pretty peach facade. Sitting on the Marktplatz facing it, and the castle ruin above, is a great way to end your day. Though not an actual brewery, it has a long history dating back to the 1600s. It was bought by the Riemhofer family in 1841 and though no longer in their ownership, it serves as their unofficial old-town brewery tap and a swan still adorns their labels. It is now run by the Sollinger family, who also own the Gasthof Zur Post next door. Noted as much for its food as its beer, it has a bustling atmosphere at mealtimes, and on nice days, the outdoor seating fills up quickly.

The actual brewery you saw at the beginning of the hike was once where the cooling cellars were located. In the days before refrigeration, they were built into the sides of hills to keep the beer cold to avoid spoilage.

Beers on tap: Riemhofer Schwanen-Weiße, Riemhofer Helles Vollbier and Riemhofer Zwickl.

PRACTICAL INFORMATION

Schwan Riedenburg, Gasthaus & Hotel
Marktplatz 5
93339 Riedenburg
+49 9442-1272
www.schwan-riedenburg.de

Open Wednesday to Sunday 10:00 am to 10:00 pm
Friday only 4:30 pm to 10:00 pm
Closed Monday and Tuesday
but the neighboring Zur Post is
open those days and some of
the Riemhofer beers are
available there, as well.

Rooms are available and
they can be booked
on their website.

ZWIESEL

THROUGH THE BAVARIAN FOREST IN SEARCH OF DAMPFBIER

LOWER BAVARIA

▷⋯ STARTING POINT	⋯✕ DESTINATION
BRÄUSTÜBERL ZWIESEL, ZWIESEL	**BRÄUSTÜBERL ZWIESEL, ZWIESEL**
🍺 BEER	🔲 DIFFICULTY
1. DAMPFBIERBRAUEREI DAMPFBIER	**HIKE** 🚶
⛰ MAP	
ATK25-I18 **ZWIESEL**	⏱ DURATION OF THE HIKE **7.5 KM 2–2.5H**
🔍 HIGHLIGHTS	〰 ELEVATION GAIN
BAVARIAN FOREST, SCHWARZER REGEN RIVER, OLD BRICK BREWING CHIMNEY OF THE DAMPFBIERBRAUEREI ZWIESEL	ASCENT: 240 M DESCENT: 165 M

5.0%
ALCOHOL CONTENT

DAMPFBIER; TOP-FER-
MENTED SPECIALTY
BEER REPORTED TO GIVE
OFF STEAM DURING THE
FERMENTATION PROCESS

AMBER,
OFF-WHITE HEAD

RICH MALT

FRUITY, DRY,
SLIGHTLY SOUR,
DRY FINISH

BITTERNESS

SWEETNESS

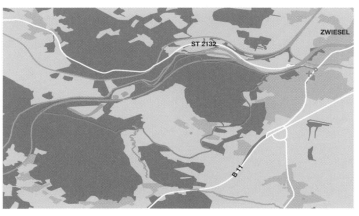

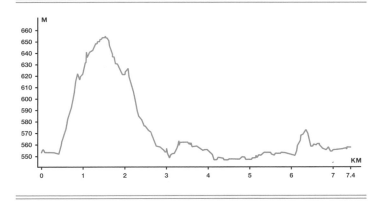

DESCRIPTION OF THE ROUTE

The Bavarian Forest is a large swath of heavily treed hilly terrain close to the Czech border. Only a relatively small part of it is the Bavarian Forest National Park but even the areas not designated so are quite beautiful and full of recreational possibilities. Zwiesel is one of the most accessible gateway towns with a fair array of accommodation and dining possibilities. It is also home to the 1. Dampfbierbrauerei, where steam beer was revived in Bavaria. While most of the more noted trails are in the Bavarian National Park, this nice route just on the edge of town provides some river views and forested paths. It is perhaps more noted for winter recreational sports. For example, the Bayerwaldloipe, a 150 kilometers long cross-country skiing trail, runs through Zwiesel.

Zwiesel is serviced by frequent trains from Plattling, which is well-connected to Munich, Regensburg and Passau. The trip from Munich is about 2.5 hours but is shorter from the other two origin points.

Coming out of the Bräustüberl Zwiesel, you can admire the old brick chimney of the 1. Dampfbierbrauerei just across the street before going left on Regener Straße. At the corner, go left on Langdorfer Straße and walk past a large home improvement center on your left. Just beyond it, there is a series of trail signs. You're going left here, initially on the long-distance Flusswanderweg but also a town pedestrian path at this point. Walk along the pleasant path with the Schwarzer Regen River flowing to your right. You'll come to a small junction with trail numbers 6 and 10 going left but you will continue straight on the 21 and 20. Go under the overpass, after which is another larger trail junction. To the right is Trail 21 (also the Flusswanderweg) – this is your return route. Instead, go on the left fork to follow the Panoramaweg 14. Once in the forest, you'll see signs for both the 14 and 21. Trail 21 is the circuit you'll be doing. The trail will lead you left towards a parking area and then right with an apartment complex on your left, before going back into the forest.

Once back in the forest, the trail goes up gently with occasional signs on the trees. Out in a clearing, you will come to a fork – take the right side of it, soon it will become a forested gravel road. Exiting this stretch of forest, you'll pass a bench and start walking towards a village. At the end of this path, go left to walk through Zwieselberg. After crossing one street you'll leave the small village and at a T with a larger road, go left. Follow this to a small path on your right, marked with a 21 sign. You'll be leaving the Panoramaweg 14 here. Go through a few trees and once on the other side, veer right across an open area. If you look straight across, you'll see a tree and next to it, a small post. Walk towards it and you'll see the post has the Trail 21 sign on it. Go right on an asphalt road and follow it past a forest and a junction for Trail 6. Continue straight and when you see another 21 sign pointing you left just after the 3 kilometer mark, take the unpaved road through a brief forested section. This will come to an open area with a stream flowing through it. It looks like you should skirt the forest, but if you look closely, you'll see a 21 sign on a tree just on the edge of the forest. Enter there but do not go straight. There is a path there, but it is quite wet at times and even has a few pond-like puddles. Instead, look closely to your left and you'll see a somewhat overgrown narrow path. Once you get on it, it is very distinct and there are some signs along the route. Take this all the way to a gravel road and go right onto it. Follow this road to a stone overpass for the railroad line. Walk through the opening and on the other side, go right to follow the 21 sign. You'll also be back on the Flusswanderweg now. This is a nice stretch through the forest. It follows the river, though not alongside it. You'll cross a small bridge and come to a gravel road, where you'll take a well-marked left.

After passing a small development, the unpaved road will take you along the river, much closer this time. There are some turnoffs to actually walk right along it but these are quite narrow. Depending on the time of year, they can be overgrown, so if you don't want to follow this, remain on the gravel road. They come back to the road not far up the path anyway. Continue on this route, following the river until the marked right just after the 6 kilometer mark. This will bring you through a forest to a train track crossing.

On the other side of the tracks, you'll veer left to get closer to the river again before coming to a junction. This is the first big one where you began Trail 21. Now, go left to walk under the same overpass you walked under earlier. Follow the river back to Langdorfer Straße and turn right, followed by another right on Regener Straße to bring you back to the Bräustüberl Zwiesel.

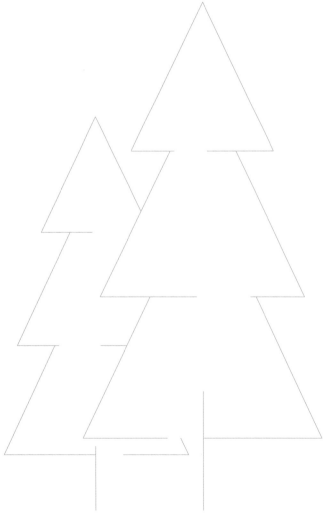

BRÄUSTÜBERL ZWIESEL

Sitting across from the 1. Dampfbierbrauerei Zwiesel W. Pfeffer is the cozy Bräustüberl with its green tile oven and pleasant outside seating area. A lot has changed at the brewery since they decided to revive an old recipe in 1989. Wolfgang Pfeffer founded his brewery in 1889 and unsurprisingly called it Pfefferbräu. He had to deal with a lack of hops and wheat in the Bavarian Forest and made his brew with barley malt, less hops and a top fermenting yeast – unusual for non-wheat beers in Bavaria. It was done in open fermentation tanks, with bubbles forming on top, which burst to give an impression of steam (Dampf) rising.
Over the course of time, the beer fell out of favor and with hops not as scarce, Pfefferbräu brewed a pilsner. For their 100th anniversary, they decided to make a commemorative Dampfbier, and it was so popular, it became part of their regular line-up. While most locals probably drink their Helles now, the brewery is most known worldwide for this beer and so the name was changed to showcase it. The beer is still matured in cellars built deep in the rocks adjacent to the brewery.

Beers on tap: 1. Dampfbierbrauerei Zwiesel Dampfbier, 1. Dampfbierbrauerei Zwiesel Export Hell. Bottled National Park Pils, Hefe Weißbier and seasonals.

PRACTICAL INFORMATION

Bräustüberl Zwiesel
Regener Straße 6
94227 Zwiesel
+49 9922 6686
www.braeustueberl-zwiesel.de

Open daily 9:30 am to 2:00 am

Brewery website: www.dampfbier.de

BÖBRACH

ALONG THE RIVER TO ECK

LOWER BAVARIA

▷⋯ STARTING POINT

BRAUEREI-GASTHOF ECK, ECK (BÖBRACH)

⋯✗ DESTINATION

BRAUEREI-GASTHOF ECK, ECK (BÖBRACH)

🍺 BEER

WILDERER DUNKEL

⛰ MAP

ATK25-I17
VIECHTACH

🔀 DIFFICULTY

HIKE

🕑 DURATION OF THE HIKE

6.5 KM
1.5–2H

🔍 HIGHLIGHTS

BAVARIAN FOREST, SCHWARZER REGEN RIVER, ST. NIKOLAUS CHURCH IN BÖBRACH, RURAL FARMLAND

〜 ELEVATION GAIN

ASCENT: 180 M
DESCENT: 180 M

 DUNKLES

 UNFILTERED CHESTNUT, OFF-WHITE HEAD

 CHOCOLATE MALT

 MALTY, DRY, HINT OF CHOCOLATE, BITTERSWEET FINISH

BITTERNESS   SWEETNESS

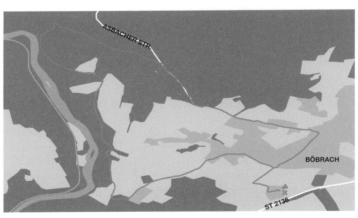

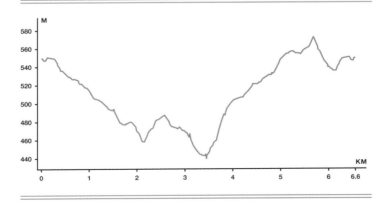

DESCRIPTION OF THE ROUTE

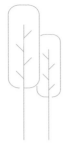 Böbrach is a pleasant town scenically set in the Bavarian Forest, heading towards the Czech border. With its relative proximity to the Bavarian Forest National Park, it makes a nice base if traveling by car. Of course, if you love great brewpub hotels, staying here makes even more sense. While the more noted trails are within the national park boundaries, with long-distance routes like the Goldsteig, there are some nice ones nearby as well. The route described takes you down to the Schwarzer Regen River and out into the countryside for some fine views.

Böbrach is not an easy place to get to by public transportation. The nearest train station is in Teisenach, which involves a few changes to reach. From there, most buses are call buses that must be pre-arranged. For this reason, Böbrach is a place best visited by car.

Coming out of Brauerei-Gasthof Eck, go right, through the Biergarten to wrap around the restaurant and hotel. You will be between it and the beer market and distillery on your left. There is a large events room straight on. When you see an opening to your right, go through it. On your right is a covered open structure full of old horse-drawn carriages and wooden wheels, giving the place a Wild West kind of feel. Just past it, go immediately right to walk along the outside of the complex. At the end of the building, veer left into an open field. Straight across it, you'll see a lone tree. Walk towards it on a somewhat worn path in the grass. Once there, you'll see a small shrine. Go right to walk along a more worn path towards the road. When you reach an asphalt road named Wieshof, you'll see signs for the Panoramaweg 11. Go left to follow this route initially. When you come to the first intersection, take a left on Lindenweg. You will start to see signs for Trail 10 – this is your circuit. Follow this through a small residential area and then past a spa hotel on your left before the trail bends right and ducks briefly into a forest. You will come out into an open area and skirt the forest on your left and open farmland on your right. You'll notice that you are not only on Trail 10 but also the long-distance Flusswanderweg, as the Schwarzer Regen River is to your left, though not always visible.

Continue on this mostly straight route as it passes through a mix of forest and open areas, always following the signs for Trail 10 and the Flusswanderweg. Just after the 3 kilometer mark, the trail gets close to the river and you can take a detour over to it for a closer look. About a half kilometer more up the trail, you will cross a small foot bridge and come to a junction. To the left is the continuation of the full Trail 10 circuit as well as the route of the Flusswanderweg. Instead, go right to follow Trail 10 back to Böbrach. Not far up the trail, go right over another small foot bridge to cross the same stream. This is where you'll rejoin the full 10 circuit. You've just taken shortcut. Continue following Trail 10 as it climbs upward until you come to an asphalt road. Go right on it – there are trail signs just up the road for trails 10 and 5. Follow this until it veers left, becoming Asbacher Straße just before the 5 kilometer mark. Continue on this paved road past Lindenweg towards the center of Böbrach. You'll see its church in the near distance. Just before the church, there will be a pedestrian path on your right. It is also marked with a Panoramaweg 11 sign pointing you to the right. If you'd like, go check out the church and return here. Otherwise, head down the pedestrian path which turns into Fichtenweg. Follow this all the way to Wieshof, the road you started on. On the other side of the road is the continuation of the Panoramaweg. Take it back up across the field to the lone tree. Go left there and follow the path back to Brauerei-Gasthof Eck.

BRAUEREI-GASTHOF ECK

This country Inn is a destination in itself, with brewery tours, beer seminars, an onsite distillery and museum, beer market, and banquet halls suitable for large events like weddings. The restaurant is a sprawling affair, and the Biergarten has some large old trees providing ample shade. Founded in 1462, they've maintained traditional methods, including the use of open fermentation tanks. Along with traditional Bavarian dishes, they have a few fish and a couple of vegetarian and even vegan options. They also pride themselves on their desserts, including a homemade pancake dish served with plum compote, from a recipe from 1658.

Their Wilderer Dunkel has won a gold medal at the European Beer Star competition, and their new Heller Saphir Bock is a craft beer take on a traditional style, made with Hallertau Saphir hops.

Beers on tap: Eck Wilderer Dunkel, Eck Lager Hell, Eck Heller Saphir Bock. Seasonals: Eck Festbier (June 15th to September 15th), Eck Maibock (May).

PRACTICAL INFORMATION

Brauerei-Gasthof Eck
Eck 1
94255 Böbrach
+49 9923 84050
www.brauerei-eck.de

Open Wednesday to Sunday 10:00 am to around 10:00 pm
Closed Monday and Tuesday

Rooms are available and can be booked on their website, the booking part of which is also available in English.

UPPER PALATINATE

FALKENBERG TO NEUHAUS

ON A QUEST FOR ZOIGL ON FOOT

 UPPER PALATINATE

▷⋯ STARTING POINT	⋯✕ DESTINATION
FALKENBERG ST. PANKRATIUS CHURCH	**ZUM WALDNAABTAL HOTEL, NEUHAUS**

🍺 BEER	🗺 DIFFICULTY
ZOIGL	
🗺 MAP	**HIKE** 🚶
ATK25-E14	⏱ DURATION OF THE HIKE
NEUSTADT A.D. WALDNAAB	**14 KM** **3–4H**

🔍 HIGHLIGHTS	∿ ELEVATION GAIN
WALDNAABTAL, BUTTERFASS, COMMUNAL BREW HOUSES, NEUHAUS CASTLE, ZOIGLS-TUBEN	ASCENT: 199 M DESCENT: 184 M

ZOIGL

AMBER, UNFILTERED

FRUITY, GRAINY

FRUITY, DRY, BITTER

BITTERNESS   SWEETNESS

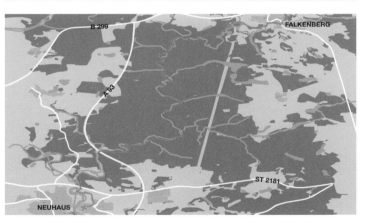

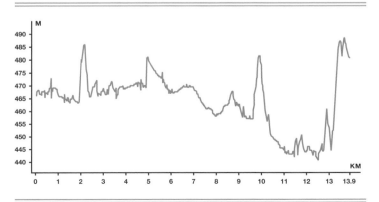

DESCRIPTION OF THE ROUTE

The Waldnaabtal Nature Reserve is a more than 300 acre protected area centered around its namesake river the Waldnaab. Located between Falkenberg and Neuhaus in the Upper Palatinate, this incredibly lush slice of paradise is the primary draw of an area known to beer aficionados for its Zoigl. Little known outside the German-speaking world, Zoigl is garnering more attention with the promotion of Germany's longest hiking trail, the 660 kilometer Goldsteig which opened in 2007. The Goldsteig passes through some incredible scenery, but it's doubtful any section is as spectacular as the stretch that will bring you between two of the five authentic Zoigl producing towns.

Buses to Falkenberg (Oberpfalz) from Wiesau run on a regular basis, but some are designated AST, meaning you have to call in advance as they don't run unless someone is utilizing it at that given time. Try to use the regular buses if you can to make things simpler. The trip will take about 10 minutes. Alternatively, if you're keen to see more of the Goldsteig, it also passes just outside Wiesau to Falkenberg.

The bus drops you off right in the old town on the Marktplatz. Falkenberg is a lovely town with a hilltop castle, so it's worth spending a night there if you can. If not, before you start your hike, it's worth a short detour to see the communal brew house at the foot of the Falkenberg Castle, just a short stroll up Wiesauer Straße. From the Marktplatz, you'll also see the beautiful St. Pankratius Church. Look for Schönfichter Straße and proceed down it. Soon you'll see the smaller street Am Netzbach on your right. There are lots of trail signs, too. The Goldsteig one has a yellow S on it. You will be following this very well-marked trail the entire way.

Am Netzbach soon becomes Am Steg before it crosses over the Waldnaabtal River. From the small bridge, gaze back for great views of Falkenberg, including the castle looming up on the hill. Follow the road to the Premenreuther Straße, go left and look immediately for Färbergasse and then go left again. This route is well-marked with S signs. You'll follow Färbergasse along the river for a bit before it veers away. You'll come to a hiker's parking lot which you'll proceed through, following the Goldsteig signs. The first part skirts the river before ducking into the forest. You will have some nice, shady sections on this trail, and you'll be following the river, though at times you will veer away from it. This is a very winding river so if you followed it exactly, it would be a very long route! The Kammerwagen is a good place for a break if you need one. This large granite formation resembles an old train wagon. There are write-ups about most of the sights on the trail, though only in German. After your break, continue along the trail through a very lush part of the forest. You'll pass some lesser sights such as the Amboss, the Sauerbrunnen and one

formation that does indeed look like the profile of a man with a large nose. These little diversions are great for kids and do make the route go by more quickly, even for adults. The best of the lot is the Butterfass. This one is worth a stop – if you're carrying a big pack, take it off and proceed down a set of stone steps to have a better look. The river rushes over the often moss-covered rocks, making for a very relaxing sound. If you have it to yourself, take a seat and enjoy.

From the Butterfass, it's a short scenic meander to the Blockhütte, an old hiking hut located just beyond the main bridge that crosses the river. This is a great place for a real break, especially if you're hungry. On the way in, you'll see the original old building to your right. It's been well-preserved as a tourist attraction of sorts but in no way would it be big enough to handle the hikers coming through now at busy times. The more modern, though still log cabin-style, building is just ahead. If it's cold, you'll enjoy the cozy interior with its green ceramic wood-burning stove. If the weather is fine, sit outside in what has to be one of the most scenically situated beer gardens in Germany, resplendent with a working water wheel. Hot meals are excellent and though not on tap, they have a commercially bottled Zoigl on offer. From there, you can continue on this side of the river on the Uferpfad (bank path), which requires better footwork but is good fun. If you do, meet up with the Goldsteig downriver after crossing a small bridge.

This route will continue on the Goldsteig. If you've stopped at the Blockhütte, retrace your steps back to the bridge and cross it. Following the S signs, head right on the wide path. As it follows the river, this is a pretty stretch, too. You'll see some wooden steps and ladders on the other side, which is the Uferpfad. Before you know it, you'll be at the cute little wooden bridge coming out from the Uferpfad. Continue along the wide, well-marked path as it hugs the river. There are few choices on this route, so enjoy the green Waldnaabtal. You'll come to a junction at one point, but again, signs prod you along the Goldsteig nicely and even give you the distances to Neuhaus. It's relatively flat until you come to a narrow path through a forest, where it rises up before dropping you back down to the river. Once you emerge from this section, you'll see an overpass ahead. Continue first towards and then under it. This is probably not the most beautiful section of the trail and can be jarring after coming out of what is a beautiful paradise. No worries as you'll soon be in an open, pretty valley. Take note of the religious retreat on your right. At this point, Neuhaus is only a couple of kilometers away. There are a few forks, but those that pop up are marked, so follow the S signs. Not far after going under a second overpass, you will come to a small fork. The left goes uphill to Neuhaus and the right to Windischeschenbach. If staying in the latter, go that way. It's also the quickest route to the train station there. The Goldsteig goes through Neuhaus so continue that way. It's a bit of a trudge, and on hot days it can be exposed to the sun at times.

You'll come into Neuhaus on Demeshofweg which soon comes to a T. Go right and continue on the Demeshofweg. At the intersection, go right on Marktplatz. Even through town, the Goldsteig is signed. At the end of the Marktplatz, on your right, is the Zum Waldnaabtal Hotel. This makes for a pleasant place to spend the night. Grab a shower and head out for a much deserved Zoigl.

ZOIGL

For those who know little about Zoigl, it is a very special area of the brewing world. Traditionally, towns in this area would have a communal brew house, where residents could take turns making their own beer. If there was enough, they'd share with neighbors. They would possibly have shared snacks, too. At one point, the six-sided star was hung outside the house to show who had Zoigl. This star is composed of two triangles. The first stands for the ingredients of beer: water, hops and barely. The second is for the three elements: water, fire and air. It was once very difficult to find Zoigl but its makers have become much more organized now. One group called "Echter Zoigl" has a website that is invaluable in this search. They also promote the idea that real ("echter") Zoigl has to follow certain criteria. It's not a protected designation like Champagne, but their argument is logical and, for me, has a lot of merit. To be real Zoigl, it must be made of only the top triangle ingredients and be heated by the natural element of fire. It must also be made in a communal brew house. There are five remaining towns in the Upper Palatinate that follow this protocol, two of which are Neuhaus and Windischeschenbach. Your starting point in Falkenberg is a third. If you had a peek at the communal brew house there, then you've already seen one. The particularly different thing here is the wort (brewed liquid concoction from water, barley and hops) is brought to the Zoiglstuben, where yeast is added for fermentation. It is pumped up right from the tanks in the cellar at the Zoiglstuben.

ZOIGLSTUBEN

The modern day Zoiglstuben are businesses – but the best truly do retain the homey atmosphere of people inviting friends over to share. They are often in houses, and old-style kitchens are part of the décor. Some offer mostly cold and simple warm snacks but others offer bigger meals. Great value is the common denominator. The biggest collection of them is certainly in Neuhaus and Windischeschenbach but take turns opening throughout the year. Generally speaking, there is almost always one in each town open on any given weekend but sometimes there are more. The twin capitals of Zoigl also have the advantage of having one place offering real Zoigl every day except Saturday. So, if you can't get there on a weekend, this is your best shot at having Zoigl. While Zum Weißen Schwan is a fine restaurant with excellent food (and is even part of the Echter Zoigl association), it doesn't quite capture the Zoiglstube atmosphere. So, check out the Echter Zoigl website, plan accordingly, and get ready to enjoy one of the most authentic beer experiences left in the modern world.

PRACTICAL INFORMATION

Gasthof Zum Weißen Schwan
Pfarrplatz 1
92670 Windischeschenbach
+49 9681/1230
www.schwanerer.de

Monday to Friday from 5:00 pm
Sunday and holidays for lunch, closes at 3:00 pm
Closed Saturday

They also offer rooms and are very centrally located.

You will notice Zoigl signs everywhere in these two towns. Some are commercial breweries while others are not part of the Echter Zoigl association, which doesn't mean they are not good. In fact, the association even says on their website that other Zoigl is not bad. Some are not Zoigl in the sense that they do not follow the established protocols above. Other less commercial outlets might follow some of the protocols, but are not part of the association. By all means, try whatever you fancy and comes your way, but seeking out the Zoiglstuben on the website supports them, and all of the ones I've been to have been great.

There are five additional Echte Zoiglstuben in addition to Zum Weißen Schwan in Windischeschenbach. There are six Echte Zoiglstuben in Neuhaus. Consult the website to find out their schedules and opening hours.

Echter Zoigl association: www.zoiglbier.de

FALKENBERG

HILLTOP CASTLE AND COMMUNAL BREW HOUSE

UPPER PALATINATE

▷··· STARTING POINT

MARKTPLATZ, FALKENBERG

🍺 BEER

ZOIGL

⛰ MAP

ATK25-E14

NEUSTADT A.D. WALDNAAB

🔍 HIGHLIGHTS

FALKENBERG CASTLE, ST. PANKRATIUS CHURCH, THE OLD TOWN HALL OF FALKENBERG, RURAL LANDSCAPE

···✗ DESTINATION

MARKTPLATZ, FALKENBERG

▦ DIFFICULTY

HIKE 🚶

🕐 DURATION OF THE HIKE

5 KM
1.5–2H

〰 ELEVATION GAIN

ASCENT: 127 M
DESCENT: 127 M

ZOIGL

 LIGHTLY FILTERED
AMBER

 GRAIN,
MALT

 FRUITY,
HOPPY,
DRY

BITTERNESS   SWEETNESS

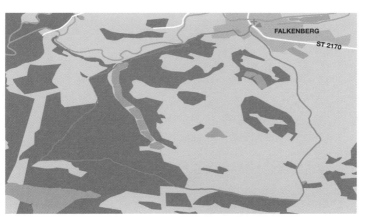

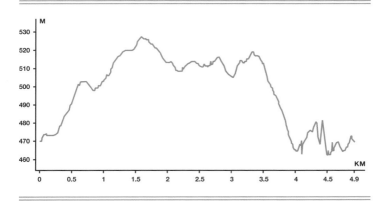

DESCRIPTION OF THE ROUTE

Falkenberg is a pretty market town in the Upper Palatinate with a hilltop castle and a scenic riverside location. The market square features an impressive stone church and old town hall, but what sets it apart from other such places in Bavaria is its communal brew house. The Upper Palatinate has five such places but Falkenberg's is surely the most scenic. It is a great place to tackle one of the most beautiful sections of the Goldsteig, but there are also other nice trails nearby. The added lure of Zoigl makes Falkenberg a great place to spend a night or two.

Buses to Falkenberg (Oberpfalz) from Wiesau run on a regular basis but some are designated AST, meaning you have to call in advance as they don't run unless someone is utilizing it at that given time. Try to use the regular buses if you can to make things simpler. The trip takes about 10 minutes.

Falkenberg Rundweg 5 starts just on the edge of the old town center. From the Marktplatz, go straight on Schönfichter Straße, taking note of the pretty stone St. Pankratius Church to your right. As the street bends to your left, look out on your right for Bodenreuther Weg and turn right onto it. The street veers left – follow the small asphalt road for a little under a kilometer. At the fork, take the left side, more of a dirt track at this point. Once on the trail, you'll see a small sign with a number 5 affixed to a tree on the left side of the trail. That's the route you're following. You're soon in open farmland, veering right and then left. At the T, you'll go right and skirt a small forest. The trail briefly enters an open area before delving into a larger forest. In this forest, you will also see some red dot trail signs.

The trail veers left before coming briefly into the open where you will again skirt the forest and then make a relatively quick hard right at about the 3 kilometer mark. Follow this path through the next section of forest. When you reach the next open area, the 5 trail merges with the red X route. Not long after that, you will come to the Hammerka-pelle, a very small chapel. At that fork, stay to the right and continue through that forest until you come to a small pond on your right. You're also on the 1 trail so there are a lot of trail signs. Soon after the pond, you can continue on the 5 trail, but there is a small turn on your right for the 1 trail and red X route. If you decide to take this detour, follow this narrow route for a short time and you'll end up at a small bench with an opening in the trees that affords great views of the Falkenberg castle. Continue along the 5 trail until you arrive at some steps that lead to a religious display. If you're interested, check it out and then come back to the trail and continue down it to finish off the circuit. It will turn into Holzbrunnenweg. Keep your eyes to the left for more nice views of the castle. At the end of the road, go right on Kalvarienbergweg. You won't be on this for long. Look for your first left and take it. Up at the end of this street is Bodenreuther Weg, where you started the circuit. Once there, go left and take another left at Schönfichter Straße to get back to the old town center. It's time for a Zoigl!

ZOIGLSTUBEN

Zoigl is a special part of the brewing world using communal brew houses and strict protocols with regard to ingredients and process. There are five towns in the Upper Palatinate that produce Zoigl: Neuhaus, Windischeschenbach, Mitterteich, Eslarn and Falkenberg. While it's most easily experienced in the twin towns of Neuhaus/ Windischeschenbach, there's no denying the beauty of Falkenberg and the many hiking trails around it. Zoiglstuben are small places that make Zoigl in communal brew houses and serve them onsite about once a month. It is best to consult a Zoigl calendar to find out which places are open on any given weekend (e.g. the Echter Zoigl website, www.zoiglbier.de). If that sounds hard, once upon a time you had to wander the streets and look for a Zoigl star hanging from houses dispensing it.

There are two Zoiglstuben in Falkenberg recognized by the Echter Zoigl site, and another one I am including since I was there when the owner was making his Zoigl in the communal brew house. The website also makes it possible to find Zoigl on just about every weekend of the year.

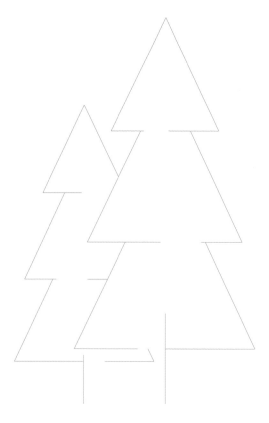

PRACTICAL INFORMATION

Kramer-Wolf
Tirschenreuther Str. 4
95685 Falkenberg
+40 9637-328
www.zoigl-kramer-wolf.de

Friday to Monday 10:00 am (check the Zoigl calendar for which weekends it is open)

Schwoazhansl-Zoigl
Tirschenreuther Str. 7
95685 Falkenberg
+49 172 9106756
www.schwoazhansl-zoigl.de

Friday & Monday from 5:00 pm
Saturday & Sunday from 3:00 pm (check the Zoigl calendar for which weekends it is open)

This last one is not part of the Echter Zoigl group so consult their own website for the schedule:

Wolfadl-Zoigl
Gumpener Weg 1
95685 Falkenberg
+49 157-72067495
www.wolfadl-zoigl.de

Friday to Monday 10:00 am to 11:00 pm

REGENSBURG

VIEWS OF THE OLD TOWN CENTER FROM ACROSS THE RIVER

UPPER PALATINATE

▷⋯ STARTING POINT	⋯✕ DESTINATION
DOME OF ST. PETER, REGENSBURG	**BRAUEREIGASTSTÄTTE KNEITINGER, REGENSBURG**
🍺 BEER	⌗ DIFFICULTY
KNEITINGER DUNKEL EXPORT	**WALK** 🚶
⛰ MAP	
ATK25-I13	⏱ DURATION OF THE HIKE
REGENSBURG-NORD	**2 KM 30–45MIN**
🔍 HIGHLIGHTS	〰 ELEVATION GAIN
DOME OF ST. PETER, CORN MARKET, DANUBE RIVER, STONE BRIDGE	ASCENT: 0 M DESCENT: 0 M

 DUNKLES

 CHESTNUT,
ROCKY TAN HEAD

 MALT,
LIGHT HOPS,
SLIGHT CHOCOLATE

 RICH MALT,
UNDERLYING HOPS,
ROAST, CHOCOLATE

BITTERNESS   SWEETNESS

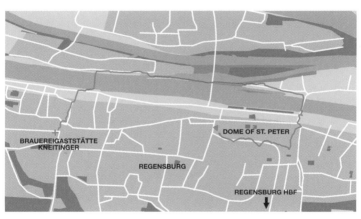

BRAUEREIGASTSTÄTTE
KNEITINGER

REGENSBURG

DOME OF ST. PETER

REGENSBURG HBF

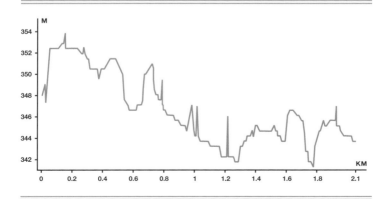

DESCRIPTION OF THE ROUTE

Regensburg never seems to enter the realm of first choice tourist towns in Bavaria, but that's okay for those who have fallen in love with its charming old town center and hauntingly beautiful cathedral. While very much part of the Upper Palatinate, it has strong ties to Lower Bavaria due to its geographic location, and its proximity to the Altmühltal makes it a good base for exploring that region. Those who do venture there all flock to the renowned Dome of St. Peter, but it seems many miss the islands that lie in the Danube, awaiting exploration. This walk takes you there and gives you great views of the Regensburg old-town center from the other side.

Regensburg is serviced by frequent trains from Munich and Nuremberg, the trip taking about 90 minutes and 1 hour respectively.

After exploring the interior of the Dome of St. Peter, walk along the Domplatz towards the Alter Kornmarkt (old corn market), once the center of grain trade and now a charming square. Admire both the Roman Tower and Duke's Courtyard. As you continue straight Domplatz will become Pfluggasse. Almost immediately, turn left onto Erhardigasse, a narrow cobblestone lane. At the end, go down a small set of stairs to emerge on St.-Georgen-Platz. Go left and cross the Eiserne Brücke on the left-hand side, where you'll have pretty views of the Danube. On the other side of the bridge, go left on a small footpath that brings you down to the river's edge. Walk along it towards the old stone bridge for a different perspective of one of Regensburg's iconic symbols. Walk under the bridge and on the other side will be a peaceful area. If it's a nice day, locals will be sunning themselves or enjoying a picnic. Continue straight, and at the end of this narrow peninsula, cross the small foot bridge to the mainland. At Badstraße, go left. As you walk along this stretch, you will have perhaps the best views of Regensburg to your left. There is a grassy area next to the path, another popular spot for locals. At the pedestrian bridge (Eiserner Steg), go left to cross back over the Danube. There are great views from the bridge too. On the other side of the bridge, go right on Holzländerstraße, followed by a quick left on Rehgäßchen, a narrow alleyway that widens to a regular street. Continue straight and it will open up onto Arnulfsplatz. On your right, just across the square, is Brauereigaststätte Kneitinger.

BRAUEREIGASTSTÄTTE KNEITINGER

There's been a brewery at this location since 1530 but the Kneitinger family didn't come into the picture until 1861. The new brewer developed their renowned Bock, the tapping of which is still a yearly event each fall. After three generations, the sole and childless heir formed a charitable foundation, and after her death in 1991, owner-ship passed on to it. Even without the touching story, what remains is admirable. The various pubs tied to the brewery are individually run, and the most traditional of the lot is the one at Arnulfsplatz, lovingly referred to as "Mutterhaus" (mother's house). It was opened in 1892, and though renovated over the years, it has kept its timeless charm. It's a sprawling place with lots of rooms. The inside courtyard is covered but retains a bit of an outside seating feel. If you want a real Biergarten, you'll have to head to the Kneitinger Keller up on Galgenberg.

Noted for their fine Bavarian cuisine as much as their beer, the "Mutterhaus" serves full hot meals from 11:00 until well into the evening, and is a popular place for functions and family celebrations. They also host the first of the many Kneitinger Bock beer tapings on the first Thursday in October, when a team of goats pull a cart with a wooden barrel of the precious cargo through the old town to the old pub.

Beers on tap: Kneitinger Edel-Pils, Kneitinger Dunkel Export. Seasonal Bock.

PRACTICAL INFORMATION

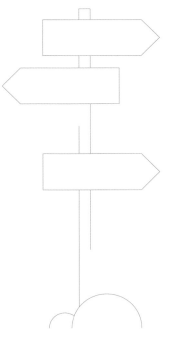

Brauereigaststätte Kneitinger
Arnulfsplatz 3
93047 Regensburg
+49 941 524 55
www.knei.de

Open daily 9:30 am to midnight

Kneitinger Keller
Galgenbergstraße 18
93053 Regensburg
+49 941 76680

Open daily 9:00 am to midnight

Full restaurant is open all year
but the large Biergarten is only
open in warmer months.

MIDDLE FRANCONIA

UEHLFELD

WALKING ON THE PATH OF THE STORKS

MIDDLE FRANCONIA

▷··· STARTING POINT

BRAUEREIGASTSTÄTTE PRECHTEL, UEHLFELD

···✗ DESTINATION

BRAUEREIGASTSTÄTTE PRECHTEL, UEHLFELD

🍺 BEER

PRECHTEL SCHNAPPERLA

🗺 MAP

ATK25-F07

NEUSTADT A.D. AISCH

🔠 DIFFICULTY

WALK 🚶

🕐 DURATION OF THE HIKE

**7 KM
1.5–2H**

🔍 HIGHLIGHTS

STORK NESTS, CARP PONDS, JAKOBUS CHURCH, RURAL SCENERY, AUTHENTIC FRANCONIAN BIERKELLER

〰 ELEVATION GAIN

ASCENT: 45 M
DESCENT: 45 M

KELLERBIER

LIGHTLY FILTERED
GOLDEN

MALT,
GRAIN

FRUITY, DRY,
SOME GRAIN,
SLIGHTLY BITTER FINISH

BITTERNESS   SWEETNESS

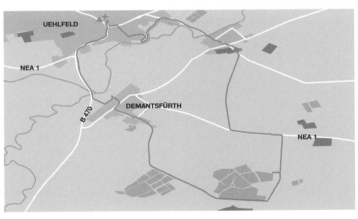

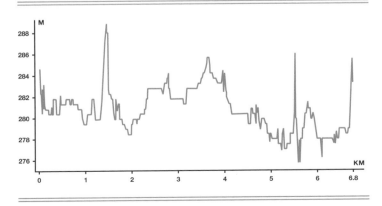

DESCRIPTION OF THE ROUTE

Uehlfeld is on the well-promoted Bierstraße that runs along the Aisch River between it and Bad Windsheim. The Aischgrund region of Middle Franconia has a gentle and pretty landscape and is most noted for its carp. Fittingly, there are numerous carp ponds dotting the area and the two breweries listed here specialize in serving carp. For those not interested in trying the local delicacy, they have many other choices as well. If you are piqued to sample it, go in months with an "R" in them, as that is when the fish is surely available and freshest. It's also noted as a nesting area for storks, hence the name of today's hike, and you'll quite possibly see some with nests right in the small town.

There is fair bus service from the Neustadt (Aisch) train station to Uehlfeld (the Uehlfeld Kirche stop is closest to the breweries). Neustadt (Aisch) has good connections to Nuremberg. It's about a 90 minute trip, half that by car. If you're contemplating other breweries on the Bierstraße, a car is probably preferable.

Coming out of the Brauereigaststätte Prechtel on Hauptstraße, take note of the pretty Jakobus Church across the street and then head left down the main street. At the first street, turn left on Kirchenstraße. Follow this to a T and go left on Raiffeisenstraße. This soon forks – go to the right, around the curved part of the street. Once around it, look for signs for the Storchen-Lehrpfad on your left. They are colorful with a drawing of a stork on them. There's also a small wooden bridge. Cross it and turn left to walk along the Aisch River on a tree-lined path. It veers left and then right as you follow along the Mühlkanal. At the end of the path, go right on Mühlenstraße. Though not a super-busy street, always be careful when crossing. Thankfully part of the route is along a raised wooden pathway and off to the left of the street. It's a bit like walking in the Scandinavian parks, albeit not as remote. You'll cross over the Aisch River and walk through the small farm village of Voggendorf before coming to another street. Cross it, and the Voggendorfer Bierkeller is on your left. It's perched up on a small hill with nice views over the valley, so it's worth a stop. There are some cool old beer storage cellars off to the side, built into a hill. If the Bierkeller is open, they will have Prechtel Schnapperla on tap. If not, or you're saving yourself for the brewery, continue past the Bierkeller and take the first right onto an unnamed farm road marked with the Storchen-Lehrpfad sign. Follow it to the next major farm road, then follow the signs to the left and then a relatively quick right, also marked. Down this road, there are some large ponds on your right and smaller ones to your left. At the last and largest one, you'll turn right and walk along it. At the turn, you'll be about halfway back to Uehlfeld.

The route back is straight forward. At the end of the pond you'll veer right onto another farm road that ends in a T where you go right again. You get nice views of Uehlfeld from here – keep your eyes open for flying storks which frequent the area. This road curves left as it enters Demantsfürth, a small suburb of Uehlfeld. As you exit the small village, there's a low observation tower, best suited for children, for a slightly elevated view. If not interested, turn left and then right to the main road. Go right on the 470, there's a pedestrian path on the bridge as you cross the Aisch River again. There's a bicycle path that mirrors the road back into Uehlfeld on the other side. As it curves to the right, it becomes the Bahnhofstraße, which turns into Hauptstraße as it curves left. You'll be back at the Brauereigaststätte Prechtel before you know it. If you've already been there, rather than turn with Hauptstraße, go straight on Burghaslacher Straße. Brauerei-Gasthof Zwanzger is immediately on right. If you're wise, you'll have reserved a room there so you can enjoy both breweries at your leisure.

BRAUEREIGASTSTÄTTE PRECHTEL

Founded around 1900, Brauereigaststätte Prechtel has a homey atmosphere and seems very much a village pub. Both times I was in town, however, it was very busy – probably due as much to their great food as their beer. Though they specialize in carp dishes, I had a smoked pork dish both times. It was that good! My wife was with me the second time and agreed I'd not exaggerated (something I'm prone to do!). They also have a nice outside seating area. Their main Biergarten is just outside town, on the edge of the small village of Voggendorf. This is where they serve their Schnapperla (Kellerbier) on tap. I'd specifically come to try it at the source and was sad to find it only in bottles. I've yet to be there during Bierkeller season so it will be a good reason to return. I did, however, have their Kirchweihbier from a bottle and it was excellent. It was to be tapped the following week at the annual Kirchweih.

Beers on tap: Prechtel Hopfenstoff. Bottled Schnapperla, Schmankerl Weiße and seasonals like their lovely Kirchweihbier.

PRACTICAL INFORMATION

Brauereigaststätte Prechtel
Hauptstraße 24
91486 Uehlfeld
+49 9163-228
www.brauerei-prechtel.de

Open daily at 11:00 am
Closed Monday
From May to September, no hot meals in the evening due to the
Bierkeller being open.

Voggendorfer Bierkeller
Mühlenstraße
91486 Uehlfeld
+49 9163 441 or call the brewpub on +49 9163 228

Open Monday to Thursday at 5:00 pm
Friday and Saturday at 3:00 pm
Sundays and holidays at 11:00 am

There is a little information, such as announcements about the
Bierkeller's events on the brewery website. It is right on the Storchen-
Lehrfpfad so finding it shouldn't be a problem. It's only open from May
to the end of August and only in good weather as there is no indoor
seating.

Brauerei-Gasthof Zwanzger
Burghaslacher Str. 10
91486 Uehlfeld
+49 9163 959756
www.brauerei-gasthof-zwanzger.de

Open from Whit Sunday to mid-October:
Tuesday 4:00 pm
Wednesday to Friday 11:00 am
Saturday 10:00 am
Sunday 10:00 am to 8:00 pm
From mid-October to Whit Sunday:
Same as above except at 4:00 pm
Tuesday to Thursday and at 10:00 am Friday

The second of the town's breweries is
equally good and has the bonus of having
rooms. They also have a fair selection of
beers including some craft beers so
spending the night might be a good idea,
especially if you come by car.

UPPER FRANCONIA

GRÄFENBERG

TOP OF THE FÜNF-SEIDLA-STEIG®

UPPER FRANCONIA

▷⋯ STARTING POINT

LINDENBRÄU, GRÄFENBERG

🍺 BEER

LINDENBRÄU VOLLBIER

⛰ MAP

ATK25-E10 & ATK25-F10

EBERMANNSTADT & ECKENTAL

🔍 HIGHLIGHTS

THUISBRUNN CASTLE, GEORG BREHMER BREWING MUSEUM, GASTHOF SEITZ, FARMLAND SCENERY, FOREST LANDSCAPE

⋯✕ DESTINATION

LINDENBRÄU, GRÄFENBERG

🎲 DIFFICULTY

HIKE 🥾

🕐 DURATION OF THE HIKE

12 KM
2.5–3H

〰 ELEVATION GAIN

ASCENT: 279 M
DESCENT: 276 M

5.2%
ALCOHOL
CONTENT

OLD-STYLE FRANCONIAN
LAGER BREWED WITH
AN EIGHT-HOUR BOIL,
ONE-WEEK COLD
MATURATION AND
LAGERED FOR SIX WEEKS

AMBER,
ROCKY HEAD

MALT,
HOPS

SOFT, FRUITY, SLIGHT
BITTERNESS, CLEAN DRY
FINISH

BITTERNESS   SWEETNESS

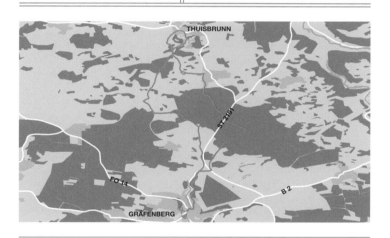

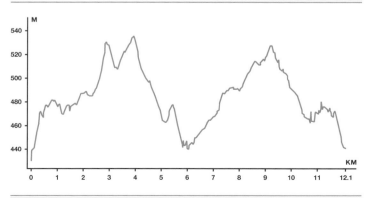

179

DESCRIPTION OF THE ROUTE

 The Fünf-Seidla-Steig® may not be the oldest beer hiking circuit in Bavaria, but it's very likely the most popular. It's not hard to see why – with five great breweries, a well-marked trail, a hilltop castle, half-timbered houses and a varied landscape, it really has it all. The various trails that make up the circuit have likely been used for hundreds of years and have even been marked for recreational use for quite some time now. However, the idea to put them together in order to link all the breweries didn't come about until 2008, when the defunct brewery in the Gasthaus Seitz started brewing again. The Greater Nuremberg Travel Network (VGN) jumped on the bandwagon to promote the trail's accessibility by public transportation, which helped boost awareness. Another good marketing aspect was the catchy and self-descriptive name: "Fünf" for the five breweries; a Seidel is a beer mug typical of the area, with a side handle and is generally a bit rounded and stout; "la" is a suffix attached to words in the Franconian dialect to connote small and Seidlas are only a half liter; Steig refers to a steep path or track. Soon enough, people from Nuremberg were flocking there on weekends to get out in the countryside, enjoy the fresh air, and of course, the great beer. Needless to say, you won't be alone if you do this on a nice weather weekend or any holiday, but that's part of the fun. It's a bit like a beer festival where everyone hikes from stand to stand. Yet another well-thought-out marketing ploy was having a stamp card. You collect a stamp from each of the five breweries and when completed, you can buy a Fünf-Seidla-Steig® mug at a reduced price.

While the circuit can be, and usually is, completed in one day, with five breweries and around fifteen different beers to potentially try, saying it can seem rushed is an understatement. So, I've cut it in half. The below description is the upper part of it.

Gräfenberg is serviced by frequent trains from Nuremberg so this can be easily done as day trip from there.

Coming out of Lindenbräu, go left on Am Bach. At the end of the street, you'll see a yellow building on your left. It's the Brewery Museum dedicated to the late Georg Brehmer, the original brewer at Lindenbräu. Turn right here on Kasberger Straße. This becomes Büttnersberg after you pass Egloffsteiner Straße. Take the first left onto an unnamed street that has multiple trail signs, including the colorful one for the Fünf-Seidla-Steig®, featuring some mugs with hills as their background. This small path joins with Am Michelsberg. You will then come to a fork; both sides have the same name which is initially confusing. Take the left side, following the trail signs. This soon veers right and then enters a nice forest as you continue to climb, marred slightly by the sounds of a quarry on the left-hand side. When you pass this, you crop back down to street level. This is a trail junction. Going to the right is the regular Fünf-Seidla-Steig® route, but you'll come back on that. Instead, go straight on the larger, much busier road. You'll see a sign for the Variante Rundweg über Neusles, with the same symbol as the regular Fünf-Seidla-Steig® signs. You're not on the big road for long, crossing it and looking for signs on your left for the trail. The street is Alte Egloffsteiner Straße. This initially mirrors the main road but isn't as busy, and you'll quickly veer left off the street onto the dirt track. This is all before the 2 kilometer mark and you're out in a pretty open area – especially nice during the fall foliage season. After the open area, you will skirt a forest on your right before briefly going into it. As you emerge from it, the trail veers left and you'll be on a farm road. This soon comes to an asphalt street which you will turn right onto and follow into the small village of Neusles. Walk through it and go right on the large street, looking for the smaller path on your left. Go left onto the unnamed but well-marked path. This is probably the prettiest part of the route, with a nice mix of open areas and forests, accentuated by mossy rocks. After passing a Christmas tree farm on your right, you will come to a T at the 5 kilometer mark. You are now leaving the Variante and going back on the Fünf-Seidla-Steig®. You'll want to go left here to go towards Thuisbrunn. You will then come to an intersection and the signs will send you right to Thuisbrunn, a slightly shorter route, but if you continue straight, uphill, you'll get some nice views. Follow the brick road up, under the electrical wires and at the top of the hill, go right. This will take you right to Thuisbrunn, and as you round the corner, you'll get great views of the castle. As you walk a bit further, the full Thuisbrunn skyline with the castle and church come into view. You will then go downhill and at the main road, take a right. Gasthof Seitz is on your right. This is home to Elch-Bräu, the newest brewery on the route. You will probably be hungry at this point, or at least thirsty. The Biergarten is one of the best on the circuit and is generally packed. Dive in and enjoy. Don't forget your stamp!

When you're done, continue past the brewery and go right. Not unusual for these parts but confusingly, all the streets have the same name: Thuisbrunn. You'll be walking with the brewery on your right and will notice their whiskey distillery with the moose head logo. Continue on this road, and when you come to a fork, take the well-marked right side. This will bring you back to the intersection you smartly went uphill at for the views. This time, go left and follow the now familiar hiking signs. At the next fork, take the left side again to remain on the Fünf-Seidla-Steig® and avoid going back on the Variante you came in on. At around the 7 kilometer mark, you'll see an unmarked path on your left. This is a much-used shortcut to Brauerei Hofmann. If it's a busy day, you'll see people coming down the path but even if you don't, go left and follow the obviously well-trodden trail. If you miss it, no worries. You'll take a marked left at the intersection, followed by a left to get there. Either way, you'll end up at Brauerei Hofmann, and even if you're not ready, you'll have to have a beer to get a stamp. Their Dunkles is a can't miss even if you're not collecting.

Coming out of Brauerei Hofmann, go left – not back on the shortcut route. Follow this to a larger road and carefully cross it. You'll walk by an idyllic private half-timbered home before ducking into one of the greenest stretches of the route. This meanders a bit before coming to an asphalt street. Cross it and look for trail signs. You will more or less cross a small dirt parking area and go left back into the forest. Just after the 9 kilometer mark, keep your eyes out to your right for the turn. It's well-marked and says Gräfenberg is 3.5 kilometers on the Fran-kenweg, also part of the Fünf-Seidla-Steig® during this portion. Not too much longer after that, you will come out into an open field. As you reach the main road, you will veer left and soon cross it a bit away from the busy intersection. On the other side, cross a small open field before turning left into the forest and by the quarry again. This is the same trail you started on, so follow it back to Gräfenberg, making a right on Büttnersberg and a left on Am Bach this time. Lindenbräu is on your right. Get your stamp right away, you're going to forget otherwise!

LINDENBRÄU

Though a relative newcomer on the block, having been founded in 1932, Lindenbräu remains perhaps the most traditional, still serving their renowned Vollbier from a gravity dispense barrel. Draped in hops and with a gorgeous old green tile oven, it is also the most atmospheric pub on the route. The courtyard seating area is bustling late in the day on weekends, but the most charming spot, if you're lucky enough to get one, is under the Linden tree where a few wooden benches and tables get their shade from the brewery's namesake.

There's a good cold snack menu and a fair amount of warm meals. Their daily specials often feature an excellent Schäuferla (pork shoulder), the signature dish of Franconia. If all this weren't enough, they do their own malting of the grains and have a distillery on site as well.

This is another family-run enterprise. The late Georg Brehmer, brewer and life of the old-world pub passed away in 2000, but his daughter has ably taken the reigns, becoming one of three female brewers on the Fünf-Seidla-Steig®. Her husband is now doing most of the brewing, as the pub has become quite busy in the wake of the now-noted beer hiking circuit. Though their Vollbier is considered one of Franconia's best, they've expanded their line-up in recent years and even won a medal for their Hefeweizen. The icing on the cake is that they have rooms – but book well in advance.

Beers on tap: Lindenbräu Vollbier, Lindenbräu Pils and Lindenbräu Zwickl. Bottled: Lindenbräu Hefeweizen. Seasonal: Lindenbräu Bock during Lent and Lindenbräu Festbier before Christmas.

PRACTICAL INFORMATION

Lindenbräu
Am Bach 3
91322 Gräfenberg
+49 9192 348
www.lindenbraeu.de

Open:
Monday 4:00 pm to 10:00 pm (closed mid-November to mid-March)
Tuesday to Friday 11:00 am to 10:00 pm
Saturday 10:00 am to 10:00 pm
Closed Sunday

Rooms available and information on their website along with Betriebsurlaub (vacation dates). Rooms can be booked via e-mail but it's best to call, especially if on short notice.

Gasthaus Seitz-Elch Bräu
Thuisbrunn 11
91322 Gräfenberg (Thuisbrunn)
+49 9197 221
www.gasthof-seitz.de

Open Tuesday, Friday, Saturday & Sunday from 10:00 am
Closed Monday, Wednesday and Thursday

Brauerei Hofmann
Hohenschwärz 16
91322 Gräfenberg (Hohenschwärz)
+49 919 2251
www.brauerei-hofmann.de

Open Wednesday to Sunday 10:00 am to 9:00 pm
Closed Monday & Tuesday

Brauereimuseum Brehmer
The Georg Brehmer Brewing Museum has no regular opening hours. Appointments must be arranged in advance: +49 919 2348.

WEISSENOHE

BOTTOM OF THE FÜNF-SEIDLA-STEIG®

UPPER FRANCONIA

▷··· STARTING POINT	···✕ DESTINATION
WEIßENOHE TRAIN STATION	**WIRTSHAUS KLOSTER-BRAUEREI, WEIßENOHE**
🍺 BEER	🀱 DIFFICULTY
ALTFRÄNKISCHES KLOSTERBIER	**HIKE** 🚶
🗺 MAP	
ATK25-F10 ECKENTAL	⏱ DURATION OF THE HIKE
	5.5 KM 1.5–2H
🔎 HIGHLIGHTS	〰 ELEVATION GAIN
KLOSTER WEIßENOHE, ST. BONIFATIUS CHURCH, MAIN SQUARE OF GRÄFENBERG, FOUNTAIN STATUE OF THE RITTER WIRNT	ASCENT: 210 M DESCENT: 210 M

OLD-STYLE
FRANCONIAN
LAGER

AMBER,
CREAMY HEAD

MALT,
SLIGHT CHOCOLATE

MALTY, SOME CHOCOLATE,
UNDERLYING HOPS,
DRY, BITTER FINISH

BITTERNESS

SWEETNESS

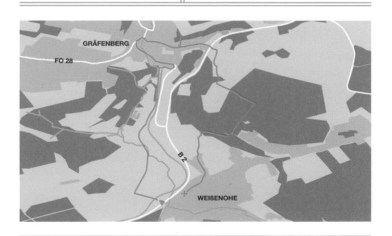

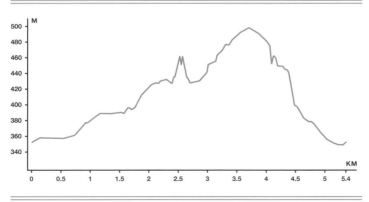

DESCRIPTION OF THE ROUTE

Kloster Weißenohe is a former Benedictine monastery dating back to around 1050, and there is indication that a brewery has been on site since then, too. Many believe it to be the oldest brewery in Franconia. It weathered many tough years before succumbing to secularization in the early 1800s. Many of the buildings were destroyed but a core area was sold into private hands in 1827 and has remained in the same family ever since. The monastery's church is still in use for services and is a tourist draw to those visiting the brewery's fine restaurant. Some good fortune came its way when the Fünf-Seidla-Steig® was created, with many people starting or finishing their trek here.

Weißenohe is serviced by frequent trains from Nuremberg and is an easy day trip.

The station at Weißenohe is only a platform, and coming off it, you could get to Kloster Weißenohe most easily by going right. In fact, probably everyone disembarking from the train there will do just that. This hike will take you in the other direction, so take a left and cross the tracks. Go straight on Am Neuacker until it comes to a T. Take a right on Sportplatzstraße. It basically takes you all the way to Gräfenberg and mirrors the train tracks much of the way. People use it as a shortcut between the two towns, most typically at the end of the hike. Chances are if you're doing it early, you won't see anyone on it. You'll soon see the station to your right as the route comes to an end. Turn right onto Bahnhofstraße and follow it until you see a smaller path on your left. Take that rather than the street, then on the other side, go left and follow Bahnhofstraße all the way into town. As it bends right, it will merge with Guttenburger Straße. Continue on Bahnhofstraße as it veers right. If you continue straight, you'll be on Am Bach and the brewery Lindenbräu will be on your left. If you haven't already been there, by all means check it out. If you have, go right on Bahnhofstraße which soon veers left and becomes the Marktplatz. It's a cute little square with some half-timbered buildings. The fountain is adorned with a statue of the Ritter Wirnt, a lyrical poet/singer revered as the first son of Gräfenberg. Continue along this road and it becomes Bayreuther Straße, which will lead you through the town's medieval gate. On the other side of it is Friedmann's Bräustüberl on your right, one of the five breweries on the Fünf-Seidla-Steig®. Stop in for their lovely Pils – if you're hungry, it's a great place to eat.

When finished, continue along Bayreuther Straße and look on your left for signs for the Biergarten zum Bergschlösschen. The street is called Jägersberg. It's a steep climb, but beyond the Biergarten is a nice viewpoint with a memorial. The Biergarten is Friedman's other outlet and features Sigi's Lager on tap. There are nice views so, if it's open, it's worth a stop. Head back down the stairs to the main street and make a left to follow Bayreuther Straße once again. On your left will be the actual Brauerei Friedmann, but they don't have a tasting room so keep going to the fork, veering right to go towards the large busy street, Nürnberger Straße. Carefully cross it and look for an opening on the other side for the Fünf-Seidla-Steig®. It leads to steps that will take you up for good views of Gräfenberg. At the top, go right on Sollenberger Straße. Follow this through a residential area until it bends to the left. Both forks are called Sollenberger, but there are Fünf-Seidla-Steig® signs pointing you towards Weißenohe, your destination. This leads to a brief forested section as it veers right and then left, before opening up into farmland. Follow this to the intersection and go right. You'll skirt another open field and walk between two fenced-in areas before ducking into the forest again as it veers right. You'll make a left to stay on the path which will turn into Mönchs-bergstraße, leading you into the outskirts of the town of Weißenohe. This becomes Gräfenberger Straße as it winds to the right, ending at Sollenberger Straße, where you will turn right. It's soon the Haupt-straße and the Wirtshaus Klosterbrauerei Weißenohe is on your left.

WIRTSHAUS KLOSTERBRAUEREI WEISSENOHE

Though the monastery hasn't been in operation for over 200 years and has been in private hands for nearly as long, when you walk through the archway you could be forgiven for thinking otherwise. Of course, that would be on a quiet day during the week. On busy weekends, though, you're unlikely to encounter a monk sharing a brew with the throngs of tourists.

The church is straight on and is well worth a peek. On your right is the charming Biergarten and on your left, the atmospheric old restaurant. Both are quite nice, but if it's busy, you might not have a choice so grab a seat and celebrate the end of your hike.

It's claimed to be the oldest brewery restaurant in Franconia, but that might be a bit misleading since there were many closures over the years, including a relatively recent and long one. Due to hard times and the war, it closed in 1943 and remained so until the year 2000. The restaurant was refurbished just in time for the Fünf-Seidla-Steig®'s inception some eight years later and is now one of the most popular stops on the renowned route.

In addition to their full range of traditional beers, they make some craft beers, one of which (Green MONKey) has become so popular that it's not only joined the regular line-up but is generally on tap in the Biergarten too.

Beers on tap: Altfränkisches Klosterbier and three others, including possibly Bonifatius Dunkel, Eucharius Pils, the aforementioned Green MONKey, and the seasonal Bonator Doppelbock.

As you can see, there are lots of good beery reasons to spend the night in Weißenohe, but if you are headed back to Nuremberg, walk back out that archway and go left on Hauptstraße. This winds to your right and brings you to the main road (Bundesstraße). Carefully cross it and on the other side is the Weißenohe platform you started the hike from.

PRACTICAL INFORMATION

Wirtshaus Klosterbrauerei Weißenohe
Klosterstraße 20
91367 Weißenohe
+49 9192 63 57
www.das-wirtshaus-klosterbrauerei-weissenohe.de

Open Wednesday to Friday from 11:00 am
Saturday & Sunday from 10:00 am (from 11:00 am in winter)
Closed Monday & Tuesday

Friedmann's Bräustüberl
Bayreuther Straße 14
91322 Gräfenberg
+49 9192 992318
www.friedmanns-braeustueberl.de

Open Wednesday from 5:00 pm
Thursday & Friday from 11:00 am
Saturday from 10:00 am
Sunday 10:00 am to 8:00 pm
Closed Monday & Tuesday (but open all holidays, even if it's on a Monday)

Biergarten zum Bergschlösschen
Am Michelsberg 36
91322 Gräfenberg
+49 162 589 06 90

Open from May to September only:
Friday 4:00 pm to 9:30 pm
Saturday, Sunday & holidays 2:00 pm to 9:30 pm

THUISBRUNN TO LEUTENBACH

THE CASTLE RUIN TRAIL

UPPER FRANCONIA

▷··· STARTING POINT	···✕ DESTINATION
GASTHOF SEITZ ELCH-BRÄU, THUISBRUNN (GRÄFENBERG)	BRAUEREI-GASTHOF DRUMMER, LEUTENBACH (OBERFRANKEN)

 BEER

DRUMMER DUNKLES VOLLBIER

 DIFFICULTY

HIKE

 MAP

ATK25-E10 & ATK25-F10

EBERMANNSTADT & ECKENTAL

🕐 DURATION OF THE HIKE

9 KM
2-3H

 HIGHLIGHTS

CASTLE RUIN OF THUISBRUNN, CASTLE RUIN OF BURGSTALL SCHLOSSBERG, RURAL SCENERY, ST. MORITZ CHAPEL

〰 ELEVATION GAIN

ASCENT: 190 M
DESCENT: 300 M

CLASSIC
FRANCONIAN
LAGER

AMBER,
OFF-WHITE HEAD

GRAIN

BALANCED, HOPPY,
MALT BASE,
DRY BITTER FINISH

BITTERNESS

SWEETNESS

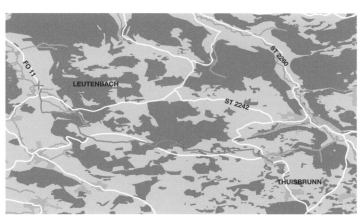

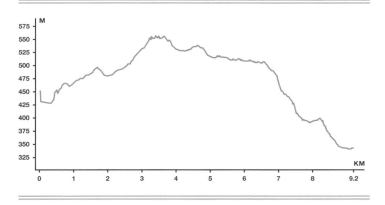

DESCRIPTION OF THE ROUTE

 Franconian Switzerland is renowned for the number of small breweries that densely dot its landscape. Traveling by public transportation can create the illusion of distance between them but a good map will reveal otherwise. This is a great trail connecting the Fünf-Seidla-Steig® and the many trails in the Leutenbach (Oberfranken) area. It's not only a good way to get from point A and point B but also a fine scenic route in its own right.

Thuisbrunn is at the northern extreme of the Fünf-Seidla-Steig® and this hike works best if you can spend the night there. Otherwise, doing it on a weekend or public holiday is best.

Thuisbrunn is serviced by regular but limited buses from Gräfenberg, which is well-connected to Nuremberg. On weekends and public holidays, the direct buses take as little as 10 minutes. During the week, it's more complicated and some of the buses are call buses. You will have to prearrange them and it requires some German to do so. It's easiest to use regular buses if possible.

If you've arrived by bus from Gräfenberg, you will be just up the street from Gasthof Seitz. You will likely be able to see the castle up on the hill, so make your way towards it. The Gasthof, also known as Elch-Bräu, will be on your left-hand side. With the Gasthof at your back and the castle in sight above you, go left on the main road out front. Walk with the castle to your right. Follow it for a short distance. There are some small hiking signs with a green circle. This will be your initial route. You'll see a bus stop on your right as the road bends left. Just before you leave the village, you'll see a large sign saying that Egloffstein is 3 kilometers away. There will also be a biking sign and on the pole will be a green circle hiking sign. Go right there. Not far up this road, on your left-hand side, is a small set of wooden steps. There's an old wooden sign for Knoll-Leite and a smaller new one with a flower inside a black circle. Go up the steps to find a junction for the Leitenweg. This is the circuit that the flower sign is for. You will want to go left. Follow it to a brick farm road and go right on that. Take this road up to another left. There are signs on the right-hand side of the turn. You will already be leaving the Leitenweg and returning to the green circle trail. It also follows a second trail with a yellow diagonal line on it. Take the left and you'll be on a wide gravel road. This is all before the 1 kilometer mark.

You'll be out in the open countryside now with pretty views in all directions. Continue straight, and even when turns or forks are obvious, there will be green circles to point you in the right direction. Around the 2 kilometer mark, look to your right and up high on the hill is a small red and white flag for Franconia. That's the Schlossberg, where you're headed. You'll go through one intersection before coming to a very well-marked right. Take this and walk towards the forest ahead. Once there, duck into it to your right when you see a large tree with a green dot on it. You will also see red X signs. At the top of this path, go left. Follow this through the pretty forest, and before the 3 kilometer mark, make a well-marked right. You will soon come to a junction. Continuing straight will eventually bring you to Leutenbach but there is a side trail to your right. This leads to the Burgstall and is well worth the small climb to get there. You'll be at the Schlossberg-Anlage before you know it. There are some picnic benches and it's a cool shady spot for a break. Go through the entrance and follow the obvious trail to the Burgstall. There are some steps and wooden walkways. It's a fun trail, and from the top, you'll have views into the valley you just walked through. When you're done, head back to the junction from which you came.

Once there, go right and follow the green dot signs through the forest. When you come to a small junction, go to the left on the yellow dot trail and leave the green circle trail behind. This leads to the main road, where you'll go right. Carefully cross it first as you'll be looking for the trail on that side. Walk up the somewhat busy road and you'll see the occasional yellow dot and come to a well-marked left. It has a yellow dot and says that Leutenbach is 4.5 kilometers away. Ortspitz is also listed as 2 kilometers away – your next focal point.

Follow this through a small stretch of forest before coming out in open farmland. Continue straight, and you'll soon be walking through a pretty orchard. You'll come to an asphalt road just before the 6 kilometer mark; cross it and continue straight on the other side. This veers right before coming to another street. Take a right here to head into Ortspitz. Walk through the small village and keep your eyes open for your route to the left. It's at about the 6.5 kilometer mark.

Although it is well-marked, it is nearly impossible to see when coming from this direction. It's a dirt path and in spring there are lilacs in bloom. When you walk past it and look back, you'll see a yellow dot sign saying St. Moritz is 600 meters away. Follow the path downhill to an open grassy area. You'll see St. Moritz Chapel in the not-too-far distance. Walk towards it, staying on the left side of the meadow. When you come to a small hiking trail junction, veer left to stay on the route to Leutenbach, now only few kilometers away. Just up this gravel path, you'll see some wooden stairs going down on your right. Go down them to remain on the route. This is a very pretty section that goes along a brook and has some limestone formations. There's an atmospheric picnic area down there, which you will appreciate if it's a very hot day. When this part of the trail ends, you will walk through a well-marked forest, following the yellow dots.

You'll pass some cellars built into the hill on your left along the way. These were the forerunners of refrigeration. Just before the 8 kilometer mark, you will come out into the open and have views of Leutenbach to your right. At the main road, turn right to head into town. This is Mittelehrenbacher Straße. As you walk along it, look ahead to your left to see the Walberla, a flattish hill and the north peak of the Ehrenbürg. There are hikes up and around it from town. Continue straight; the road becomes Am Pfarrgarten after the intersection. Keep going straight on this road – it crosses another intersection before becoming St.-Moritz-Straße. This ends at Dorfstraße, where you will veer right. Brauerei-Gasthof Drummer is just up the street on your right.

BRAUEREI-GASTHOF DRUMMER

Founded in 1738 by the Drummer family, who are still very much at the helm, Brauerei-Gasthof Drummer is a great old traditional pub with a green tile oven and a low-beamed ceiling. Their truly homestyle cooking features all the Franconian standards, including the increasingly rare Bauchfleisch mit Bohnen (pork belly with beans). This pairs well with their Dunkles Vollbier, a hoppy treat. The Biergarten out back is a great spot to enjoy your post-hike celebratory beer.

This is not a place you would be likely to stumble across – it took me 20 odd years to do so, even though I'm always on the lookout for new breweries. I first had their beer at the yearly Fränkisches Bierfest in Nuremberg. This is a great event which features an amazing array of Franconian beers along with a small selection of international ones. It's set in the moat around the medieval old town, about as atmospheric a beer festival as you'll find.

Beers on tap: Drummer Dunkles Vollbier, Drummer Helles Lager.

PRACTICAL INFORMATION

Brauerei-Gasthof Drummer
Dorfstraße 10
91359 Leutenbach
+49 9199 403
www.brauerei-gasthof-drummer.de

Open Tuesday, Wednesday & Friday
11:00 am to 2:30 pm & 5:00 pm to 10:00 pm
Thursday 11:00 am to 2:30 pm
Saturday 11:00 am to 10:00 pm
Sunday & holidays 11:00 am to 3:30 pm

Rooms available but reservations can only be made by phone.

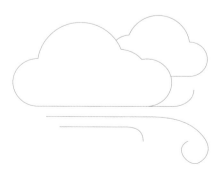

LEUTENBACH (WALBERLA)

OVER THE WALBERLA AND THROUGH THE WOODS TO THE RODENSTEIN WE GO

UPPER FRANCONIA

▷··· STARTING POINT	···✕ DESTINATION
BRAUEREI-GASTHOF DRUMMER, LEUTENBACH (OBERFRANKEN)	**BRAUEREI-GASTHOF DRUMMER, LEUTENBACH (OBERFRANKEN)**
🍺 BEER	🎲 DIFFICULTY
ALT VOLLBIER DUNKEL	**HIKE**
⛰ MAP	
ATK25-E10	🕐 DURATION OF THE HIKE
EBERMANNSTADT	**7 KM 2H**
🔍 HIGHLIGHTS	〰 ELEVATION GAIN
WALBERLA, ST. JAMES THE ELDER CHURCH, RODENSTEIN, ST. WALBURGIS CHAPEL, HALF-TIMBERED HOUSES OF DIETZHOF, EHRENBÜRG	ASCENT: 290 M DESCENT: 295 M

5.0%
ALCOHOL CONTENT

CLASSIC
FRANCONIAN
LAGER

CHESTNUT,
OFF-WHITE HEAD

MALT,
A TOUCH OF LICORICE

ROAST MALT, HINT OF
LICORICE, HOPPY DRY,
BITTER FINISH

BITTERNESS

SWEETNESS

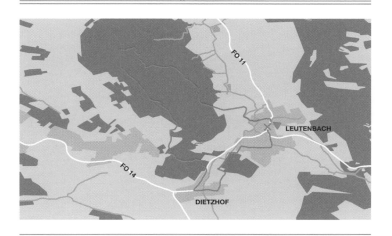

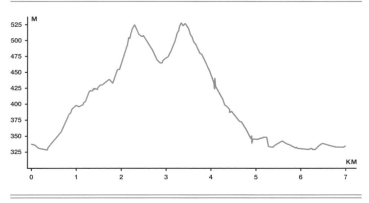

DESCRIPTION OF THE ROUTE

The Ehrenbürg is an impressive flattish twin-peaked hill in Franconian Switzerland with a history dating back to 4000 BCE. Some evidence of pagan worship and sacrifices has been excavated from its hauntingly beautiful grounds. Today, it provides great recreational opportunities like hiking and cycling. There are trails around it and across the flat plateau that connect Walberla and Rodenstein but the Walburgiskapelle (St. Walburgis Church) that sits atop and dates from the 17th century is a reminder of its religious roots. There is a Walberla-Fest each spring, reportedly the oldest of its kind in Germany, dating back to the 9th century. It's likely to have evolved from pagan spring rituals but let's not let that interfere with the task at hand: going on a beer hike.

Leutenbach (Oberfranken) is serviced by regular but limited buses from both Forchheim and Gräfenberg (Oberfranken) during the week and on Saturdays. On Sundays, it is a call bus and must be prearranged. The trip takes around 15 minutes from Forchheim, easily reached on lines between Nuremberg and Bamberg.

Coming out of Brauerei-Gasthof Drummer, go right on Dorfstraße. At Ehrenbürgstraße, go left, and as you walk along it you will see the Kirche St. Jakobus der Ältere (St. James the Elder Church) on your right with its distinctive tower. Continue straight and you'll soon pass a pond on your right. There are nice views of the church, often reflected in the pond from the far end of it. Past the pond, the road forks and you'll go right to continue on Immergrundstraße. You will start to see numerous hiking signs. One is for the Rundweg Walberla – red with a white circle and a depiction of the twin-peaked hill within it. The other is a half red triangle/ half white triangle. This is the IFS-Weg, a long-distance route headed towards Kirchehrenbach. Your initial route will be on both of these. It's very well-marked and initially on asphalt. As you gain elevation, you will get nice views of the valley and some rocky outcroppings of the Walberla. You'll soon be in the forest as you continue to climb. You will come to an automobile gate just after the 1 kilometer mark.

There is a side path going up from the left side of it, but you will pass the gate instead and stay on the main, wider unpaved road. The route continues with both trails intertwined, but when you eventually come to the fork where they diverge, take the left side. The other route would get you to the top but in a less direct way, wrapping around the Walberla first. This one has you there in no time. Once on top, you will pass some great rock formations as you make your way along the flattish top. Once down the far end of the Walberla, there are some viewpoints before you veer left towards the St. Walburgis Church. Just past the church, you'll come to a trail junction with many signs pointing in what seems every direction. You want to head towards the Rodenstein – it's only a half a kilometer away. The very obvious route dips down as you make your way back across the opposite side of the Walberla. You can see the crucifix atop the Rodenstein straight on. From its orientation, you won't be surprised when the path starts going back up as soon as it bottoms out. It's a fair grade with barriers on the sides, not to protect you from falling but to protect the adjacent areas from erosion. When the Walberla-Fest is on, there are thousands of people up here. On top, next to the crucifix, there's a nice bench. Take a seat and enjoy the valley below and the expanse of this marvelous butte.

When you're done, continue on to find the route dropping down on the other side. Follow signs for Dietzhof, your next destination. It's called the Jubiläumsweg 1914 on the sign. You'll pass a junction that could take you on the Walberla-Rundweg in the other direction to go around it, but keep following the signs for Dietzhof. You'll see the pretty church of Schlaifhausen as you drop down. When you come to a road with a small parking area, cross it and look for the trail on the other side. It says Dietzhof is 1 kilometer away. The route is marked with a horizontal red stripe and a yellow vertical one, both on white back-grounds. It's a dirt path that drops down from the parking area to a lush stretch of forest. Follow this until the two routes diverge. Take the left side to stay on the red stripe trail, also marked with a K, for Kulturwanderweg (cultural hiking trail). This continues down to a large road, where you go right. Follow this into town. At the first intersec-tion, take a left on Dietzhof. Brauerei und Gastwirtschaft Alt is just ahead on your right.

BRAUEREI UND GASTWIRTSCHAFT ALT

Brauerei und Gastwirtschaft Alt is housed in a lovely old half-timbered building, and though founded in 1886, the history of the town, and quite possibly brewing here, goes back a lot further. Within the barn out back, where the brewery now stands, there are two old barrel-vaulted ceilings, remnants of Dietzhof Castle, with a recorded history dating back to the early 1400s. With royals on the premises, it's likely there was beer. At any rate, the Dietz family has been brewing and running their timeless old pub for five generations, with particular attention paid to keeping things as close to the old days as possible. It's another low-beamed ceiling affair, with the requisite green tile oven giving it a cozy air. Their Schäuferla (pork shoulder) is legendary, and people flock here for their traditional Brotzeit (cold and warm snacks). Students from nearby Erlangen have a long history of making excursions here, and records show they have been coming to the Walberla-Fest since the 18th century. There's a small Biergarten out back but sitting in this history-filled room seems the best place to quaff their tasty dark brew.

Beers on tap: Alt Vollbier dunkel, Alt Vollbier hell

Sadly, the Dietz family doesn't have rooms for you to spend the night in and, to my knowledge, no one else in the village does either. So, when you're ready, it's time to head back to Leutenbach.

Coming out of Brauerei und Gastwirtschaft Alt on the street you arrived on, go right to continue on Dietzhof. At the first intersection, go left on the bike path to Leutenbach. It says it's only 1.7 kilometers. Follow this through the back of the village to a T. Go left there, followed by a relatively quick right. This trail is parallel to the main road on your left and passes pleasantly through open fields. It goes right and left before becoming Am Langen Bach. You'll already be on the outskirts of Leutenbach. At the first intersection, go right on Rosenau. Follow this to Mittelehrenbacher Straße and go left on it. Go straight, passing one intersection where the street becomes Am Pfarrgarten. Continue on this through another intersection, where the street turns into St.-Moritz-Straße. This soon ends at Dorfstraße where you will go right. Brauerei-Gasthof Drummer is just up the street on your right.

PRACTICAL INFORMATION

Brauerei und Gastwirtschaft Alt
Dietzhof 42
91359 Leutenbach (Dietzhof)
+49 9199 267
www.brauerei-alt.de

Open Wednesday to Friday 5:00 pm to 11:00 pm
Saturday 4:00 pm to 11:30 pm
Sunday 11:30 am to 11:30 pm
Closed Monday & Tuesday

Brauerei-Gasthof Drummer
Dorfstraße 10
91359 Leutenbach
+49 9199 403
www.brauerei-gasthof-drummer.de

Open Tuesday, Wednesday & Friday
11:00 am to 2:30 pm & 5:00 pm to 10:00 pm
Thursday 11:00 am to 2:30 pm
Saturday 11:00 am to 10:00 pm
Sunday & holidays 11:00 am to 3:30 pm

Rooms available but reservations can only be made by phone

LEUTENBACH (HETZELSDORF)

A TRIP FROM LEUTENBACH OVER THE REISBERG TO HETZELSDORF AND BACK

UPPER FRANCONIA

▷··· STARTING POINT

BRAUEREI-GASTHOF DRUMMER, LEUTENBACH

🍺 BEER

HETZELSDORFER FRÄNKISCHES VOLLBIER

 MAP

ATK25-E10
EBERMANNSTADT

👁 HIGHLIGHTS

ST. MATTHEWS CHURCH IN HETZELSDORF, REISBERG, ST. JAMES THE ELDER CHURCH IN LEUTENBACH, ROLLING HILLY LANDSCAPE

···✕ DESTINATION

BRAUEREI-GASTHOF DRUMMER, LEUTENBACH

 DIFFICULTY

HIKE

🕐 DURATION OF THE HIKE

9.5 KM
2.5–3H

〜 ELEVATION GAIN

ASCENT: 315 M
DESCENT: 330 M

CLASSIC
FRANCONIAN
LAGER

 AMBER,
MASSIVE ROCKY HEAD

 FLORAL HOPS,
SLIGHT CHOCOLATE

 DRY, FRUITY,
UNDERLYING HOPS,
BITTERSWEET FINISH

BITTERNESS

SWEETNESS

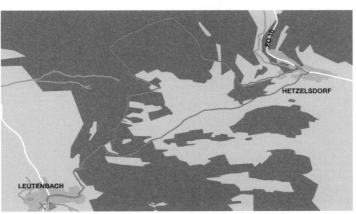

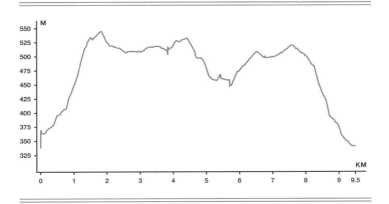

DESCRIPTION OF THE ROUTE

Though the small village of Hetzelsdorf is cute enough, and its St. Matthews Church has an atmospheric setting, it's not likely it would draw many tourists – but nonetheless, it does. They are primarily hikers and cyclists who come to enjoy the surrounding Franconian Switzerland landscape its nestled in and to visit the old-world brewpub there that serves up one of the region's most renowned beers. Since there is nowhere to spend the night in the quaint hamlet, this route takes you from nearby Leutenbach in a circuit over the Reisberg, all the while passing through the scenery the area is noted for.

Leutenbach (Oberfranken) is serviced by regular but limited buses from both Forchheim and Gräfenberg (Oberfranken) during the week and on Saturdays. On Sundays, it is a call bus and must be prearranged. The trip takes around 15 minutes from Forchheim, which is easily reached on lines between Nuremberg and Bamberg.

Coming out of Brauerei-Gasthof Drummer, go right on Dorfstraße. At the first intersection, you'll see St. James the Elder Church on your left. Take a right on Am Köppel. There are some hiking symbols on the pole of the street sign. The initial part of your route is on the yellow dot and red diamond trails. Follow the paved road as it winds to the left and then look on your right-hand side for the unpaved road. The red triangle trail sign says Hetzelsdorf is 3.6 kilometers away. The yellow dot one says Reisberg is 5.3 kilometers away. You're going to the latter first. Walk up the path until you come to a well-marked left turn. You'll also be on the red circle trail for a short stretch. This section is flat as you walk along a cherry orchard to your left with views of the Walberla through the trees. This path leads to a wider road, take it to the right for a short time. It will bring you to a trail junction where you will leave the red circle trail. Take the right side to remain on the yellow dot/red triangle trails. Reisberg and Hetzelsdorf are the two destinations. Follow this up through the forest. You'll pass some great mossy rock formations en route. This is all within a kilometer of Leutenbach.

When you come to a trail junction with a bench, you will leave the red triangle trail and continue straight on to follow the yellow dot trail to Reisberg. This is largely forested, but there are some views into the valley and towards the Walberla in the openings. This comes to a T trail junction, where you will take the well-marked left to remain on the yellow dot trail. Just up the trail, there is a junction for the red dot trail, but remain on the yellow dot trail: Reisberg is your destination.
This route soon joins the red circle trail as you walk around the Reisberg. This flat area has a lovely weathered pine forest. At the next junction, go right to follow the yellow dot/red dot trails. Another junction will come up quickly, the red X trail to Pretzfeld, but continue on the red dot: Hetzelsdorf is your destination. Follow the path down through the forest, and when you come to the curve of a paved road, go left and continue into the village. You'll soon have a nice photo opportunity on your left of St.-Matthäus-Kirche (St. Matthews Church). At the T, go left to find Brauereigasthof Penning-Zeissler on your right.

BRAUEREIGASTHOF PENNING-ZEISSLER

You probably wouldn't even see Brauereigasthof Penning-Zeissler if you weren't looking for it. The trees out front provide ample shade for their small but charming Biergarten. Interestingly, when the pub is closed, they leave cases of beer off to the side, along with a bottle opener, and you pay for them on the honor system. Such is life in small-village Franconia and it's much appreciated by the cyclists and hikers who happen by to sadly find the doors shuttered. When the weather's good, it's tough to top it for your post-hike thirst-quencher. There's no table service in the Biergarten, so head inside to grab a beer and check out the timeless old pub, often packed with people who come here specifically for their highly quaffable amber brew. On Sundays, they have various roast lunches but their regular menu is limited to simpler cold and warm snacks. Their mixed cold cuts plate is tasty but it seems Bratwurst is their specialty, judging by all the plates of it that are served.

Beers on tap: Hetzelsdorfer Fränkisches Vollbier, Hetzelsdorfer Pils plus seasonal Maibock and Festbier.

Every time I come here I lament their (and the village's) lack of overnight accommodation. So, when you're ready to head back to Leutenbach, go left outside the pub and walk past the road you entered town on to the next junction. You'll go right there on the red diamond trail, for Leutenbach and Kirchehrenbach. At the first fork, go left following the red diamond sign. When you come to a second fork just before the 6 kilometer mark, take the right side to Leutenbach. You'll pass some other side trails but stay on the red diamond trail. You'll cross an intersection with the red X trail but continue straight on the red diamond. You'll be crossing open farmland and orchards. At the next fork, take the left side. At the foot of the next forested section there's a fenced-in house and a sign pointing you towards Leutenbach. On the other side of this brief stretch, you will come to another trail junction. There's a shelter on your left. It was covered in wisteria when we last walked through. There's also a picnic bench. Go right on the main trail, a red diamond sign saying both Leutenbach and Kirchehrenbach. Follow this wide path to the next junction. This is the beginning of the circuit, so you should remember it, it has a bench. Go left here on the yellow dot trail to Leutenbach. This is the route you walked up from town on. Keep your eyes out to the left and you should catch a glimpse of some rock outcroppings, one with a crucifix atop. Take the trail back towards town, following yellow dot signs. When you get to Dorfstraße, go left and Brauerei-Gasthof Drummer will be on your left.

PRACTICAL INFORMATION

Brauereigasthof Penning-Zeissler
Hetzelsdorf 9
91362 Pretzfeld (Hetzelsdorf)
+49 9194 252

Wednesday to Friday from 4:00 pm
Weekends & public holidays from 11:00 am

BÜCHENBACH

BOTTOM OF THE BIERQUELLENWANDERWEG

UPPER FRANCONIA

▷··· STARTING POINT	···✗ DESTINATION
BRAUEREI-GASTHOF HEROLD, BÜCHENBACH (B. PEGNITZ)	**BRAUEREI-GASTHOF HEROLD, BÜCHENBACH (B. PEGNITZ)**
🍺 BEER	🁢 DIFFICULTY
BÜCHENBACHER BECK'N BIER	**HIKE** 🚶
⛰ MAP	
ATK25-E11	⏱ DURATION OF THE HIKE
PEGNITZ	**10.5 KM** **2.5–3H**
🔍 HIGHLIGHTS	〜 ELEVATION GAIN
ST. VITUS CHURCH, LEUPS CHAPEL, RURAL FARMLAND, HILLY LANDSCAPE	ASCENT: 290 M DESCENT: 285 M

4.6%
ALCOHOL CONTENT

DUNKLES MADE WITH HALLERTAU AROMA HOPS

**DEEP AMBER,
OFF-WHITE ROCKY HEAD**

**SLIGHT CHOCOLATE,
GRAIN,
HALLERTAU HOPS**

**MALTY, UNDERLYING HOPS,
TOUCH OF CHOCOLATE,
DRY BITTERSWEET FINISH**

BITTERNESS   **SWEETNESS**

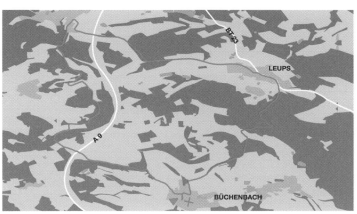

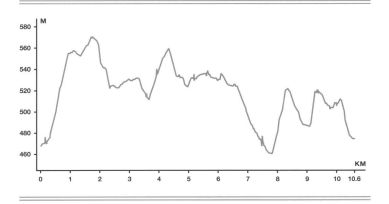

DESCRIPTION OF THE ROUTE

The Bierquellenwanderweg is one of the older beer hiking circuits in Bavaria. It's also one of the longer ones and features four breweries, two of them truly old-world Franconian classics. Though you can tackle it easily enough in a day, it can seem a bit rushed if you do. There is a convenient makeshift trail that cuts it in half, and if you are planning to stay in Trockau (perhaps the most conveniently located town), you can easily do both in two days. Its close proximity to Bayreuth and its neighboring autobahn makes for a somewhat mixed experience, but the beauty of the landscape itself is undeniable when you're away from the road. The villages themselves are small-town affairs and the brewpubs, when not crowded with weekend hikers, are frequented almost entirely by locals. Stepping into one is like stepping back in time – places like this are sadly a dying breed. If you only have time for half of the circuit, the below description will get you to my two favorite breweries on it in an easy 10-kilometer hike.

While the hike can be started in any of the three towns on the route, I am going to describe it from the Brauerei-Gasthof Herold. If you can get a room in the popular brewpub, it's a great place to end your hike and you can enjoy their beer at a leisurely pace. To my knowledge, there isn't anywhere to stay in Leups, and even though there are many accommodation options in Trockau, there is no brewery there.

Büchenbach (b. Pegnitz) is serviced by limited call buses from Pegnitz and Bayreuth. These operate a bit like pre-set taxis but go at set times and appear on the German transit websites and apps. If unaccustomed to using them, it would be easier to use a regular taxi but these should be arranged in advance as well, especially if your German is limited. Another option is to get a regular bus to Trockau or Leups. This is an area perhaps best visited by car, especially if you can get a room at Brauerei-Gasthof Herold.

Coming out of Brauerei-Gasthof Herold, you will see signs for the Bierquellenwanderweg right away. These have a typical beer mug of the area on them. Go left and follow Marktstraße until you come to Kosbrunner Weg. This is where the trail splits. You will be going towards Trockau and Weiglathal, about five and eight kilometers away, respectively. Turn right, beer mug signs marking the way. You will be out of the village before you know it and going through a brief tree-lined section before heading into open farmland. You'll have nice views of the St. Vitus Church to your right. You will turn left into a forest and back out into the open, all before the 1 kilometer mark. You will then walk along a fenced area towards the highway. This is perhaps the least pleasant part of the hike. Once there, you walk through well-marked underpass. This part is asphalt but you will only remain on it for a short time. Coming to a three-way fork, take the middle prong onto a farm road. This plunges into a forest which then

comes to an open area before you go right and skirt along it. There are numerous signs pointing you in the right direction as these were trails before the beer circuit was set up. You'll cross the open area just after the 2 kilometer mark and come to a T at a road. There is a sign, more or less saying Trockau is in either direction. Though slightly shorter to your left, you will want to go right to remain on the Bierquellenwanderweg. When in doubt, follow the yellow mugs. The trail passes through a forest before emerging at the curve of a larger road, where you will go left and follow the big curve. This winds 180° before going left. Follow its natural progression and turn right at the T where it ends. Stay on this road into the outskirts of Trockau. You will come in on Bodendorfer Weg, and if you are planning on doing the full circuit in one day, go left to remain on it and go through Trockau.

While Trockau is a nice enough place to stay and there are a few places to eat, unless you're planning on doing so, there's not a lot to see. The castle is a private residence so you can't go onto the property to get a good look at it. Otherwise, when you come to the intersection, go right instead of left and look for signs for Leups. This is the Bierquellenwanderweg "kurze Variante" (short route) and is marked with brown beer mugs. It's a shortcut across the circuit. Leups is only 2.6 kilometers away. You'll take a fairly quick right, followed by a left. Both turns are well-marked. At about the 5 kilometer mark, you'll be headed right for the highway again but it's a high overpass that you'll quickly walk under. On the other side, you'll quickly come to a playing field with seating and a kiosk. Walk through it, or the parking lot and continue on the other side into the forest. This ends at a larger road at around the 6 kilometer mark, where you will go left. Stay on this road all the way into Leups. It's only about a kilometer away. When you come to the main street in town, go right. You will now be back to the yellow mug signs of the main Bier-quellenwanderweg again. Brauereigasthof Gradl is just up the street on the left-hand side, after you pass the small Leups Chapel. No one could fault you for dropping in for their amazing dark beer at this point. Besides, you're only a few kilometers from the finish.

If not, continue straight on this road to the end of the small village. As small as it is, this is a fairly busy road so be careful crossing it. Thankfully, you won't be on it for long. As it veers left, you will veer right with a few beer mugs pointing you towards the forest ahead. At the mouth of the forest is a pretty crucifix and a sign saying Büchenbach is 4 kilometers away. Of course, half of it is uphill. After you exit this forested section and finish the first part of the climb, you will go left and skirt the trees before going back into them. There are ample beer mug signs whenever there is a turn to be made. When you come to a larger road, you will go left onto it and look for the biggest of the yellow beer mug signs on your right-hand side. I guess a lot of people followed the main road in the past but it's hard to miss the turn now. Go right and back into the forest on the smaller path.

This is the second part of the climb, but it's short. You'll veer to your right once out of the forest and follow this country road back into Büchenbach. You will get nice views of the valley from it and soon see the St. Vitus Church looming in the not-so-far distance. At about the 10 kilometer mark, you will take the natural left onto St.-Veit-Berg. You will get a closer look at the church to your left as you enter the village, but the road goes right as you follow it. At the Marktstraße, go left to return to your starting point. Brauerei-Gasthof Herold is waiting.

BRAUEREI-GASTHOF HEROLD

Brauerei-Gasthof Herold is the kind of place that makes Franconia a special place for beer because so little has changed here. The craft beer scene in America sprang from what had become an overly industrialized brewing world where beer was no longer "crafted" but merely produced. Well, these guys never went that way. The Herold family has been crafting beer the same way for 400 years. They also make their own meats and bake their own bread. The menu is simple but of great quality. Their Bratkartoffeln (roasted potatoes) are fabulous, as are all the butchered products. Locals pack the place, especially when they have full hot meals, but this isn't all that makes it such a gem. The bar area is particularly atmospheric, with pewter-topped beer mugs on display and an ever-rare gravity dispense barrel on the counter top. The brewer mans it himself and every beer is perfectly poured. His pride in his craft is evident.

Beers on tap: Büchenbacher Beck'n Bier. Seasonal Maibock (May) and Weihnachtsbock (before Christmas).

PRACTICAL INFORMATION

Brauerei-Gasthof Herold
Marktstraße 29
91257 Pegnitz (Büchenbach)
+49 9241 3311
www.beckn-bier.de

Open Wednesday to Monday 9:00 am to 10:00 pm
Closed Tuesday

Rooms available. Pricing is on their website but you'll need to call to reserve, and I suggest you do it well in advance if you're looking for a warm weather weekend.

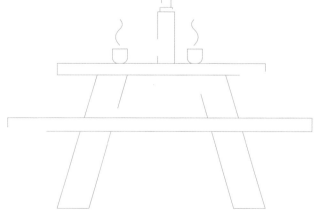

LINDENHARDT

TOP OF THE BIERQUELLENWANDERWEG

UPPER FRANCONIA

▷··· STARTING POINT	···✕ DESTINATION
BRAUEREI & LANDGASTHOF KÜRZDÖRFER, LINDENHARDT	**BRAUEREI & LANDGASTHOF KÜRZDÖRFER, LINDENHARDT**

🍺 BEER	🔲 DIFFICULTY
LEUPSER DUNKEL	**HIKE**

🗺 MAP	
ATK25-E11 PEGNITZ	⏱ DURATION OF THE HIKE **13 KM** **3-4H**

🔍 HIGHLIGHTS	〜 ELEVATION GAIN
CHURCH OF ST. MICHAEL, LEUPS CHAPEL, FARMLAND SCENERY, ZUM FICHTA BIERGARTEN	ASCENT: 260 M DESCENT: 260 M

DUNKLES FROM AN OLD
FAMILY RECIPE

LIGHTLY FILTERED
DARK CHESTNUT,
ROCKY TAN HEAD

MALT,
SLIGHT CHOCOLATE

PRONOUNCED HOPS, DARK
CHOCOLATE AND MALT,
LONG DRY BITTER FINISH

BITTERNESS   SWEETNESS

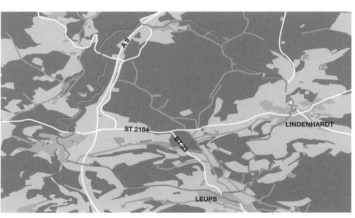

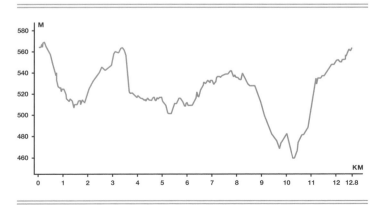

DESCRIPTION OF THE ROUTE

While the Bierquellenwanderweg can be tackled in a day, the breweries on the route are worth more time. With a convenient divider trail called the "kurze Variante" (short route), it makes it easy enough to spread it over two days. The top half of the circuit is perhaps the more scenic and takes in three of the four breweries. Conveniently, one of them offers rooms. The below description will start and finish there. Lindenhardt is a pretty little village on the edge of the lush, dense forest home of the Rotmainquelle, one of the sources of the Main River.

Lindenhardt is serviced by limited regular buses as well as call buses from Pegnitz and Bayreuth. These operate a bit like pre-set taxis but go at set times and appear on the German transit websites and apps. If unaccustomed to using call buses, it would be easier to use regular ones, especially if your German is limited. This is an area perhaps best visited by car, especially if you can get a room at Landgasthof Brauerei Kürzdörfer.

Coming out of the Landgasthof, go left on Brauhausgasse. You'll walk by a small cemetery on your right before coming to an intersection where you'll continue straight. This initial part of the route is on asphalt and is also part of not only the route to the Rotmainquelle but also the Jakobsweg (Way of St. James). You will leave those when you come to a fork. Take the left side, a smaller unpaved road marked with a yellow beer mug. The trail veers left and you soon take a well-marked right, after which it veers left again. When you come to a larger gravel road, go right. This wide path is easy to follow but still mostly in the forest. After a bit more than a kilometer, you will come to another large road. Go left again and you'll be going into Weiglathal. This is a very small village but home to a great old pub called "Zum Fichta," which dates back to 1870. They no longer brew their own beer; it's now contract-brewed but still lagered on the premises. It's a

216

very tasty beer, and their Biergarten, redesigned in 2013, is the nicest one on the Bierquellenwanderweg.

Leaving "Zum Fichta," go through the parking lot towards the overpass. This is a busy street so cross it carefully. Go under the overpass and look for signs on the left side of the road. Take the well-marked left and follow the gravel road parallel to the highway for a very short stretch before making another marked right. This is a very pretty forest which briefly coincides with the Fränkischer Gebirgsweg. When it forks, take the left side, leaving the long-distance route behind. You'll see some green numbered signs, which are shorter loops that take in various villages. You will come to an asphalt road – cross it and continue on the other side. This part is mostly forested but skirts an open area and any turns that need to be made are well-marked with the yellow mugs and ones for Trockau, your next stop. When the trail emerges onto an asphalt street, go left and walk on it briefly. Look across the road to your right and you'll see a small opening with the mug symbol, so you can now get off the road and go into town on a more pleasant path. You'll soon be on Am Anger – follow it as it winds right and left before becoming Marktplatz. You'll now be in the center of Trockau. There is a small castle but it's a private residence and cannot be visited. There are a few places to eat and have a beer, as well as a butcher serving small snacks. Continue through the Marktplatz to the fork and take the left side, Bodendorfer Weg. You'll see more yellow mug signs pointing you to Büchenbach. This would be your destination if doing the full circuit but you'll leave Bodendorfer Weg (and the regular Bierquellenwanderweg) at Hohenweg and continue straight. This route is marked by brown beer mugs – the Bierquellenwanderweg kurze Variante. This is all asphalt and the route will veer right and then a more distinct left. These turns are well-marked with brown mugs.

You'll be walking towards a high overpass now, and if you look under it, in the distance you will be able to see the church in Lindenhardt. You won't be headed that way just yet. Your next stop is Leups. Walk under the overpass and continue straight. You'll come to a playing field with some seating and a kiosk. Walk through it, or its parking lot and enter the forest on the other side. Walk through this pretty green section on a gravel road leading to a larger asphalt one. Go left and follow this all the way to Leups. When you come to the main street, go right. You'll walk by the Leups Chapel on your left and not far beyond that is Brauerei-Gasthof Gradl.

BRAUEREI-GASTHOF GRADL

Brauerei-Gasthof Gradl is another Franconian classic, much like Brauerei-Gasthof Herold in Büchenbach on the lower portion of the Bierquellenwanderweg. It's a similar simple set up, resplendent with a gravity dispense barrel. The brewer is often pouring his wares in perfect form. The menu is simple but goes perfectly with their one beer on tap – a marvelous Dunkles that locals, hikers, and cyclists obviously love. They also brew a dark Bockbier for May 1st and around Christmas but neither seems to last very long. I did have it once on May 1st, but this past year, it was gone by the middle of the month. It was so good, I'd specifically returned in May in hopes of having it again. The Gasthof is a real family affair. I was once served by a young boy, who couldn't have been more than 10 years old and plainly enjoyed what he was doing and being part of the family business. It's a heartening thing to see when so many small breweries are closing down in Franconia due to the inability to find workers. The Wolfring family have been at it since 1683, and if we're lucky, the young boy who served me will be the brewer one day.

Once you manage to pry yourself from this beery paradise, go back up the main street the same way you came in. At the fork, take the right side. You'll be back on the yellow beer mug trail and a sign will say that Lindenhardt is 2.5 kilometers away. Follow the main road out of town but stay on the right-hand side as you'll soon be leaving it. At the turn is a crucifix and an old wooden Bierquellenwanderweg sign. This one says your destination is 3.5 kilometers away. I have to admit, it feels more like the latter. It veers left and enters a forest before opening up into some fine farmland scenery. You skirt some forests and make a few well-marked turns. When I recently walked through, the rapeseed plants were gloriously in bloom, a vast field of bright yellow.

As you get close to town, you'll pass a fenced area, often with a few horses grazing. Just past it, go left onto an asphalt road and you'll also see Jakobsweg signs again. This becomes Leupser Weg as it winds right and brings you into Lindenhardt. When you come to the intersection with Marktstraße, cross the main road and continue on the other side, where it becomes An der Kirche. You'll see the lovely St.-Michaels-Kirche (Church of St. Michael) on your right. Once past the church, go right, and at Brauhausgasse, turn left. The actual Brauerei Kürzdörfer is on your right-hand side as you walk towards the Landgasthof, where you hopefully have a room for the night awaiting you.

LANDGASTHOF & BRAUEREI KÜRZDÖRFER

This big log cabin affair has a scenic location across from a pasture where horses often roam. It's a close race between it and "Zum Fichta" for the nicest outside seating. They also have the largest food menu of the four breweries on the Bierquellenwanderweg, and most importantly, they have rooms and a nice Dunkles on tap.

PRACTICAL INFORMATION

Brauerei-Gasthof Gradl
Leups 6
91257 Pegnitz
+49 9246 247
www.leupser.de

Open Wednesday to Monday from 10:00 am
Closed Tuesday

Landgasthof & Brauerei Kürzdörfer
Brauhausgasse 3
95473 Creußen (Lindenhardt)
+49 9246 221
www.brauerei-kuerzdoerfer.de

Open Tuesday to Sunday 11:00 am to 10:00 pm

Information about their rooms is available
on their websites in German but it's probably
best to call and inquire.

Wirtshaus Weiglathal "Zum Fichta"
Weiglathal 1
95503 Hummeltal (Weiglathal)
+ 49 9246 491
www.weiglathal.de

Open Tuesday to Sunday from 10:00 am
Closed Monday

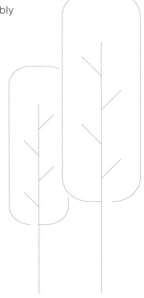

POTTENSTEIN

TO THE CAVE OF THE HUNGRY HARE

UPPER FRANCONIA

▷⋯ STARTING POINT	⋯✕ DESTINATION
BRAUEREI & GASTHOF MAGER, POTTENSTEIN	**BRAUEREI & GASTHOF MAGER, POTTENSTEIN**
🍺 BEER	⌗ DIFFICULTY
MAGER DUNKEL	**HIKE**
🗺 MAP	
ATK25-E11	🕐 DURATION OF THE HIKE
PEGNITZ	**5.5 KM** **1.5–2H**
🔍 HIGHLIGHTS	〰 ELEVATION GAIN
POTTENSTEIN CASTLE, ST. BARTHOLOMÄUS CHURCH, HASENLOCH, ROCKY OUTCROPPINGS	ASCENT: 170 M DESCENT: 165 M

DUNKLES

**MAHOGANY,
TAN HEAD**

**MALT,
HINT OF CHOCOLATE**

**RICH MALT, SOME CHOCO-
LATE, UNDERLYING HOPS,
DRY BITTER FINISH**

BITTERNESS   **SWEETNESS**

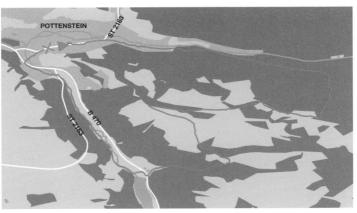

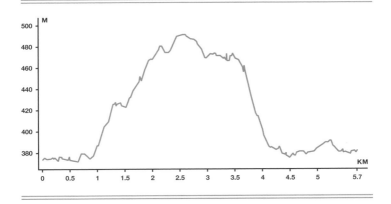

DESCRIPTION OF THE ROUTE

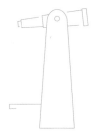

Pottenstein is one of the main gateway towns to the Fränkische Schweiz (Franconian Switzerland). In many ways, its half-timbered architecture and rocky outcroppings nestled in green hills are the iconic images associated with a region filled with both natural and man-made wonders. With a hilltop castle, numerous caves, an abundance of trails, and two breweries, Pottenstein is a worthy spot for at least a few days of exploration.

Pottenstein is serviced by regular buses from both Ebermanns-tadt and Pegnitz. Pegnitz is easily reached from Nuremberg and Bayreuth. Ebermannstadt is well-connected with Forchheim.

Coming out of Brauerei & Gasthof Mager, you will have a great view of the St. Bartholomäus Church just across the street. It's worth a stop either before or after the hike (you'll finish up here later). Go left on the Hauptstraße and you will see many half-timbered buildings along the route, especially at the main square. The street comes to an end at a fork, take the right side called Löhrgäßchen. You'll see hiking signs with a green dot for the Waldtempel (forest temple) and Hasenloch (rabbit hole). The road will soon fork again; this time, take the left side to remain on Löhrgäßchen. At just under one kilometer from the brewery, there will be another fork. Take the right side to head up a narrow path, well-marked with the green dot sign. This is a pretty, lush trail with lots of ups and downs that brings you to the Hasenloch, an interesting cave with an odd and gruesome legend attached to it, whereby a boy was mangled by a spirit of some kind disguised as an injured hare. After investigating the somewhat spooky-looking cave a bit, continue along the trail and you'll come to a turn for Felsenbad, still on the green dot trail.

You'll soon pass the simple stone Hofmann Chapel and be walking towards the Schullandheim Hostel. Before you get there, cut back hard to your left and towards the Felsenbad. At around the 4 kilometer mark, you will come to the public swimming area and can take a dip if you've brought your swim suit. If not, carefully cross the busy road (470) and there will be a cafe on another small lake that rents boats. It's a scenic spot worth a stop, with some rocky scenery as the Felsenbad's backdrop. When you're ready to go, head through the parking lot and look to your left for green dot signs. They point you towards the Rodelbahn Bergstation.

This is a nice little stretch that mirrors the river that runs along the main road and is also part of the Frankenweg, a long distance route through Franconia. You'll be mostly in the shade, and at one point you will go under the Rodelbahn riders as they whiz by overhead. There are nice views to your right of the rocky outcroppings the region is noted for. As you climb a bit, there will be some nice shots of Pottenstein's castle to be had, too.

When you leave the path, you will cross a busy road and go left onto Nürnberger Straße, which brings you back to town. You'll pass Wagner Bräu as you do. This former brewery has their beer contract-brewed and has a lovely Biergarten nearby. Cross the busy 470 to get a closer look at the atmospheric old building and to remain on Nürnberger Straße. This becomes the Hauptstraße and you will go right to stay on it and get back to the city center. Before you know it, you'll be back at Brauerei & Gasthof Mager and their marvelous dark brew.

BRAUEREI & GASTHOF MAGER

The Mager family has been doing it all in this very location since 1774, and they somehow manage to straddle the fine line of tourist restaurant and village pub quite well. The half-timbered building sets the tone, and the interior, while lacking frills, exudes an atmosphere of bygone days. Homemade meals are great value with their Schäuferla (pork shoulder) and Roulade (beef rolls) featuring authentic tasty sauces. It's busy at mealtimes with both locals and tourists. There's a small outside seating area out back as well. Though their big seller appears to be their Pils, their Dunkel is one of Franconia's best and matches well to their sauce-laden meal entries. It was another find from Graham Lees' *Good Beer Guide to Munich and Bavaria* (CAMRA), who gave it a rare top 4-star rating. I first had it in 1997 and am glad the brewpub has weathered the times well – it's now one of only two breweries in the once three-brewery rich town. All this and they even have rooms to sweeten the deal!

Beers on tap: Mager Dunkel, Mager Pils and Mager Helles. Bottled Mager Märzen and seasonal Festbiers.

PRACTICAL INFORMATION

Brauerei & Gasthof Mager
Hauptstraße 15–17
91278 Pottenstein
+49 9243 333
www.brauerei-mager.de

Open in summer Monday to Sunday from 9:00 am
Thursdays only to 3:30 pm
Winter hours vary, consult their website

Rooms available, pricing on website is in German only.

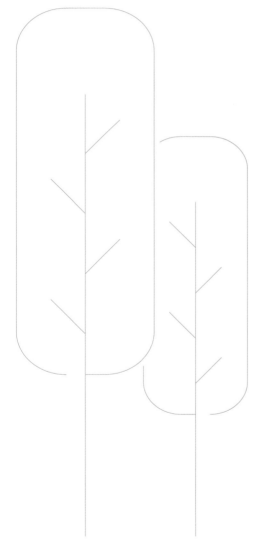

OBERAILSFELD

VIEWS OF RABENSTEIN CASTLE
FROM THE PROMENADENWEG

UPPER FRANCONIA

▷··· STARTING POINT	···✕ DESTINATION
HELD-BRÄU, OBERAILSFELD	**HELD-BRÄU, OBERAILSFELD**

 BEER

HELD-BRÄU ALTFRÄNKISCHES
BAUERNBIER DUNKEL

 DIFFICULTY

HIKE 🚶

⛰ MAP	

ATK25-E11
PEGNITZ

🕐 DURATION OF THE HIKE

7.5 KM
2–2.5H

🔍 HIGHLIGHTS

RABENSTEIN CASTLE, CRAGGY ROCK
FORMATIONS, ST. BURKARD CHURCH,
SOPHIE'S CAVE, LUDWIG'S CAVE

〰 ELEVATION GAIN

ASCENT: 330 M
DESCENT: 290 M

DUNKLES

DEEP CHESTNUT,
TAN HEAD

LICORICE,
CHOCOLATE

RICHLY MALTY, SOME LICO-
RICE, HINT OF CHOCOLATE,
BITTERSWEET FINISH

BITTERNESS   SWEETNESS

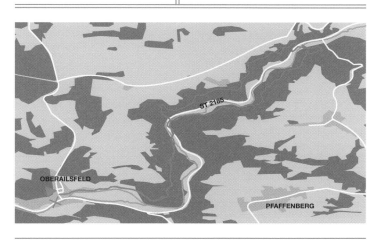

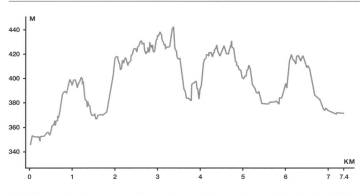

DESCRIPTION OF THE ROUTE

 Oberailsfeld is a pretty hamlet in Franconian Switzerland, with rocky outcroppings above and numerous trails emanating from it. For all the scenic beauty surrounding it, there is little in the way of a tourist infrastructure in the sleepy village. Thankfully, Castle Rabenstein is a short hike away, and if staying overnight in a castle is on your bucket list, you're in luck! What the village does have is a great brewpub, and don't be surprised if everyone in the area is in there enjoying their renowned dark beer.

Oberailsfeld is serviced by limited buses on weekends and holidays from Pottenstein, which is well-connected to Nuremberg. Believe it or not, this particular bus is for tourists and takes in castles and breweries in the area. It is therefore an express bus and takes less than 15 minutes from Pottenstein. Aside from this bus, it's an area best visited by car.

Coming out of Held-Bräu, cross the main street to find many hiking trail signs. You're going to be following the blue cross one called the Markgrafenweg/Burgenweg. Rabenstein Castle is only 2.5 kilometers away. Follow the street through the quaint neighborhood. You'll quickly be out of town and will pass some rocky outcroppings on your left. When you come to a fork, take the very well-marked left side towards Rabenstein Castle. Continue up and into the forest as the route meanders past ample blue cross signs and mossy rock formations. When you come to a small junction, follow signs for Rabenstein Castle. You're going to walk to and then through the rock formation straight ahead. On the other side of the cave-like tunnel, you drop down to a small bridge. Cross it and follow the signs veering you left towards a major road. Carefully cross it and walk along the right side of it to a parking area for the Promenadenweg, the 5-kilometer circuit you're about to start. Walk through it and follow the bend of the road. Once around it, you will have views of the back of the castle already. Cross back over the street, looking for the very visible hiking signs on the other side. You'll see that Rabenstein Castle is only 0.8 kilometers away now. The symbol for the hike is a green rook. Follow the path up, using steps at some points. As it rounds and comes into the open, you will see a cool-looking overhanging rock at a trail junction. Continue straight and walk under it towards the castle, it will be quite close now. In fact, it's just up ahead on the right-hand side. To your left, up a short path is the castle restaurant, a nice Biergarten, a falconry, and public toilets.

Just past the bridge of the castle, you'll see more hiking signs. Follow the Promenadenweg towards Sophienhöhle (Sofie's Cave). This is a great stretch crossing large boulders that you will walk around or between. When you come to a junction, there is a choice between the Bequemer Weg (comfortable way) or going straight on. Go straight for some viewpoints even better than the cave. There are covered benches too. Continue on towards the cave. It's a big and popular one with an admission charge. Just past the cave, you'll come to another junction. Go right to drop down some stairs, following the Promenadenweg sign towards Ludwigshöhle (Ludwig's Cave). Down at street level, you'll cross the same road you did earlier, just a kilometer or so away. You'll go through another parking lot for the cave and cross a brook on a small wooden bridge. On the other side are steps to bring you up to the cave. This one is smaller but it's free. You can bypass it and stay on the trail, or once inside the cave, there's a shortcut through a hole to rejoin it. It's up to you. Either way, you'll soon be making your way back up the other side of the valley on the Promenadenweg.

You'll be heading towards Rabenstein over Neumühle. It's another great section with intermittent views to your right, including the chapel in Klausstein, perched up high. Continue along this route towards the Schneiderloch with partial views of the castle to your right. Walk through the short arch-like cave and emerge through the "needle-hole" and down the steps. Once on the other side of the hole, you will have fantastic views of Rabenstein Castle. There's a bench there to savor them from. The rest of the route rounds the bend of the road, and you'll soon be at the first parking lot for the Promenadenweg. Cross the street and the small bridge you crossed earlier. Follow the blue cross route back to Oberailsfeld, a little more than a kilometer away. When you emerge from the forest and see St. Burkard Church in the not-so-far distance, you'll know Held-Bräu is close, too.

HELD-BRÄU

Founded in 1860, it seems little has changed at Held-Bräu since then, including one of the nicest green tile wood-burning stoves in Franconian Switzerland. A low-beamed wooden ceiling and old clock round out the picture. A small menu of full hot meals is available on weekends and holidays, but both their warm and cold snacks are every bit as good. A favorite is a homemade Glasfleisch, and though meat in a glass jar might not sound appetizing, I can assure you it very much is. Served with some of the best roast potatoes you'll find anywhere, it's a meal I get nearly every time I go. It's not a big place so don't be surprised to find it quite full. In warmer months, there is an ample outside seating area, including a covered stone-walled area. Their Bauernbier Dunkel is renowned throughout the area and people make their way here specifically for it.

Beer on tap: Held-Bräu Altfränkisches Bauernbier Dunkel, Held-Bräu Helles Bier, Held-Bräu Weizen (in summer). Seasonal Bock (during Lent) and Weizenbock (Advent season).

PRACTICAL INFORMATION

Held-Bräu
Oberailsfeld 19
95491 Ahorntal (Oberailsfeld)
+40 9242 295
www.held-braeu.de

Open Friday to Tuesday from 10:30 am
Closed Wednesday and Thursday

Burg Hotel (Burg Rabenstein)
Rabenstein 33
95491 Ahorntal
+49 9202 9700440
www.burg-rabenstein.de

BREITENLESAU

THE CASTLE AND BEER TRAIL

UPPER FRANCONIA

▷··· STARTING POINT

BRAUEREI-GASTHOF KRUG, BREITENLESAU

🍺 BEER

KRUG-BRÄU LAGER

△ MAP

ATK25-E10
EBERMANNSTADT

🔍 HIGHLIGHTS

WAISCHENFELD CASTLE, AN OLD MILL, WIESENT RIVER, ST. MARTIN'S CHURCH, RURAL AND FOREST SCENERY

···✗ DESTINATION

BRAUEREI-GASTHOF KRUG, BREITENLESAU

▦ DIFFICULTY

HIKE 🚶

⏱ DURATION OF THE HIKE

13.5 KM
3-4H

〜 ELEVATION GAIN

ASCENT: 300 M
DESCENT: 290 M

5.0%
ALCOHOL
CONTENT

DARK LAGER MADE WITH
A SPECIAL MASHING
PROCESS INVOLVING A
VARIETY OF MALTS

DEEP CHESTNUT,
OFF-WHITE ROCKY HEAD

MALTY,
SOME CHOCOLATE

MALTY,
SLIGHT CHOCOLATE, DRY
BITTERSWEET FINISH

BITTERNESS

SWEETNESS

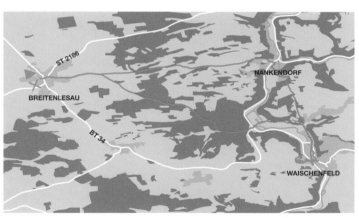

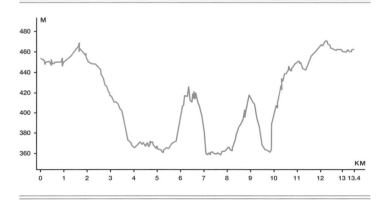

DESCRIPTION OF THE ROUTE

 The Fränkische Schweiz or Franconian Switzer-
land is one of the prettiest areas in northern
Bavaria, with hilltop castles and jagged rocky
outcroppings dotting the otherwise green
rolling hills that are typical of the landscape.
Add to this, a great abundance of small
breweries and you have a tough-to-beat beer
hiking Mecca. One trail is called the Burg-und-
Bier-Pfad (castle and beer path) and on the relatively
short circuit you'll get one castle and three breweries to back up its
name.

**There is regular but limited bus service from Ebermannstadt,
which has good connections to Forchheim but plan your route
carefully. This is an area more easily visited by car.**

Since the area is a bit remote and there is a lot to do and many
breweries to check out, you might want to consider staying over for a
couple of nights. Since only one of the breweries has rooms, I suggest
Krug-Bräu in Breitenlesau and will describe the circuit from there. If
you are beginning from either of the other two towns, it's easy to
follow from there as well.

Coming out of Krug-Bräu, cross the street and go left. There will be
hiking signs with a yellow circle pointing you towards both Nankendorf
and Waischenfeld. At the first street, turn right. Follow this all the way
out of town and into the countryside. You'll come to a fork at just
under one kilometer, take the right side of it to stay on the yellow
circle trail. You would get to Waischenfeld either way, but this is the
longer route and saves Nankendorf for the return part of the circuit.
This is a pleasant, bricked farm road that passes across a field before
ducking into the forest, where it becomes gravel. You will pop out of
the forest intermittently, but it's mostly a shady section. When the trail
leaves the forest for good, you will be at a large busy road. Cross it
carefully and look for a small bridge on the other side. This bridge will
bring you over the Wiesent River. Follow the road over the open green
area towards the village ahead, and once you reach it, go right. Follow
this dirt road a short distance until it forks. Take the right fork, which
is a much narrower path. There are trail signs and an arrow to point
you in the right direction. Follow this route to another street called
Fischergasse and turn right onto it. Follow Fischergasse all the way
into Waischenfeld. This is an atmospheric little tourist town, with the
Wiesent River flowing through it and the castle ruin high up on a hill to
your right. There's a small bridge before the center, but I like going all
the way to the larger one where you can take some nice photos.

At the bridge, you can do a few things. Head over the bridge and look
for green circle signs for the Burgweg. This will take you up to the

castle ruin. While perhaps more impressive from down below, it's a fun, steep excursion up to reach it and it does afford nice views over the town. But if you're not up for that, continue straight and Fischergasse becomes Vorstadt and Brauerei Heckel will be on your left. It has limited opening hours, but it's about as authentic a Franconian brewpub as you'll find and the beer is super. In fact, if it's not open but will be soon, head up to that ruin and come back. It's worth it!

When you're done visiting Waischenfeld, head back out of town the same way you came, up Fischergasse. When you get back to where you came into town, do not go left but take the left side of the fork of Mönchsgrund. It's well-marked with a Brauereienweg sign as well as one for the Höhenweg to Nankendorf, which is only 1.5 kilometers away. It's also part of the Fränkischer Gebirgsweg. This is a pretty stretch that rises up, and from there, you get nice views of the valley. There are some rocky hills to your right where you will often see sheep feeding. The logo for the brewery in Nankendorf is a lamb, so it's an appropriate entrance to town. Just before you enter, you'll pass a cute, tiny chapel on your left, built in 1718. When you leave the trail, you'll go left on well-marked Auberg and enter the pretty little village of Nankendorf. Continue on as the street bends before coming to a scenic bridge across the Wiesent River once again. There's an old mill and some rocky outcroppings to your right. Once over the bridge, take the first right to stay on the route and then the first left to reach Brauereigaststätte Schroll, otherwise known as "Zum Weißen Lamm" or the White Lamb. This homey little pub is always surprisingly busy – one sip of their marvelous dark Landbier and you'll understand why. If in season, their Bockbier shouldn't be missed. There's a small, sunny outside seating area out back, so head there and enjoy.

When you're done enjoying the White Lamb, it's time to head back to Breitenlesau. Cross the busy street out front and look for Kirchberg. There are also hiking signs for the Brauereienweg as well as a red/white triangle sign heralding Breitenlesau as being only 3.5 kilometers away. It's a bit of an uphill road but it levels out soon enough. Be sure to look back for views of Nankendorf and a pretty picture of the St. Martin's Church if the light is right. You'll leave Kirchberg just as you leave town and remain on the unnamed road, following trail signs for Breitenlesau. You'll be out in rural scenery with a few short patches of forest. It's a fairly flat stroll back to where you started, and if it's late afternoon and the sun is going down, there's a beautiful glow to the countryside. Continue straight to reach town and Krug-Bräu.

BRAUEREI-GASTHOF KRUG

Krug is a fairly big regional player, but the brewpub maintains a traditional feel despite being quite crowded on good weather weekends. With its close proximity to many beer hiking trails, excellent food, and a good-sized selection of beers, it's not hard to see why. Housed in a half-timbered house, the inn is perhaps best enjoyed while sitting in their outside seating area with the rather large, modern brewery on display as well. Krug has been a family enterprise since its inception in 1834 so they obviously know what they are doing. Their beers are now available in a few key foreign markets as well as around Franconia. Their dark Lagerbier is one of those "can't miss" regional beers.

Beers on tap: Krug-Bräu Dunkles Lagerbier, Krug-Bräu Pils, Krug-Bräu Weißbier and Krug-Bräu Urstoff. Bock in season.

PRACTICAL INFORMATION

Brauerei-Gasthof Krug
Breitenlesau 1b
91344 Waischenfeld (Breitenlesau)
+49 9202-835
www.krug-braeu.de

Open Wednesday to Sunday and holidays 9:00 am to 11:00 pm
Closed Monday and Tuesday

Rooms available but are in high demand so book in advance.

Brauerei-Gaststätte Schroll "Zum Weißen Lamm"
Nankendorf 41
91344 Waischenfeld (Nankendorf)
+49 9204-248

Open Wednesday to Monday 9:00 am
Closed Tuesday

Brauerei Heckel
Vorstadt 3
91344 Waischenfeld
+49 9202-493

Open Tuesday to Friday 4:30 pm to 10:00 pm
Saturday 9:30 am to 1:00 pm
Sunday and holidays 10:00 am to 12:30 pm and 4:30 pm to 10:00 pm

AUFSEß

GUINNESS WORLD RECORD HOLDER OF MOST BREWERIES PER PERSON

UPPER FRANCONIA

▷··· STARTING POINT	···✕ DESTINATION
BRAUEREIGASTHOF REICHOLD, HOCHSTAHL	**BRAUEREIGASTHOF REICHOLD, HOCHSTAHL**
🍺 BEER	🔢 DIFFICULTY
REICHOLD LAGER	**HIKE** 🥾
⛰ MAP	
ATK25 D10	⏱ DURATION OF THE HIKE
HOLLFELD	**14 KM 3-4H**
🔍 HIGHLIGHTS	〰 ELEVATION GAIN
UNTERAUFSEß CASTLE, EASTER FOUNTAINS IN SEASON, RURAL COUNTRYSIDE, ROCKY OUTCROPPINGS, THE CHURCH IN HOCHSTAHL	ASCENT: 245 M DESCENT: 241 M

AMBER LAGER

LIGHT AMBER
TO DEEP GOLDEN,
CREAMY HEAD

GRAIN

BALANCED BETWEEN
GRAIN MALT AND HOPS

BITTERNESS

SWEETNESS

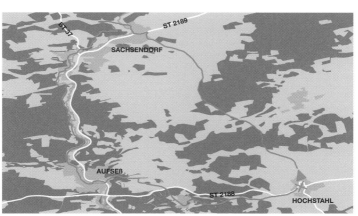

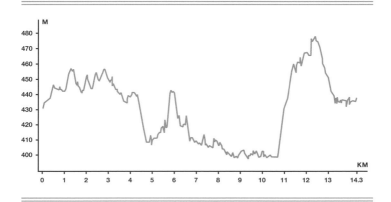

239

DESCRIPTION OF THE ROUTE

While Franconia is well-noted for its brewery density, Aufseß in particular is abundantly blessed. According to the *Guinness Book of World Records*, in the year 2000, it had the most breweries per person. To be fair, the town of Aufseß has only one but there are three more villages with breweries within the same postal code. As a point of reference; there are fewer than 1,500 people in the combined area. To better help you explore this area, the community of Aufseß has conveniently utilized hiking paths already in place and created their very own Brauereienweg (brewery path). Due to its relatively short length and the rolling landscape it traverses, it is understandably popular.

There is very limited bus service from Bamberg. A better point of entry is Ebermannstadt, easily reached by S-Bahn from Forchheim. Even from there, bus service is better on weekends. It is a great area to visit by car as the area around Aufseß is rich with sights and even more breweries. Getting from area to area by public transport takes some advance planning and lots of patience but it can be done.

You can start the Brauereienweg in any of the villages along the route, but Hochstahl and Aufseß are the most convenient if you don't have a car and both have brewpubs with accommodation. They are both quite good but since I like Reichold in Hochstahl a bit more, my directions will start from there. Coming out from the brewery's lovely outdoor seating area, you will go to your left. You'll see signs for the Brauereienweg going in both directions, and since it's a circuit, you really can't go wrong. I like going counterclockwise as it gets the longest stretch without a brewery in first, saving a cluster of them for the finish. Look for signs for Sachsendorf and proceed out of the village. When you come to a fork in the road, take the left side. This section is the red dot trail as well as the Brauereienweg. The trail is very well marked, another reason for its popularity. You will cross some open farmland before entering an all-too-brief-if-it's-a-hot-day stretch of forest. Exiting it, you come to another fork; take the left side again, leaving the red dot trail. Continue on the Brauereienweg along this stretch. At the next two forks, keep right for both. You'll skirt a few more forested sections but it's pretty much straight ahead to Sachsendorf. When you get to the Hauptstraße, go left to find Brauereigasthof Stadter. They only brew one beer, but it's a winner. Their homemade pan-fried Schnitzel is justifiably popular as well.

After your short break, it's time to hit the trail. You can retrace your steps to the Hauptstraße but it's uphill, and you can just as easily

continue on the street in the opposite direction until you reach Schloßstraße. There's a cute little chapel on the corner, and during Easter, its fountain is beautifully decorated with colored eggs. Take a right onto Schloßstraße. Not that I want to confuse you, but if you went back in the other direction, you would also reach Schloßstraße, but would need to take a left. I mention this because if you ask for directions, you might get either one of these options. My suggestion is slightly shorter and just as scenic as it takes in the little chapel. At one point not far up the road, they merge and you continue along their now-joint trajectory. When the road forks, take the left side. Not long after, you will take a left into the forest but on a much narrower trail. This trail goes back in the direction you've come from before zigzagging back to follow the flow of the valley.

You exit this pleasant stretch in Neuhaus and go left onto the larger street, which curves a bit. When you see Talstraße, turn right onto it. You'll see signs for Aufseß at this point. It's only about 3 kilometers away. Follow Talstraße and keep your eyes to your left and you'll see a pretty group of rock outcroppings, and if you are lucky, some climbers scaling them. Make a right onto a smaller road marked by the Brauereienweg signs. Soon after that, go left on a small footpath. Follow this to a T, and go left towards Mühlengrundstraße. Go right on Mühlengrundstraße and then take another quick right onto a smaller path. Follow this pretty stretch which mirrors the Aufseß River. It winds a bit along with the flow of the river, and eventually it becomes Neuhauserstraße, where you will go slightly left. Continue on to a fork and take Brunnengasse which becomes Soldatenweg. The names of the streets aren't so important because everything is very well marked. You walk through a cute little village and soon start to see the Unteraufseß Castle in the distance. At the end of the road, go left on Burggraben, cross the bridge over the Aufseß River and then turn right on Im Tal. The Brauereigasthof Rothenbach is just up the street on your right. Set at the foot of the Unteraufseß Castle, it must be one of the most scenically situated breweries in Germany. They have a fair assortment of beers on tap and have been brewing since 1886. Don't go too crazy, you still have two more breweries on your route!

Exiting the brewpub, cross the often busy Im Tal and look for Brauereienweg signs as well as ones for Heckenhof, about 1.4 kilometers away. You will end up on Hochstahler Straße, which starts off a bit steep before it becomes a narrower path and takes you through some rural countryside, often on small roads. You will follow the signs to the right and soon cross the ST 2188 (caution: it can be quite busy at times), where you will see signs for the Kathi-Bräu parking lot. This part is on the road and is popular with not only cyclists but also large groups of motorcycle enthusiasts. You're soon rewarded with one of the cutest brewpubs in all of Bavaria, in a great old stone building with a super-popular but all-too-small Biergarten. Dating back to 1498, their one regular beer, a Dunkles, is one of the most beloved on this circuit. If their Bock is available, you'll find it goes well with their home-baked cakes. Go on, have one! You've hiked a fair amount by now and deserve it. Besides, you only have a short stroll back to your starting point.

Continuing on the path the Biergarten is on, go left at the end of the road. Follow signs for Hochstahl and the Brauereienweg as you wind through the small village of Heckenhof. You're soon on a gravel road that takes you through open fields and some sections of forest. This emerges onto the ST 2188, but there is a bicycle/pedestrian path that runs alongside the road. It's a short stroll with the lovely church looming in the distance. This brings you back to Brauereigasthof Reichold, and if you've planned well, you have a room awaiting upstairs.

BRAUEREIGASTHOF REICHOLD

Brauerei Reichold, founded in 1906, is the new kid on the block on the Brauereienweg but is nonetheless one of the most popular, especially for their varied menu of Franconian specialties offered all day and a fair assortment of beers. You won't go wrong ordering a Schäuferla (pork shoulder) here. The family-run enterprise also offers rooms, making it an ideal home base for your stay.

Beers on tap: Reichold Lagerbier, Reichold Zwickl, Reichold Dunkelbier and Reichold Weizen. I've not tried the Weizen but all the others are well-crafted. I tend to drink the Lagerbier and find it refreshing after a long day of hiking.

PRACTICAL INFORMATION

Brauereigasthof Reichold
Hochstahl 24
91347 Aufseß (Hochstahl)
+49 9204 / 271
www.brauerei-reichold.de

Open April through October:
Monday from 5:00 pm (November through March: closed on Monday)
Tuesday and Wednesday closed
Thursday through Sunday 8:00 am to 11:00 pm

Brauerei-Gastwirtschaft Kathi-Bräu Heckenhof
Heckenhof 1
91347 Aufseß (Heckenhof)
+49 9198/277

Open Monday through Friday 11:00 am to 7:00 pm
Saturday, Sunday and holidays 9:00 am to 7:00 pm

Brauereigasthof Stadter
Hauptstraße 26
91347 Aufseß (Sachsendorf)
+49 9274/81 93
www.braulehrer.de

Open Tuesday from 5:00 pm
Wednesday through Friday from 10:00 am
Saturday, Sunday and holidays from 9:00 am
Closed Monday (if Monday is a holiday, it's closed on Tuesday)

Brauereigasthof Rothenbach
Im Tal 70
91347 Aufseß (Aufseß)
+49 9198/929 20
www.brauereigasthof-rothenbach.de

Open daily 11:00 am through 10:00 pm (mid-April to mid-October,
check website for winter hours)

Rooms can be booked on their website.

HUPPENDORF

A JOURNEY TO FRANCONIAN BREWING LEGEND HUPPENDORFER

UPPER FRANCONIA

▷··· STARTING POINT	···✕ DESTINATION
BRAUEREI GRASSER, HUPPENDORF	**BRAUEREI GRASSER, HUPPENDORF**
🍺 BEER	🔢 DIFFICULTY
HUPPENDORFER VOLLBIER	**HIKE**
△ MAP	
ATK25 D10	⏲ DURATION OF THE HIKE
HOLLFELD	**16 KM 3.5–4H**
🔍 HIGHLIGHTS	〜 ELEVATION GAIN
HEROLDSMÜHLE, TUMMLERS, CHURCH	ASCENT: 280 M DESCENT: 295 M

OLD STYLE
FRANCONIAN
LAGER

 DEEP AMBER

GRAIN,
MALT,
HAY

MALT,
SLIGHT GRAIN,
DRY BITTERSWEET FINISH

BITTERNESS   SWEETNESS

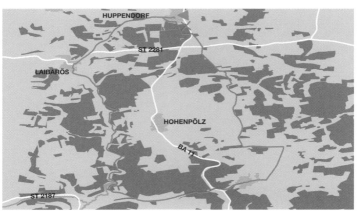

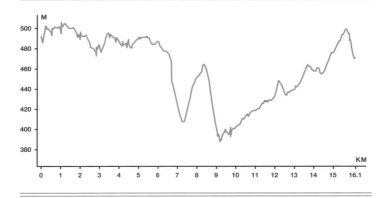

DESCRIPTION OF THE ROUTE

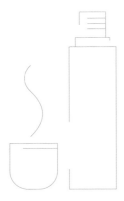

Tummler is the Franconian name for karst springs. As we all may have noticed, weather patterns have changed, and though this area was traditionally wet in late winter and spring, a recent excursion there in that season found it quite dry, despite rain the previous day. It's still a pretty valley featuring an atmospheric old mill and the possibility of running into a roaming herd of sheep, although I didn't see them on this occasion. I must say, after seeing photos of the area flooded, I wasn't as upset about it being on the dry side for the walk.

The full version of this hike is over 23 kilometers, with the southern portion featuring some fair elevation changes and can take 7 hours to complete. That's a long day, even with two breweries on the route, so I've cut it in half with this one featuring Franconian brewing legend Brauerei Grasser, more often known as Huppendorfer.

While Huppendorf can be accessed by bus from Bamberg, service is extremely limited. If it's a school holiday, it is a RUF bus (you have to call ahead to arrange pickup). For that reason, this is one area where traveling by car is much preferred.

Coming out of the brewery, go to your right. At the intersection, you will see a Schützenverein (shooting club) on your right. Make a left, following the bike signs for Litzendorf/Laibarös. Turn left at the first intersection and then take another quick left. Look for black triangular signs with a white beer mug drawn on them. At the next intersection, turn right. These streets are unnamed but marked well enough with the beer mugs. At the end of this small farm road, take the only choice: the path to the left. When it comes to an end, cross the main street and you will see a smaller road that you go right on. You are now on the blue/yellow trail called the Kapellenweg. These are two separate trails that intersect where you are now walking. You will soon cross the main road ST 2281. Fairly soon after that, you'll see a small marked side trail to your left. It's a short detour to the St. Laurentius Chapel – it's worth a peek. Continue to the point where the blue and yellow Kapellenweg split. Go straight on the yellow circle route. This winds its way to Hohenpölz but you're not headed there. Follow the black beer mug signs when they start to depart from the yellow Kapellenweg signs. Take note of the pretty church in the village of Hohenpölz as you walk along parallel to it. If you're going towards town, you are probably still on the yellow Kapellenweg trail and will need to turn around.

The church will recede to your rear as you head towards Brunn, another village. This part is fairly well marked with the beer mug signs. You will turn left at one point and then a relatively quick right soon after. At the main road, go right into the village of Brunn where you'll see the cute Church of St. Stephan and some roosters and not much else. There are some places to stay but unfortunately nowhere to eat or have a beer. Continue through the village, and once out on the main road, you will go down a steep street marked with red/white triangles on square signs for the IFS-Weg, a 100 kilometer route that cuts through Franconian Switzerland. You'll see it quite a bit in this area and it's well marked. Though an asphalt street, it's in a very pretty setting; keep your eyes to your left to catch a glimpse of the Greifenstein Castle perched high on a hill in the distance. At the bottom of the steep street, you will cross a busy road called the BA11. Carefully cross it and continue on the IFS-Weg but on a less busy street, until it turns to the left. Stop following the IFS-Weg signs at this point. Continue on the multi-marked street for a short time until you come to a three-pronged fork. Take the middle prong, marked with Frankenweg signs. This is a 500 kilometer route, but don't worry, Huppendorf isn't that far away.

You'll start to see signs for Heroldsmühle, a cute little town with an atmospheric old mill. According to its sign, the first mention of a miller here dates back to 1355. The current structure was renovated in 1975 and features one of the biggest mill wheels in Germany. After admiring it, go along the path to the right of the mill. This is marked with multiple signs, including the Frankenweg. This section is easy to follow, first through a forest and then out into a more open valley. This is the area of the Tummlers the trail is named after. As previously mentioned, it was quite dry when I walked through. Even an excursion to the larger of the two (Der Große Tummler) provided no views of water. You can see from the picture on the sign to the site that it does get wet at times.

Continue along the meandering trail as it zigzags through the pretty valley, following the Frankenweg signs with some beer mug signs thrown in for good measure. It's a pleasant stroll. You'll eventually pop out onto a small road and go right. You soon see signs for not only the Frankenweg and the beer mugs, but also your old friend the yellow Kapellenweg. Leave the street and go left. Bear right at a soon-encountered fork. At the end of trail you will come to another street; go right on it for a short bit and then another left, heading into a brief stretch of forest, all the while following all the now-familiar signs. You're heading to Laibarös now. At the end of the road, go right into town. The small town is interesting enough and features an intricate iron crucifix as you come into it. Signs lead you through to the ST 2281 where you'll make a right. The main road is marked with the black circle signs, with the occasional street sign pole on the road. There are some beer mug signs too. At the triple-pronged fork, take the middle, much smaller path, leaving the busy ST 2281 behind. This takes you all the way back to Huppendorf with black circle and beer mug signs keeping you on the right path and priming you for that beer you're bound to be ready for by now. The last bit is the same as the way you came out; make a right at the shooting club.

BRAUGASTSTÄTTE GRASSER

Founded in 1503, Brauerei Grasser has a long history in the Franconian brewing world but is nevertheless an innovative and evolving brewery – always looking to the future but remaining traditional just the same. The Grasser family took over in 1750. Their Vollbier is a regional favorite, and you'll find it in select pubs in Bamberg, but there's no better place to taste it than at their bustling brewpub in the small farming village of Huppendorf. People travel from miles around to down a "Huppi" or two. With such a popular brew in their line-up, it would be easy for them to rest on their laurels, but they craft a full selection of regular beers as well as one of the biggest ranges of specialties you'll find in a small countryside brewery. It's no wonder it's a Franconian brewing legend.

In addition to the brewery and restaurant, they have their own distillery, butchery, and the best thing of all, rooms! It's a hands-on family-run enterprise with everyone doing their part, so it's not likely to have to close its doors anytime soon. They generally offer a simple hot menu during the week along with their great cold platters. Their broiler chicken is top-notch. On Sundays they have amazing roast meals, but they have recently cut back on how often they offer this. Huppendorfer takes pride in using local ingredients with barley grown by surrounding farmers which they have malted in Bamberg at Weyermann, or in Kulmbach at Zeitler. Hallertau full hops are generally used but they utilize other varieties for more subtle flavors, too. The water of their town comes from the region between Heroldsmühle and Laibarös, the valley you just walked through to get here!

Beers on tap: Huppendorfer Vollbier, Huppendorfer Pils, Huppendorfer Weizen, Huppendorfer Zwickl, plus a rotating seasonal including Josefibock, Märzen, Export, Grachäds, Kathreinbock, Weihnachtsfestbier and Winterweizen. I've had all of the seasonals on tap except the Winterweizen – most are excellent and some are amazing. It is a destination in itself.

PRACTICAL INFORMATION

Braugaststätte Grasser
Huppendorf 25
96167 Königsfeld (Huppendorf)
+49 9207/270
www.huppendorfer-bier.de

Closed Monday and Tuesday
Open Wednesday to Saturday 9:00 am to 10:00 pm

Sundays are more complex and it's best to check the schedule
("Termine") on their website, but generally every other Sunday, they
have hot lunches (well worth seeking out and expect it to be very
busy). On those Sundays, they follow their regular hours of 9:00 am to
10:00 pm. On Sundays without hot midday meals, they are open from
3:00 pm to 10:00 pm. They are also quite good about posting their
vacation dates; check in advance so you won't be disappointed.

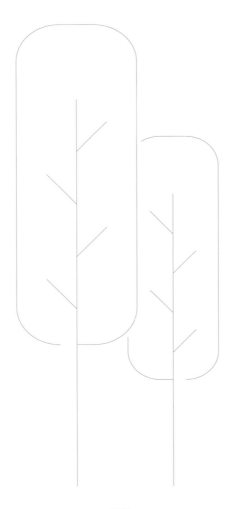

OBERLEINLEITER

GREAT GRAFENSTEIN CASTLE VIEWS FROM THE PANORAMAWEG

UPPER FRANCONIA

▷··· STARTING POINT

BRAUEREI-GASTHOF OTT, OBERLEINLEITER

🍺 BEER

OTT ORIGINAL OBALADARA

🗺 MAP

ATK25-E10
EBERMANNSTADT

···✕ DESTINATION

BRAUEREI-GASTHOF OTT, OBERLEINLEITER

▦ DIFFICULTY

HIKE 🚶

🕐 DURATION OF THE HIKE

11 KM
2.5-3H

🔍 HIGHLIGHTS

GREIFENSTEIN CASTLE, KREUZSTEIN, RURAL SCENERY

〰 ELEVATION GAIN

ASCENT: 350 M
DESCENT: 330 M

DUNKLES

LIGHT CHESTNUT,
ROCKY, OFF-WHITE HEAD

MALT,
FAINT CHOCOLATE

CHOCOLATE MALT,
UNDERLYING HOPS, DRY
BITTERSWEET FINISH

BITTERNESS

SWEETNESS

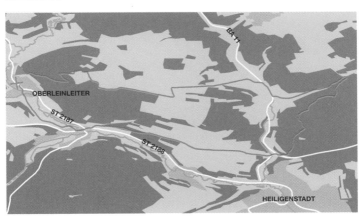

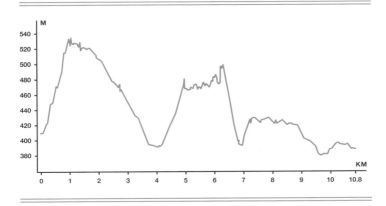

DESCRIPTION OF THE ROUTE

Oberleinleiter sits in a pretty valley in Franconian Switzerland with views of the Kreuzstein. It is on a few hiking routes that pass through it and is part of the Tummler-Wanderweg. It is also home to the fine Brauerei Ott. This route takes in part of the lower half of the Tummler route as well as the scenic Panoramaweg. You'll climb up to the Kreuzstein and have great views of Greifenstein Castle from the Panoramaweg.

Oberleinleiter is serviced by regular but limited buses during the week from Bamberg. They do not run on weekends. The trip takes about 40 minutes. It is relatively close to Heiligenstadt, easily reached from Ebermannstadt. It is best to use this as a base and hike between there and Oberleinleiter. With so many great breweries in the area, it is perhaps best to visit it with a car and organize an overnight stay.

Coming out of Brauerei-Gasthof Ott, go right on the main street. The trail comes up on the right-hand side quickly. There is a sign for the Brauereienwanderweg as well as for the Kreuzstein. It's only one kilometer away but it's a steep climb. Follow this road and veer left at the garage doors straight ahead. You will then go right up an asphalt road that really picks up some elevation quickly. When you come to a T, go left. Follow this until you see a trail sign on your right for the Kreuzstein. There's also a black sign with a mug on it – this is for one of the two beer hiking circuits in the area. This leaves the asphalt but continues upward. After a short forested section, you will cross a narrow footpath over a small grassy area. On the other side, you will duck into the forest and continue your climb, following signs for the Kreuzstein.

Just before the 1 kilometer mark, you will reach the viewpoint. There's a picnic bench there to catch your breath on. Follow the black signs with beer mugs away from this area. You'll soon be skirting a forest on your left and open farmland on your right. At the next junction, go right, towards Basaltbrüche. This is both a red dot and a green horizontal stripe trail. Follow this across the field and when it comes to the trees, it will veer left. Walk along the edge of the forest. When you leave the trees behind, you will come to a T – it's around the 2.5 kilometer mark. Go left there, followed by a relatively quick right. This road will take you to Reckendorf and has red dot signs. Follow it straight before it bends right, and then left before it meets the main road. Take the marked right here and follow this street into Reckendorf. At the intersection, there will be a bus stop and some red dot signs. Go left here to walk through the small town, which you will soon exit. Stay on this asphalt road for about 750 meters, looking for the trail on your right-hand side. It's black with a beer mug on it. There are other hiking signs, too. One is for the Gotische Kapelle and has a red dot and sideways red triangle on it. Follow this dirt path up into the forest and take the first right. Follow the red symbol signs as the route meanders through the lush forest. This is the nicest stretch of trail in the area. You'll come to an overgrown ruin of an old Gothic chapel on your right. Further along the trail you will come to a narrow section with some nearly vertical rocks on your left-hand side. Follow the route as it curves around to your left to meet another trail junction at around the 6 kilometer mark. Go right here, and start to follow a different Brauereienweg. It's a white sign with red lettering and says Heiligenstadt-Leinleitertal on it. The trail almost immediately forks, and you will take the right side to go towards Heiligenstadt. There are numerous other signs that keep you on the well-worn path. There's a vertical red stripe one as well as some triangles with numbers in them. Follow the path down to an asphalt street. On the other side of the road, the path continues straight and goes to Heiligenstadt, but you go right instead and head through the village of Neumühle. This route is marked with a white sign with a horizontal green stripe. The road bends to the left and you will pass by a bus stop. Right after that, on your right-hand side, you'll see a sign with a green stripe pointing you towards Oberleinleiter. It's a narrow paved road that goes up fairly steeply but levels out soon enough. This is the Panoramaweg, and if you look to your right, you'll have grand views of Greifenstein Castle. Continue on this straight, flat, paved path, enjoying the panoramic views the route is named after. Remember to occasionally look back as the castle looks great from a distance. You'll cross an intersection with signs saying Burggrub is 1.5 kilometers away, straight on.

You'll come to a fork, take the left side of it to remain on the Panoramaweg. Follow this down, and just past the 9 kilometer mark you'll come to an asphalt road, go left here. This quickly brings you to a major road – go right here to make your way into the small village of Burggrub. You'll walk by Gasthof Hösch on your right and continue on the road; as it bends left you'll cross it. Go straight and cross the small bridge. Stay on the right-hand side of this less-busy road and you'll start to see signs on street poles. Take the marked right to Oberleinleiter. It's a paved bike path, so it's an easy one kilometer walk. Once you pass the small fire station on your left, it's a pretty stretch and you'll soon see the Kreuzstein off to your right, high up on the hill. Continue to an intersection and go straight towards town. You'll pass a small war memorial just before your last turn, a left. This is the main street in Oberleinleiter and Brauerei-Gasthof Ott is just ahead on your right.

BRAUEREI-GASTHOF OTT

The Ott family has been brewing and running Brauerei-Gasthof Ott since 1822, but there's been a brewpub at this location since 1678. This bustling brewpub is the heart and soul of this small village that sees an inordinate amount of hikers for its size. The landscape surrounding the brewpub is certainly a draw but so is the great beer and food at this timeless old pub. Along with the ubiquitous Franconian dishes, there's a wide selection of daily specials, including fish dishes on a regular basis. Their specialty is broiler chicken, which comes with homemade potato salad. If you go on a weekend at lunch, you'll likely have to squeeze in on someone else's table but that's part of the fun. Chances are, they've just come off a hike, too. Jump in and grab a beer. You've probably been thinking about it since you climbed up to the Kreuzstein hours ago.

Beers on tap: Ott Original Obaladara, Ott Export, Ott Edel-Pils, Ott Hefeweizen, plus one seasonal (Ott Bock, Ott Festbier).

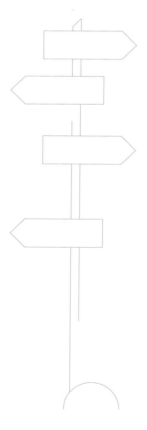

PRACTICAL INFORMATION

Brauerei-Gasthof Ott
Oberleinleiter 6
91332 Heiligenstadt i. OFr.
+49 9198 271
www.brauerei-ott.de

Open Wednesday to Sunday from 9:00 am
Closed Monday & Tuesday

HEILIGENSTADT I. OFR.

A SPEZIAL BEER AFTER A SCENIC ROUNDTRIP TO VEILBRONN

UPPER FRANCONIA

▷⋯ STARTING POINT

BRAUEREIGASTHOF DREI KRONEN, HEILIGENSTADT (OBERFRANKEN)

⋯✗ DESTINATION

BRAUEREIGASTHOF DREI KRONEN, HEILIGENSTADT (OBERFRANKEN)

🍺 BEER

AICHINGER SPEZIALBIER

🗺 MAP

ATK25-E10
EBERMANNSTADT

▦ DIFFICULTY

HIKE 🚶

🕐 DURATION OF THE HIKE

12 KM
3-3.5H

🔍 HIGHLIGHTS

MAIN SQUARE OF HEILIGENSTADT, (EASTER) FOUNTAIN (IN SEASON), NATURFREUNDEHAUS IN VEILBRONN, LEIDINGSHOFER TAL

〰 ELEVATION GAIN

ASCENT: 350 M
DESCENT: 355 M

5.5%
ALCOHOL CONTENT

OLD-STYLE FRANCONIAN LAGER

COPPER,
ROCKY HEAD

MALTY,
GRAIN

HOPPY,
FRUITY,
DRY BITTER FINISH

BITTERNESS

SWEETNESS

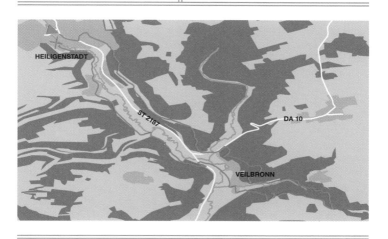

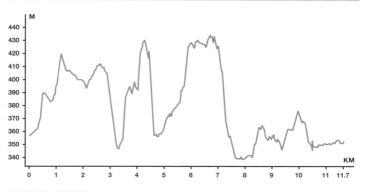

DESCRIPTION OF THE ROUTE

Heiligenstadt is a charming old market town at the base of Greifen-stein Castle and makes a great starting point for hikes in the area. It is probably best known for its impressive decoration of its square fountain just before Easter. This region has a long history of using colorful Easter eggs to adorn their fountains and brighten up their towns. Even small villages get into the act making driving through the area a pleasure during this season. You won't be alone, though, as it's well known at least to German tourists and you'll see tour buses making stops too. Even without a car, you will often pass them on hikes if passing through villages en route. Veilbronn is another popular tourist gateway town. There are nice places for walks including the Leidingshofer Tal, a lush, gently beautiful valley, perfect for casual strolls.

This route uses a few established trails to connect the two towns, taking in the highlights of each and what's along the way.

Heiligenstadt (Oberfranken) is serviced by regular but limited buses from Ebermannstadt, which is well-connected to Forch-heim. The trip takes about 20 minutes. Direct buses from Bam-berg take twice as long, are more limited, and do not run at all on weekends.

Coming out of the Drei Kronen, go right on Marktplatz and take another right at the first intersection, onto Hauptstraße. You'll see a few different hiking trail markings on the street sign poles, including one for the long distance Frankenweg. Follow Hauptstraße to the first left, Steinweg, and take it to Stüchter Berg, the next right. There will be lots of trail signs and one says Veilbronn is 3.5 kilometers away. Follow Stüchter Berg to a small set of steps. Go up them and go right on Wacholderweg. When you get to a fork, take the right side. This will bring you into the forest on a much narrower path. This is all within a kilometer from the Drei Kronen and well marked. This pretty stretch brings you to a wider unpaved road, go right there. It merges with a paved road at around the 2 kilometer mark. You walk on this a short time until you come to a fork. The paved road curves to the left, but go straight on the marked unpaved one. There will be a sign for not only Veilbronn but also the Leidingshofer Tal. There will be an open field on your left, and soon you'll be skirting a forest on your right. The next turn only has a red blaze painted on a tree, so keep your eyes to the right for the point you have to turn into the forest. It's about halfway up the field. Go right there; once you are on the path, trail signs pop up. When you emerge from the forest, you will be on a dirt track that leads you down to the main road, just across from Veil-bronn. Go left on this busy road and cross it carefully when you can. At the first right turn, there will be signs for Veilbronn. It is a paved road and the way the Frankenweg continues, but your route takes you up on the hill behind the small town.

You'll be going towards the Naturfreundehaus (Friends of Nature house). Continue straight and stay on the right side of the road, looking for a narrow path. It is well marked and goes straight up. This is the green circle trail (among others). Follow it up into the forest. Once it levels out, it's a pleasant walk. There's a pavilion to your right not far along the route. It has nice views into the valley and works you back to the main green circle trail quite naturally. Continue along the green circle route, and when you come to a T, go left. At the next junction, go right, again following signs for the obviously popular destination. It's an atmospheric stretch with lots of mossy stones and tree trunks. You'll come to a climbing park for adults and perhaps older kids too. This is part of the complex and the restaurant and hostel are to your right. The terrace of the restaurant has better views than the pavilion, and there are some mountain goats (that at first I thought were fake) on a rock right next to it. They also have the beer from Brauerei Hönig in Tiefenellern. It's a nice place for a break since you still have over half the hike to do.

There will be a set of stairs and a sign pointing to Veilbronn just next to the Naturfreundehaus. Take them down to an asphalt road and go left on it. To the right is Veilbronn but you'll be heading towards the Leidingshofer Tal, the town's main draw. This street is marked with yellow dot signs as well as ones with a sideways yellow triangle. Soon you will leave the paved road. You'll see a dirt path to your right and the two yellow symbol signs as well as one for the Frankenweg. Take that path; at its head is an information board on the Leidingshofer Tal. This is a very pretty valley with some rock formations and lots of moss for good measure. There's a babbling brook meandering through it, and you will do just the same, following the well-marked route. You'll pass a shelter on your left, and before long the yellow triangle and dot trails split. Stay with the triangle, also the Frankenweg at this point. Soon you'll see a sign for Streitberg with the yellow triangle – take that as the trail starts to gently climb. There are some wild rocky formations towards the top and a picnic table once it flattens out. Just past this rest stop there will be a trail sign with all routes veering right. Once you go a little further, you will come to a true junction. The yellow triangle trail goes right, but you will go hard right to stay on the Frankenweg. This is also the red circle route. Take this as it skirts the forest to your right. Not too far along this small stretch, you will go into the forest and soon see signs for a pavilion. This is another very short and worthy detour to some fine views. Back out on the main trail, follow the red circle and Frankenweg signs until you come to a small junction. The two routes will split, go right to follow the red circle trail.

Follow this through the forest down to the main road, where you will go right towards Veilbronn. Walk towards it, and when you come to a T, go left. Veilbronn is straight on, if you'd like to check it out. Otherwise, take the left, and on your right-hand side, you'll soon see a pedestrian path. Go right on that to continue on a parallel path to Veilbronn. You can see the large hotels that line its main street, and high up on the hill sits the Naturfreundehaus on your right. On your left is fantastic scenery too. You'll also see yellow dot and blue circle trail signs. You'll cross a bridge to go over the Leinleiterbach from which the valley takes its name and continue straight. Not much further after the bridge and before the 8 kilometer mark, you'll see an overpass. You'll also see a trail sign saying to go left before walking under it.

Follow the yellow dot, blue circle route. This will also bring you under the overpass but on a grassy path. Once on the other side, go left to walk up to street level, parallel to the other side of the overpass. Turn right on the busy road and walk along the right side of it. Just up the road, you'll make a well-marked right to continue on the yellow dot and blue circle trails. This route, however, is short-lived and not going to Heiligenstadt. So, at the next fork, DO NOT follow the yellow dot and blue circle left-hand side. Instead, continue straight on what looks like a logging road through the forest. When it comes out into the open, cross the well-worn grassy area straight on. You'll soon start seeing trail signs with a yellow horizontal stripe on a white background. These will bring you to a small asphalt road, where you'll go right. Walk towards a bridge with a building just beyond it. Cross the bridge and go left before the building. There is a yellow stripe sign and it says Heiligenstadt is 1.5 kilometers away. The old building is a pump house built in 1885. The next portion of the route is across an open field, and the path is marked with wooden posts with the yellow stripe sign. It goes towards the trees and then right to join a gravel road. You will take this to the right and follow it towards Heiligenstadt.

When you come out into the open, look high in the distance for a partial view of Greifenstein Castle. You will soon reach another asphalt road, go right on it, marked for Heiligenstadt. You'll be entering Traindorf, a small village next to your destination. Walk through the village – soon the street gets closer to the Leinleiterbach. You'll follow this brook right to Heiligenstadt. You will start to see sideways blue triangle signs along with the yellow stripe ones. On the other side of Traindorf, you'll see a pedestrian path crossing a grassy field. Take that instead of the asphalt road, following the trail signs. This will bring you to another asphalt road, where you'll go left. This is the Schätzwaldweg, a popular walking trail for locals. Follow it until you see a very well-marked right that will take you through a small city park. It's a cobblestone path that brings you right down to the river. Walk along it to the bridge, take a right to cross it and rejoin Schätzwaldweg. This becomes Marktplatz as it veers right. The Drei Kronen is on your right.

BRAUEREI-GASTHOF DREI KRONEN AICHINGER

Brauerei-Gasthof Drei Kronen Aichinger, founded in 1870, is just behind the restaurant. It's a good thing it's so close since it seems to be a one man show at times. Roland Aichinger not only brews the beer but pours it, serves food and sometimes I think he's cooking it, too. It's a simple, bustling place and the menu is full of homestyle Franconian dishes. Their lone beer is a copper classic, though I recently had a beer he collaborated on with two other local brewers and it was another winner. Across the street from the pub there is also a small self-service Biergarten. On sunny days, that might be your choice for your post-hike celebration beer.

Beers on tap: Aichinger Spezialbier. Aichinger Bock in autumn.

PRACTICAL INFORMATION

Brauerei-Gasthof Drei Kronen Aichinger
Marktplatz 5
91332 Heiligenstadt i. OFr.
+49 9198 522

Open Wednesday to Monday from 8:00 am

Rooms available but by telephone only.

Hotel-Restaurant Heiligenstadter Hof
Marktplatz 9
91332 Heiligenstadt i. Ofr.
+49 9198 781
www.hotel-heiligenstadter-hof.de

Rooms can be reserved on commercial booking sites.

BAMBERG MAHRS

DOWN THE RIVER TO MAHRS

UPPER FRANCONIA

▷⋯ STARTING POINT	⋯✗ DESTINATION
NEPTUNE STATUE, BAMBERG	**MAHRS BRÄU WIRTSHAUS & BIERGARTEN, BAMBERG**
🍺 BEER	▦ DIFFICULTY
MAHRS BRÄU "A U"	**WALK** 🚶
⛰ MAP	
ATK25-D08	⏱ DURATION OF THE HIKE
BAMBERG	**6 KM 1.5H**
🔍 HIGHLIGHTS	〰 ELEVATION GAIN
STATUE OF NEPTUNE, VILLA CONCORDIA, ST. MARTIN CHURCH, BOTANICAL GARDENS, BAMBERG OLD TOWN HALL	ASCENT: 20 M DESCENT: 50 M

UNGESPUNDETES, A BAMBERG REGION SPECIALTY UNFILTERED LOW CARBONATION BREW. BREWED WITH PERLE HOPS.

UNFILTERED AMBER

CARAMEL MALT, SLIGHT YEAST

MALT, BREAD, SLIGHTLY TART, SOME YEAST, SLIGHT BITTER FINISH

BITTERNESS

SWEETNESS

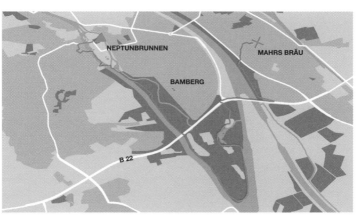

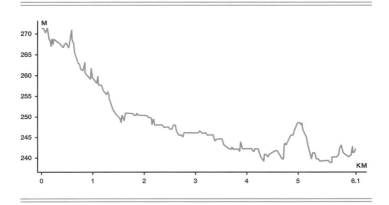

DESCRIPTION OF THE ROUTE

Bamberg is a wonderful town with a juxtaposition of architectural styles and cobblestone streets.
With seven hills to climb and as many breweries to explore, it's a town worthy of many days even before you venture out into the brewery-rich surroundings. Wandering the back streets of this marvel is one of the great joys of Franconian travel. One area that is often missed is the river area away from the renowned Old Town Hall, built surprisingly right on the flowing water. This walk guides you through this spot which is popular with locals and brings you along a more scenic route to Mahrs Bräu, surely on every beer lover's list of things to do in Bamberg.

Bamberg is serviced by regular trains from Nuremberg and is even on a few ICE express train routes.

One sight you're bound to walk by in your exploration is the statue of Neptune. Its name is "Gabelmoo" in the local dialect, meaning fork man. It is located in the atmospheric produce market between the main shopping street of Maximiliansplatz and the top tourist draw, the Old Town Hall. From the fountain, you can admire the St. Martin Church just across the square. If you haven't been inside, keep it in mind for another day. Its interior is often missed and is quite nice. Head away from the market area and church, going the other way on Grüner Markt. Turn left on Lange Straße, another great street to explore later, if you haven't already. Today, you'll only be on it for a short time as you look for an immediate right onto Habergasse. There will also be a sign pointing you towards the tourist information center. Follow Habergasse for a short time. When it turns left, it forks and you take the right side towards the river. Both are Habergasse. The part you're on will soon turn into Brucknersteg and cross the scenic river. Enjoy the views in both directions as you cross the Ludwig-Donau-Main Canal. Go left once over the bridge and then make a quick right to wrap around the tourist information center. From the center, go right and cross over the gardens out front. Carefully cross the busy Geyerswörthstraße then walk over the Bischofsmühlbrücke, a good-sized bridge. Stay on the left-hand side of it to get nice views of Klosterbräu, Bamberg's oldest brewery. Its brick chimney is easily spotted and an increasingly rare sight in the brewing world. In the other direction is Bamberg's renowned Old Town Hall.

As soon as you are over the bridge, you'll see a small parking area on your left that you need to cross to get onto the narrow Sonnen-plätzchen. This is followed by a relatively quick right onto Schimmels-gasse. These are great little back streets you're not likely to stumble across unless extensively exploring the former Jewish quarter. In fact, at the next corner, you can do just that if you go right on Judenstraße, but today, you'll need to go left onto Concordiastraße. Before you do, you can admire the Böttingerhaus, an art gallery housed in a gorgeous building. Once on Concordiastraße, take a quick left on Obere Mühlbrücke. This brings you by Klosterbräu, in case you can't wait for Mahrs Bräu. If not, stop back later – it's another great one. The street winds to the right before going left and back over the river. There's a nice little cafe there with river views. Once over the bridge, go right to remain on Obere Mühlbrücke, which soon becomes Mühlwörth as it brings you down to the river. This is a pleasant stroll along the water – keep your eyes out for the stunning Villa Concordia across it about midway up the street. Just before the one kilometer mark, you'll cross a small bridge and then you're officially in the Hain, a pretty city park that is fairly unspoiled by development. Continue along Mühlwörth as it follows the river and becomes greener. It veers away from the water as it goes around a public swimming area and the Bootshaus, a popular riverside restaurant. Stop now or keep it in mind for another time. It's a pretty spot with great beer on tap from the local Keesmann brewery. You could continue on Mühlwörth but that goes away from the river, so go slightly right to walk along the river on the unnamed narrower path. It soon comes to an open area with a small mauve pavilion. Beyond it, walk under the overpass and stay to the right to remain on the river and further explore the Hain. You'll follow this until the fork in the river.

You've been walking up the left side of the Regnitz River and now you'll walk back up the right side of it. There's a small place to rent boats at this point and it's a popular spot for locals to relax. Stay along the river until you come to a bridge. Rather than cross it (or continue straight), veer to the left to head towards the botanical gardens. Just before the 4 kilometer mark, you'll go right to skirt a small lake, another nice place for a break. Beyond the lake, you'll veer right and then go left to walk through the botanical gardens. Continue straight and into a forested section as it meanders to the left. You'll come to another overpass to walk under. On the other side, go right to exit the park and you will come to a very busy intersection. Cross it to get to the pedestrian side of the Münchner Ring as it goes over the river. Once on the other side of the river, look for the pedestrian signs that will bring you down to this side of the river. Once down the ramp, you'll walk across Neue Burghofer Straße and go right on the pedestrian path along this side of the river. You'll soon come to a kiosk with a pleasant outside seating area, but you're too close to Mahrs to stop there. Instead, veer to your right to pass it and cross the busy street before entering Burghofer Straße on the other side. Follow this until you come to a pretty, red brick church on your right. Go just beyond it, then make a right onto Wunderburg. To your left is the Keesmann brewery, worth checking out before you head back to town, but now it's time for Mahrs. It just up the street on your right. A "U" is waiting.

MAHRS BRÄU WIRTSHAUS & BIERGARTEN

Even if Mahrs Bräu hadn't been named the "Best Brewery in the World" by *Men's Journal* in 2007, this atmospheric brewpub would be appreciated by anyone who walks through its doors. Of course, it might be that more people do just that now due to its notoriety, but such is the price of fame. It's not like it was a secret to locals who do a lot of that crowding, especially on weekend midday meal days when their equally amazing food often takes precedence over their award-winning beer.

You know the pub is a classic as soon as you walk through the door. You walk into a long corridor with a windowed hatch immediately to your right. If it's crowded or you're in a hurry, order a beer through it and stand along the corridor as laborers traditionally did on the way home from work. If you have more time, and if you come here you should allot a fair amount to it, walk through the door next to the window and behold a low-beamed ceiling pub from another time. There are generally two wooden barrels dispensing the beer and the barmen wear white shirts and often waistcoats for good effect. If you see an empty spot, grab it. This is one of the best rooms to have a beer in that I've ever had the pleasure to do so. The other rooms are fine too, but this one is really a gem. It is sometimes closed on good weather days when the Biergarten just out front is operating on all cylinders. The upside is that there are more beers on tap. It's a great area, too, with leafy trees providing shade. The meals are fantastic so planning to have a meal here is a great choice and allows you time to work your way through their large selection of beers. This is one superbly run operation. They know what they're doing and have been doing it since 1670. First you'll wonder why this is your first time here, then you'll starting planning a return visit!

Beers on tap: Mahrs Bräu "U," Mahrs Bräu Helles and Mahrs Bräu Pils. Inside, they are gravity dispensed. Outside, they are from the tank served from copper fonts with more of their range offered, as well.

PRACTICAL INFORMATION

Mahrs Bräu Wirtshaus & Biergarten
Wunderburg 10
96050 Bamberg
+49 951 915170
www.mahrs.de

Open Tuesday to Saturday
10:00 am to 11:00 pm
Monday 4:00 pm to 11:00 pm
Sunday 10:00 am to 3:00 pm

BAMBERG SCHLENKERLA

A SMOKY RIVER STROLL IN BAMBERG

UPPER FRANCONIA

▷··· STARTING POINT

SCHLENKERLA, BAMBERG

🍺 BEER

AECHT SCHLENKERLA RAUCHBIER MÄRZEN

⛰ MAP

ATK25-D08
BAMBERG

🔍 HIGHLIGHTS

BAMBERG OLD TOWN HALL, LITTLE VENICE OF BAMBERG, HISTORICAL HALF-TIMBERED SCHLENKERLA BREWPUB

···✗ DESTINATION

SCHLENKERLA, BAMBERG

🏯 DIFFICULTY

WALK 🚶

🕐 DURATION OF THE HIKE

2 KM
20-30MIN

〰 ELEVATION GAIN

ASCENT: 0 M
DESCENT: 0 M

RAUCH MÄRZEN

DEEP CHESTNUT

SMOKED HAM

**RICH MALT,
BITTER,
SMOKY**

BITTERNESS	SWEETNESS

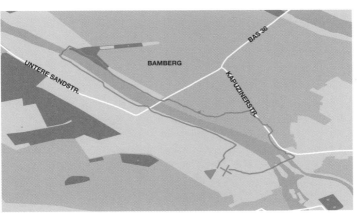

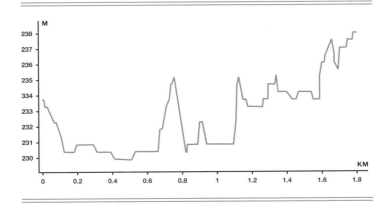

DESCRIPTION OF THE ROUTE

The term "beer Mecca" gets thrown around perhaps too casually but Bamberg is about as deserving of the title as anywhere. Blessed with 12 breweries of its own and hundreds in the surrounding area, it is sure to get the beer connoisseur salivating. Aside from the beer, Bamberg is an incredibly beautiful old town with a variety of architectural styles sprinkled along its cobblestone streets, including a half-timbered old town hall built, interestingly enough, straddling the river. You could spend days wandering the atmospheric streets.

This walk takes you on both sides the main part of the Regnitz River, which runs through the old town. While most will view the town's pretty row of half-timbered houses on the river known as "Little Venice" from the bridge crossing it, not as many seem to venture over to walk along the river itself. Even fewer do it on the opposite side. I've been going to Bamberg for over twenty years and only started doing it recently myself!

Bamberg is well serviced by frequent trains from many cities in Germany. Nuremberg, for instance is only around 40 minutes and ICE trains from Munich take an hour and 40 minutes.

Coming out of Schlenkerla, go right on Dominikanerstraße. This is a timeless old street that gets incredibly busy, so try to do this walk early in the morning to best appreciate it. At the first intersection, go right on Kasernstraße. This will take you to the river where you'll turn left on Am Leinritt. Stroll along this pleasant stretch, enjoying gorgeous views of "Little Venice" to your right. Continue straight and walk under a bridge, leaving most of the crowds behind. There are some nice, if less famous, houses across the river. At the next bridge, cross the Regnitz River and enjoy views of the old town to your right.

Once over the bridge, go right through a small city park and drop down to walk along the river on a narrow, unnamed footpath. Across the river is a beautiful white building with yellow trim – the city archives. Continue straight and go under the bridge to find a small set of stairs to your left. Go up them and turn right on Fischerei. You're walking behind the row of homes comprising "Little Venice," giving you a different perspective. Follow the street as it bends left and take a right on Kapuzinerstraße. This brings you to Am Kranen, a popular place for people to hang out along the river. Walk towards the first bridge (Untere Brücke) and to the right to cross it. On your right is one of Bamberg's iconic images, a sculpture by Polish artist Igor Mitoraj. Continue across the bridge with views of the town's lovely old town hall to your left. On the other side, the street soon becomes Dominikanerstraße. Follow it back to Schlenkerla, just ahead on your right.

SCHLENKERLA

While it's true Schlenkerla is often overrun with tourists, it is for good reason. It's about as timeless an old pub as you'll find anywhere, with lots of dark wood paneling, animal antlers and, in one of its many rooms, vaulted ceilings dating back to the 14th century. All of the rooms have a lot of character but the one immediately to your left as you come in, just oozes it. With a green tile oven as its centerpiece and two wooden barrels atop the copper bar top, it's like stepping back in time. The beer is gravity dispensed and the barrels are changed often as you might imagine. Out back is a very nice and often overlooked Biergarten. Meals are typical Franconian fare and Bamberger Zwiebeln is their specialty – an onion stuffed with ground meat and topped with bacon. They also have a great Zwetschgenbames, slices of cold smoked beef, that pairs well with their smoky beer.

Beers on tap: Aecht Schlenkerla Rauchbier Märzen. Seasonals (also on tap): Aecht Schlenkerla Fastenbier (Ash Wednesday to Easter), Aecht Schlenkerla Kräusen (June to the middle of August), Aecht Schlenkerla Rauchbier Ur-Bock (October to December), Aecht Schlenkerla Eiche (Advent season). Bottled: Aecht Schlenkerla Rauchbier Weizen, Helles Schlenkerla Lagerbier.

I hesitated to include this obvious place but it remains a special one. They produce a large line of amazing beers, even though they could brew just one. They also continue to serve them gravity dispensed when using kegs would be easier. They use actual wooden barrels rarely found in Franconia. It's not their fault that they're popular and this is not strictly a tourist place. Their Bockbier tapping in October is mobbed and I met lots of locals here then.

If you go in the late afternoon in summer, expect it to be a zoo. People line the street outside, drinking. You can go inside and get a beer from a self-service window but drinking within these hallowed walls is not to be missed. The place opens at 9:30 am. Do yourself a favor and do this walk after breakfast and go here for an early beer. Then you'll see the real old-world pub I fell in love with in 1997.

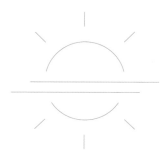

PRACTICAL INFORMATION

Schlenkerla
Dominikanerstraße 6
96049 Bamberg
+49 951 56060
www.schlenkerla.de

Open daily 9:30 am to 11:30 pm

Brauerei Spezial
Obere Königstraße 10
96052 Bamberg
+49 951 24304
www.brauerei-spezial.de

Open Sunday to Friday 9:00 am to 11:00 pm
Saturday 9:00 am to 2:00 pm

The "other" Rauchbier brewery in Bamberg, and many people's favorite, has the advantage of having overnight accommodation.

SCHAMMELSDORF

FOUR BREWERIES ON THIS RURAL AND FORESTED ROUTE

UPPER FRANCONIA

▷··· **STARTING POINT**

BRAUEREI-GASTSTÄTTE KNOBLACH,
SCHAMMELSDORF

🍺 **BEER**

KNOBLACH UNGESPUNDETES LAGER

🗺 **MAP**

ATK25-D09
SCHEẞLITZ

👁 **HIGHLIGHTS**

MARIÄ GEBURT CHURCH, MARIÄ GEBURT
CHAPEL, FOUR BREWERIES, RURAL SCENERY,
HALF-TIMBERED HOUSES IN LOHNDORF

···✕ **DESTINATION**

BRAUEREI-GASTSTÄTTE KNOBLACH,
SCHAMMELSDORF

▦ **DIFFICULTY**

HIKE 🚶

🕐 **DURATION OF THE HIKE**

15.5 KM
3.5–4H

〰 **ELEVATION GAIN**

ASCENT: 430 M
DESCENT: 450 M

UNGESPUNDETES LAGER

UNFILTERED,
DARK GOLDEN

MALT, GRAIN,
SOME GRASS,
LIGHT HOP

DRY, FRUITY,
BITTER FINISH,
LOW CARBONATION

BITTERNESS   SWEETNESS

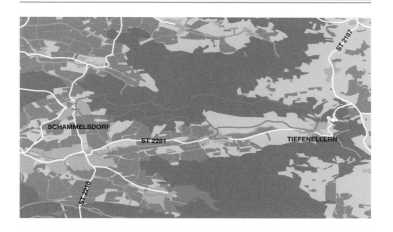

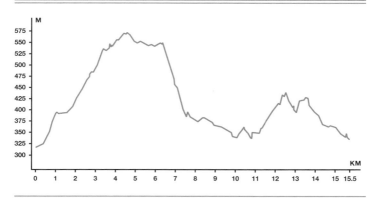

DESCRIPTION OF THE ROUTE

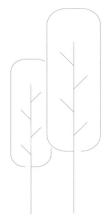

Schammelsdorf is a pleasant if unremarkable village in what is lovingly referred to as Franconian Tuscany. What it lacks in must-see sights, it more than makes up for with its surrounding landscape and proximity to many great small breweries. In fact, it is about the midway point of the 13-Brauereien-Weg, which is a bit out of the scope of this book due to its length. This hike is a loop using part of the noted semi-long-distance beer hike and takes in four of the breweries along the way. It is well marked but there are a few trails very close together and they cross each other a few times, so the description may sound more complex than the walk is. The key is to stay on the trail marked with blue diamonds.

Schammelsdorf is serviced by limited direct buses from Bamberg on weekdays and the trip takes about 20 minutes. Buses with a change in Memmelsdorf take longer. Service on Saturday is very limited and they do not run at all on Sunday.

Coming out of Brauerei-Gaststätte Knoblach, go left on Kremmeldorfer Straße and follow it as it bends to the left. Mid-bend, take a right on Haselgraben. Not far up the road, at the fork, go right onto an unpaved farm road with a blue diamond trail sign. Go with the trail as it turns left and skirts a forest before turning right and ducking into it. You'll see both blue and red diamond signs on this forested section. Just before the 1 kilometer mark, you will come to a junction. Straight on is Neudorf. Go right to stay on the blue diamond trail. As the trail bends to the left, it joins the famed 13-Brauereien-Weg that goes between Memmelsdorf and Strullendorf. Follow this route as it meanders but continue straight – the blue diamond and 13-Brauereien-Weg signs will be your guide. Around the 3.5 kilometer mark, the blue diamond and 13-Brauereien-Weg diverge. Either will get you to Tiefenellern, so if you get on the wrong one, it's not the end of the world.

The blue diamond trail has a nice viewpoint, hence our reason for heading that way. When the trail comes to a fork, stay to the left and then more or less straight to stay on the blue diamond trail. The right side would keep you on the 13-Brauereien-Weg, and go more directly to Tiefenellern. Follow this straight trail, parallel to the 13-Brauereien-Weg. It will come to a junction for Lohndorf and you will go left to stay on the blue diamond. You'll come to a more open area, skirting the forest on your right and see a viewpoint turn off before the 6 kilometer mark. Follow the small path to your right. There is a great view of Lohndorf, the place you've seen signs for. Continue along the main trail, following the blue diamonds. You'll see a turn for the Gügel but stay straight. When you come to a road called Hirtenanger, go left. This will bring you to Schlehenweg, where you will go right followed by a quick left to remain on that street. It becomes Am Altenberg just as it arrives in Tiefenellern. When you come to the Mariä Geburt Chapel, go right on Ellerbergstraße. Brauerei Hönig is just ahead on your right. If it's open, pop in for their tasty Lagerbier. Their Biergarten out back is one of the most popular spots on the 13-Brauereien-Weg.

Continue on Ellerbergstraße out of the village and you will see the trail to your right. There's a lovely stone crucifix and the blue diamond trail sign. This is a brick farm road that runs parallel to the main road before veering right to reach a higher plateau offering grand views of the valley. As you get close to the intersection you'll also have a great view of Lohndorf in the same direction, its distinctive church tower looming. When you come to an open area, there will be a parking lot for hikers on your left. To your right will be the Landhaus Lohntal, a large hotel. Just past the parking area, you can go left if you'd like to check out Lohndorf. It's probably the cutest village on the 13-Braue-reien-Weg. When you get to Ellertalstraße, Privatbrauerei Reh is to your left and Brauerei Hölzlein is to your right.

The former has no restaurant but does have a tasting room with limited hours. The latter has a great restaurant and Biergarten. Check their opening hours before making your way there. If you're not going into Lohndorf, you'll go beyond the parking lot and look for the blue diamond marking on the street sign for Lohntalstraße to your right. This goes in the opposite direction to the road to Lohndorf. Follow this across open farmland with views of the Landhaus Lohntal to your right before going back into the forest just after the 11 kilometer mark. This route meanders through the forest but is marked with blue diamond trail signs the whole way back to Schammelsdorf. When you come out into the open, you'll walk towards town and go right to enter it on Grubfeld. This crosses Dickengarten and runs into Litzendorfer Straße. Go right there and pass Stammbergstraße before coming to a fork. Go right on Kremmeldorfer Straße and Brauerei Knoblach will be immediately to your left.

BRAUEREI-GASTSTÄTTE KNOBLACH

Brauerei-Gaststätte Knoblach was founded in 1880 and is still very much a family enterprise. The Knoblachs strive to use local ingredients in their beer as well as their tasty homestyle meals. With a traditional inn feel, it's a bustling place – especially at meal times – but is also a place of beer pilgrimage, whether beer aficionados arrive on foot, bike or a bus from Bamberg. The Biergarten area is a lovely shady paradise in summer and acts as an expanded drinking area in cooler months for beer tapping events. They also have their own distillery, noted for its fruit schnapps.

Ungespundetes beer is a specialty from the area around Bamberg. Gravity dispensed beer is from a barrel with a top gas release hole that has a stopper. This can be adjusted as the barman sees fit. Traditionally, beers were lagered in wooden barrels with the same release holes and with Ungespundetes beer, the plug was taken out at least partially, to release some of the carbon dioxide build-up. This resulted in a less gassy and easier to drink beer.

Beers on tap: Knoblach Ungespundetes Lager (gravity dispensed), Knoblach Räuschla, Knoblach Hefeweizen and Knoblach Dunkles Landbier. Seasonals: Knoblach Urmärzen (February), Knoblach Sommerbier (July to September), Knoblach Bockbier (October to December), Knoblach Rauchbier (in winter), Knoblach Festbier (December).

PRACTICAL INFORMATION

Brauerei-Gaststätte Knoblach
Kremmeldorfer Straße 1
96123 Litzendorf (Schammelsdorf)
+49 9505 267
www.brauerei-knoblach.de

Open Tuesday to Friday from 3:00 pm to 11:00 pm
Saturday 9:00 am to 11:00 pm
Sunday 9:00 am to 3:00 pm
Closed Monday

Brauerei Hönig Gasthof zur Post
Ellerbergstraße 15
96123 Litzendorf (Tiefenellern)
+49 9505 391
www.brauerei-hoenig.de

Open Monday to Wednesday from 3:00 pm
Friday to Sunday from 10:00 am
Closed Thursday

Brauerei und Gaststätte Hölzlein
Ellertalstraße 13
96123 Litzendorf (Lohndorf)
+49 9505 357
www.brauerei-hoelzlein.de

Open Monday, Wednesday, Thursday, Friday
and Sunday from 3:00 pm
Saturday from midday
Closed Tuesday

Privatbrauerei Reh
Ellertalstraße 36
96123 Litzendorf (Lohndorf)
+49 9505 210
www.reh-bier.de

Open Monday to Friday 7:30 am to 6:00 pm
Saturday 8:30 am to 1:00 pm

LICHTENFELS TO VIERZEHNHEILIGEN

FROM THE TRAIN STATION TO THE MONASTERY FASTER THAN YOU CAN SAY VIERZEHNHEILIGEN

UPPER FRANCONIA

▷⋯ STARTING POINT	⋯✕ DESTINATION
LICHTENFELS TRAIN STATION	**BRAUEREI TRUNK, VIERZEHNHEILIGEN**
🍺 BEER	▦ DIFFICULTY
NOTHELFER EXPORT DUNKEL	**WALK**
△ MAP	
ATK25 C09	⊘ DURATION OF THE HIKE
LICHTENFELS	**4.5 KM 1–1.5H (ONE-WAY)**
🔍 HIGHLIGHTS	∿ ELEVATION GAIN
BASILICA OF VIERZEHNHEILIGEN, KLOSTER BANZ, STAFFELBERG	ASCENT: 160 M DESCENT: 50 M

DUNKLES MADE WITH MALT FROM BAMBERG AND KULMBACH, AND REGIONAL HOPS

CHESTNUT,
REDDISH TINGE,
DENSE OFF-WHITE HEAD

CHOCOLATE,
ROASTED MALT,
BREAD

MALT, CHOCOLATE,
HOPS IN BITTERSWEET
FINISH

BITTERNESS

SWEETNESS

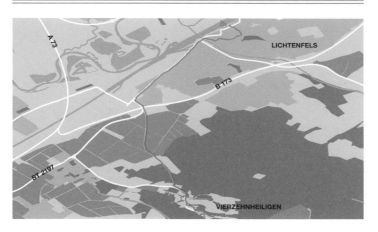

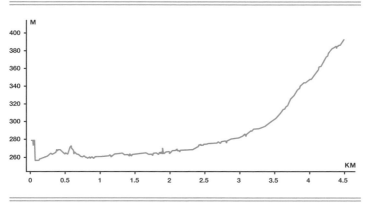

DESCRIPTION OF THE ROUTE

Vierzehnheiligen is one of the highlights of the Staffelstein region, one rich in not only beautiful landscapes but also a high concentration of great breweries. The 18th century Baroque-Rococo basilica's interior is an ornate masterpiece wowing the hordes that come to gawk in awe. It's also a place of serious pilgrimage due to an elaborate history. The fourteen holy helpers it's named after were sainted for their healing abilities. The exterior may pale in comparison, but as seen from afar, it still evokes veneration. While many arrive on tourist buses and you can reach it by public transportation or car, there's no better way to get there than by walking in on the Jakobsweg, the long-distance pilgrimage route that ends at Santiago de Compostela in northern Spain. Don't worry, your portion of the trek will be much shorter than that but will still offer views of Kloster Banz as well as atmospheric views of Vierzehnheiligen. Conveniently and unsurprisingly, there's a brewery onsite.

Lichtenfels is serviced by frequent trains from Bamberg. Some buses between Bad Staffelstein and Lichtenfels stop at Vierzehn-heiligen. Check the schedule to make sure you have a way out if you won't be spending the night.

Coming out of the Lichtenfels station, cross the street and go straight on Bahnhofstraße. At the intersection, cross Bamberger Straße and continue on Am Stadtgraben until you come to Grabenweg, where you will go right. There's a sign for the Jakobsweg on the street sign post. It's blue with a yellow scallop shell. Follow Grabenweg as it winds to the right, and when you come to some stairs on your left, climb them up to the small chapel of St. Jakob. Walk around it and then drop down the stairs on the other side and go right on Lange Straße.

Take this back to Bamberger Straße and take a left. It's a busy, modern road but there is a half-timbered house or two along the way, and if you look to your right in the distance, up high sits Kloster Banz, a former monastery. You're only on this stretch for a kilometer before you take a well-marked left on Seeleinstraße and a very quick right onto Lorenzgrund. The street sign also says Pilgerweg (pilgrim's path).

Follow this much quieter street and you will already have some partial views of Vierzehnheiligen, only a couple of kilometers away. Go under the overpass and go straight on. There's a pretty row of trees that you now walk along with great views of your magnificent church destination. Walk down this lane, with great views of the Staffelberg to your right on the horizon. You'll come to a small trail intersection with a shelter, named after the views of Kloster Banz it provides. Continue straight on to follow the Jakobsweg. This will bring you all the way to the main road, where you will go left. You'll now be on asphalt again, going uphill with the church looming straight on. On the way up, you'll see what looks like an apartment complex on your right. This is the Diözesanhaus Vierzehnheiligen, where you can spend the night. At the top of the hill is Vierzehnheiligen.

Walk to the left of the church and wrap around it. There's a visitor center on your left and you can enter the church just across the way. If the church is open, it's probably best to go in. You never know when a service might start, thwarting your photo opportunities. If a beer is more pressing, exit the scenic corridor and go left to find Brauerei Trunk.

BRAUEREI TRUNK BRÄUSTÜBERL & BIERGARTEN

Though not on their sign, Brauerei Trunk is often referred to as Alte Klosterbrauerei and it would be easy to suppose that monks may have brewed here once upon a time. The given founding date is 1803 and since then a few families have been at the helm. The Trunks have only been here since 1989, but it sure doesn't feel that way when you walk into their seemingly timeless pub. It's a real pleasant throwback with simple Franconian snacks and great beer.

All of their beers have "Nothelfer" on their label, an ode to the emergency helpers who comprise the fourteen saints the church is named after.

Beers on tap: Nothelfer Export Dunkel, Nothelfer Pils, Nothelfer Lager, Nothelfer Bio-Weiße plus one seasonal: Fastenbock during Lent, Scheffel-Trunk in spring and summer, Erntebier in September and October, and Festbier and Silberbock for the Christmas season.

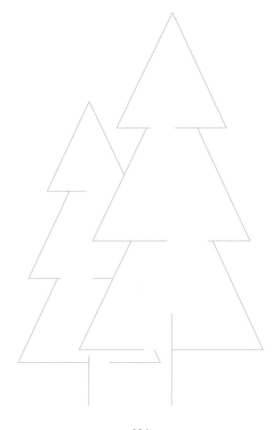

PRACTICAL INFORMATION

Brauerei Trunk Bräustüberl & Biergarten
Vierzehnheiligen 3
96231 Bad Staffelstein (Vierzehnheiligen)
+49 9571 3488
www.brauerei-trunk.de

Open daily 10:00 am to 8:00 pm

Vierzehnheiligen is a great day trip but it can also be turned into a
multi-day endeavor. You can spend the night here and continue on the
next day. With quite a few great beers to try, it's not a bad option. If
you get an early start, you can continue along the Jakobsweg down to
Loffeld the same day and enjoy the many breweries and hiking
opportunities there.

Diözesanhaus Vierzehnheiligen
Vierzehnheiligen 9
96231 Bad Staffelstein (Vierzehnheiligen)
+49 9571 9260
www.bildungshaeuser-vierzehnheiligen.de

Rooms can be booked on their website but it's only in German. They
are often on common accommodation booking sites, as well.

LOFFELD

OVER THE STAFFELBERG ON THE BLUE NORDIC TRAIL

UPPER FRANCONIA

▷···· STARTING POINT	···✗ DESTINATION
STAFFELBERG-BRÄU, LOFFELD	**STAFFELBERG-BRÄU, LOFFELD**
🍺 BEER	🎲 DIFFICULTY
LOFFELDER DUNKEL	**HIKE**
⛰ MAP	
ATK25 C09	🕐 DURATION OF THE HIKE
LICHTENFELS	**8 KM 2.5–3.5H**
🔍 HIGHLIGHTS	〰 ELEVATION GAIN
STAFFELBERG, LOFFELD, HALF-TIMBERED HOUSES, CHAPELS IN LOFFELD AND ON TOP OF THE STAFFELBERG	ASCENT: 440 M DESCENT: 303 M

DUNKLES

CHESTNUT,
CREAMY HEAD

MALT,
SLIGHT CHOCOLATE

MALT, SOFT,
SOME DARK CHOCOLATE,
BITTERSWEET FINISH

BITTERNESS   SWEETNESS

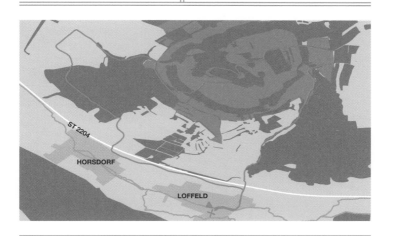

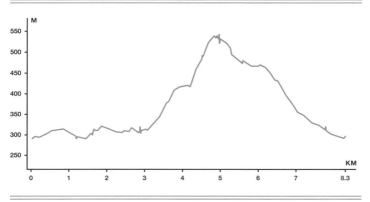

DESCRIPTION OF THE ROUTE

The Staffelberg is a large flat 500-plus meter hill in Upper Franconia. While not a high peak, it's quite a sight due to its shape. It's also a popular tourist attraction due to its proximity to many nearby sights such as Kloster Banz and Vierzehnheiligen, two hilltop monasteries. There are also numerous breweries in the area, making it a beer hiking paradise. The trail network is extensive, well marked, and designed to attract a wide variety of walkers.

Frequent trains run along the route from Bamberg to Bad Staffelstein where you can get a weekday bus to Loffeld. If you're planning a weekend trip, it's best to travel by car or bike/walk in from Bad Staffelstein on the well-posted bike trails.

This route over the Staffelberg is aimed at Nordic-walking enthusiasts but just as easily gets the beer hiker over the iconic peak and back to a very fine Franconian brewery. Starting from Staffelberg-Bräu in Loffeld, walk over the small bridge and go right on An der Lauter. Admire the beautiful half-timbered building to your right, a former school. This is a pretty little town so enjoy this pleasant stroll along its main street, taking note of the small chapel on your left as An der Lauter bends to your left, where it becomes Löwentalweg. Take this street uphill out of the hamlet of Loffeld. Before you come to the overpass, you'll notice a hiker's parking lot to your left; head that way and you start to see your first blue Nordic trail signs. The entire route is extremely well marked. Just up the road from the parking lot, you'll see a smaller trail off to your left, again marked. Take this all the way to the village of Horsdorf, about one kilometer away. It runs parallel with the road but still offers fantastic views of both the Staffelberg to your right and some pretty countryside scenery to your left. In Horsdorf, look for abundant signs beckoning you to the right and over the main road to the trail.

The route starts to climb gently and you'll notice a lot of trail markings. You're also on the yellow Nordic trail as well as one of the area's beer hiking trails. It's marked with a beer mug with the number 3 in it. You'll be following these for much of the early stages of the walk, so making the left choice at the first fork is obvious. If it's a hot day, you'll be happy to make the left at the top of the hill and enter a nice patch of forest. When you pop out, you'll head uphill once again as the trail veers to the left. You'll then follow the trail signs to the right and start to get great views of the Staffelberg on your right. Don't forget to look to your left for the equally stunning Kloster Banz. You'll soon make another right and start walking towards the Staffelberg, which you are about to climb. You'll be happy to be in another forested section as the route goes up. You'll pass a war memorial to veterans of WWI on your right as you make your way through this lush portion of trail. Once out of the trees, you'll go to your right over a more open section. To your left lies the Staffelberg, though largely obstructed by trees. Not far down the trail, the blue and yellow Nordic trails split and you go left to remain on the blue one. It starts to get steep here but take your time and enjoy the views as you make your way to the top. There are some steps to climb next but you'll find you're not quite there yet. It's a plateau, and now you can clearly see the Staffelberg as motivation for that last push. It's a very pretty spot and many walkers choose to picnic here.

Your route takes you right over the top so continue on the narrower section of trail. Once on top, you'll see a small chapel straight ahead but the blue Nordic route takes you to your left to make a half-circle of the viewpoints on that side of the peak. Enjoy the flat stroll, admiring views over the valley but keeping your eye to your right, as well, for some pretty shots of the chapel. Staffelberg's very flat stones make great viewpoints. As you round the bend and start to walk back towards the chapel, there are some fine views of Kloster Banz in the distance to your left. There's a small restaurant and Biergarten next to the chapel if you're hungry. If you're thirsty, they have fine beers from St. Georgen-Bräu in Buttenheim on tap.

You can also head over to the other side of the Staffelberg to enjoy some other views, but this route will take you downhill from the chapel area. You'll see your familiar blue Nordic trails as you head down, and at the bottom of the first section, you'll go right down some wooden steps. The trail meanders to your left before it meets up with a main trail. At this junction, follow the signs to the right. You'll see a few turn-offs from this trail, going to different locations but push on to make a right at the well-marked turn. Along with the little blue walker, there's a motivating 2 kilometer to Loffeld sign, too. You're headed down now but there are some very pretty sections of trail still to come.

As you make a second right, you may see a herd of roaming sheep to your right. I was lucky enough to have that experience, and since it was spring, some baby lambs were enjoying the sun. As you continue on, you'll see a different perspective of the Staffelberg to your right. Continue down the valley as the trail winds its way back to Loffeld. At the end, you will go under the overpass you saw at the beginning of the hike. You'll then pass the parking lot on your right and continue down the street (Löwentalweg) into the village. Make the right on An der Lauter and you can alternatively walk on the other side of the small river that runs along it. Hopefully, you saved your appetite for Staffelberg-Bräu as they have some of the very best food in the region.

STAFFELBERG-BRÄU

Founded in 1856, Staffelberg-Bräu is now a sixth-generation family business. Personifying hands-on, they are one of the hardest working families I've ever had the pleasure to observe. The current generation features a husband brewer/butcher and a wife who seems to do just about everything else. Their children more than chip in, and it's a good thing as this is one very busy brewpub. The restored half-timbered building features a cute outside seating area which offers views of the seemingly always-in-action brew kettles. Not only do they serve up great meals, they also brew one of the largest selections of beers you'll find in a small countryside brewery. They've won gold medals for quite a few of them and feature not only three regular beers on tap but also one seasonal in addition to numerous bottles. Thankfully, in addition to all this, they offer rooms at great value so that you not only get to try all their beers but can also enjoy the many hiking trails that make this such a wonderful area for the beer hiker.

Beers on tap: Staffelberg-Bräu Loffelder Dunkel, Staffelberg-Bräu Hopfen-Gold-Pils, Staffelberg-Bräu Hefe-Weißbier, plus two rotating taps.

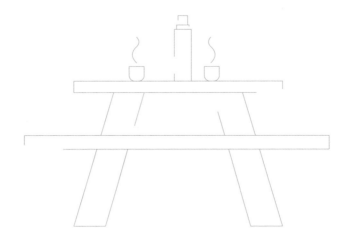

PRACTICAL INFORMATION

Staffelberg-Bräu
Mühlteich 7
96231 Bad Staffelstein (Loffeld)
+49 9573 5925
www.staffelberg-braeu.de

Open Tuesday to Sunday
10:00 am to 10:00 pm
Closed Monday

STUBLANG

THE STUBLANGER CONNECTION
ON THE #3 BRAUEREI-WEG

UPPER FRANCONIA

▷⋯ STARTING POINT	⋯✗ DESTINATION
BRAUEREI DINKEL, STUBLANG	**BRAUEREI DINKEL, STUBLANG**
🍺 **BEER**	🔢 **DIFFICULTY**
STUBLANGER LAGERBIER	**HIKE** 🚶
⛰ **MAP**	
ATK25 C09	🕐 DURATION OF THE HIKE
LICHTENFELS	**5 KM** **1.5–2H**
🔍 HIGHLIGHTS	〰 ELEVATION GAIN
ST. NIKOLAUS AND ST. GUMBERTUS CHURCH, HALF-TIMBERED BUILDINGS (AND BREWERY), VIEWS OF THE STAFFELBERG	ASCENT: 213 M DESCENT: 210 M

4.7%
ALCOHOL
CONTENT

KELLERBIER

UNFILTERED AMBER

GRAIN,
SLIGHT CHOCOLATE

MALT,
FRUITY,
DRY, BITTERSWEET FINISH

BITTERNESS   SWEETNESS

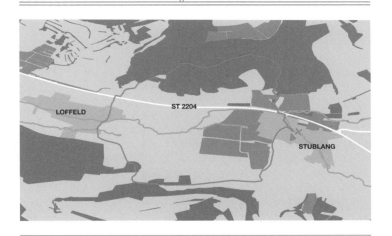

LOFFELD

ST 2204

STUBLANG

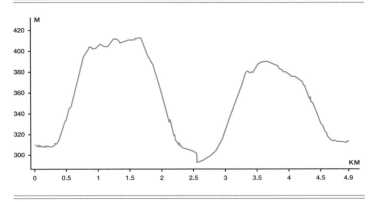

DESCRIPTION OF THE ROUTE

The Bad Staffelstein area is a top draw in Upper Franconia, a scenic slice of northern Bavaria. While Loffeld might be a bit cuter and closer to the iconic Staffelberg, Stublang is better located for checking out all the breweries in this compact, brewery-rich region. It also has the advantage of having two breweries in the town itself. While not the shortest route between the two towns, this pretty and relatively short circuit takes them both in and also gets you into the hills on both sides of the valley – both in forested sections and on open stretches, which afford great views.

Stublang is serviced by regular buses during the week from Bad Staffelstein and Lichtenfels, both of which are well-connected to Bamberg. Depending on the bus, it takes about 20 minutes. Unfortunately, there is no service on weekends. It's only a little over 5 kilometers along the bike path, so you could walk or bike in, too.

Coming out of Brauerei Stublang, go left on Am Dorfbrunnen. Walk along the stream flowing right through the village towards the pretty church of St. Nikolaus and St. Gumbertus. Before you get to the church, go left on Unterer Peunt. Follow it as it wraps back around the village and look to your left for the back of the old brewery and its tasteful logo. As you leave the residential area, you'll see signs for Loffeld, green circle trail markings, and also beer mug signs with the #3 on them. This is one of four Brauerei-Wege in the Bad Staffelstein area. You won't do the entire thing today, but in the third of the route you're going to do, you will see all three breweries left on the trail. The ones in Bad Staffelstein have all closed down. Continue up the street, which soon becomes a brick farm road. You will be gently going up and out into the countryside, with fields in both directions. You'll veer to the left before taking a distinct right, all before the 1 kilometer mark and all marked. The path is obvious so no worries. This is a pretty stretch and the elevation you've gained gives you views of the Staffelberg to your right at about 1 o'clock. You can't miss the flattish peak. Looking back slightly, you'll see the distinctive church in Uetzing. This is probably best late in the day when it seems to glow.

Continue along this elevated path. Whatever forks you come to are well marked with either green circles or #3 beer mugs, or both. After passing a short, forested section, you'll go right to cross a small, grassy area leading to another farm road. Follow this as it winds its way towards Loffeld. You'll see the Staffelstein getting closer and the small chapel in Loffeld in its foreground. This comes to a T at Dornigweg where you will go right towards town. When you get to the chapel, you make the call. You can go left on An der Lauter to walk along Loffelf's stream to Staffelberg-Bräu. It's not two minutes away and if you haven't been, it's a great place for a beer and meal. Even if you aren't quite ready, go have a look. It's housed in a fine, old half-timbered building and the old school house next to it is photo-worthy.

If not, take the rounded bend right on Löwentalweg as it goes uphill and out of the quiet hamlet. You'll come to an intersection with a parking lot on your left. Keep going straight and walk under the overpass. There's a host of hiking symbols and the green circle is among them. Just past it, take a right and keep an eye out for a fairly quick left. There are wooden signs for the Rundweg as well as the Waldweg Stublang. Again, it's not the most direct route but it's the most scenic. You're back on the #3 Brauerei-Weg again, too. The trail starts to climb and goes through a forested section before opening up, with a pretty meadow to your right – sprinkled with wildflowers when I last walked through. The views into the valley aren't too shabby from this side, either. You will then enter a lush, green forest with the few turns you need to make very well marked as you round yourself back in the direction of Stublang. It's all downhill from here, and when you emerge from the forest, you still have elevated views of the church in Stublang. Follow the path and you'll pass a small cemetery with a chapel on your left before making it down to the main road. It's surprising how busy this can be on the weekends, so carefully cross it and go left on the bike path to town. Take the first right on Frauendorfer Straße and a quick right over the small bridge. You'll walk right in front of the church, so have a look or take a moment to reflect, if you like. Go left on Kirchstraße and cross Unterer Peunt to return to Brauerei Dinkel via Am Dorfbrunnen. Your beer is waiting.

BRAUEREI DINKEL

The Dinkel brothers are proving that sometimes two heads are better than one. Founded in 1880, the old half-timbered restaurant was abandoned many years ago when the larger one with a hotel attached was built to accommodate the crowds. It remained dormant though the actual brewery has always been there. Re-opening the restaurant wouldn't make much sense, but brother Hubert has turned the great old courtyard into a Biergarten of sorts. With the picturesque old brewery and restaurant as its backdrop and centered by a big gorgeous tree providing shade, it now dispenses beer from a small doorway towards the back. They have quite a few events spread out mostly over the warmer months when they put in lots of benches and tables and serve food.

They also sell their beer to go in everything from regular bottles, larger gift-type bottles and even 5-liter kegs. Roggenbier is not an easy style to find; is a bit like a Weißbier but brewed with rye rather than wheat.

BRAUEREIGASTHOF DINKEL

The restaurant/hotel part of the family business is thriving. It's a large place, but they get a fair number of buses in so it seems to always be full, at least at main meal times. The food is great value and the menu features typical Franconian fare along with a selection of steaks. Service is pretty swift, but I guess it has to be with the turnover they get. It's not an old-world pub as I imagine the old half-timbered place attached to the brewery used to be, but it's open and doing well, preserving a great Franconian brewery for future generations. I like that both coexist now as you can get the best of both worlds: a great meal, brew, and room at the Gasthof, and an atmospheric beer in the courtyard Biergarten before or after.

Beers on tap: Stublanger Lagerbier, Stublanger Roggenbier. Bock in season.

PRACTICAL INFORMATION

Brauereigasthof Dinkel
Frauendorfer Straße 18
96231 Bad Staffelstein (Stublang)
+49 9573 6424
www.dinkel-stublang.de

Open Friday to Tuesday 10:00 am to 11:00 pm
(in December, only to 3:00 pm on Sunday)
Closed Wednesday & Thursday

Rooms can be booked on their website, which is available only in German.

Brauerei Dinkel
Am Dorfbrunnen 19
96231 Bad Staffelstein (Stublang)
+49 170 307 32 81
www.brauerei-dinkel.de

Brewery open Monday to Saturday 9:00 am to 6:00 pm
The Biergarten is open according to the schedule on their website (under Termin). It seems they are open most weekends during the day in the warmer months, later in the evening for events.

UETZING

THE CELTIC ROAD TO BEER AND SAUSAGES

UPPER FRANCONIA

▷··· STARTING POINT	···✕ DESTINATION
METZGERBRÄU, UETZING	**METZGERBRÄU, UETZING**

🍺 BEER	🌀 DIFFICULTY
METZGERBRÄU LAGERBIER	**HIKE** 🚶

⛰ MAP	
ATK25 C09 **LICHTENFELS**	⏱ DURATION OF THE HIKE **8.5 KM** **2–3H**

👁 HIGHLIGHTS	〰 ELEVATION GAIN
ST. JOHN BAPTIST CHURCH, HALF-TIMBERED HOUSES, WAY OF ST. JAMES, ALTER STAFFELBERG, CELTIC RUIN	ASCENT: 240 M DESCENT: 250 M

CLASSIC
FRANCONIAN
LAGER

UNFILTERED
AMBER

GRAIN,
FAINT HOPS

HOPPY,
BALANCED

BITTERNESS

SWEETNESS

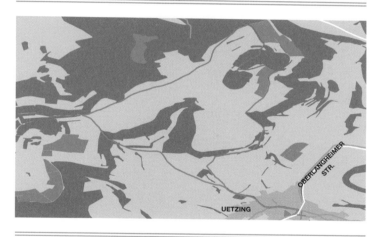

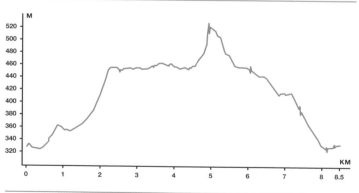

DESCRIPTION OF THE ROUTE

Uetzing is yet another gateway town to the Staffelberg region, a favorite of hiking and cycling enthusiasts. The village has a picturesque center dotted with half-timbered houses and is on a few hiking trails. Celtic tribes once called this area home and evidence of their occupation is easily found on hikes in the area. It's also home to one of the odder concepts in the brewing world: a brewing butcher.

Uetzing is serviced by regular buses during the week from Bad Staffelstein and Lichtenfels, both of which are well-connected to Bamberg. Depending on the bus, it takes about 25 minutes. Unfortunately, there is no service on weekends.

This route combines one of the area's four brewery hiking trails with part of one of its Celtic-oriented hiking trails. Coming out of Metzgerbräu, go left on Stublanger Straße, followed by another relatively quick left on Oberlangheimer Straße. At the next intersection, you can admire the statue of John of Nepomuk, a Bohemian saint, before going left on Kirchweg. You'll see a sign with a beer mug and a number two in it – the initial route of your journey. This street follows a stream called the Döberten that runs through Uetzing. Follow it as it veers left before a more pronounced right. Stay on Kirchweg and you'll see the town's church coming up. When you get to the church, Kirchweg becomes Heugasse. On the street sign post are numerous trail symbols, among them the Keltenweg (Celtic's Way) and the Brauereienweg 2. Continue straight and you'll pass some old cellars. When you come to a fork, take the left side. You will return on the other trail later. Continue on the flat path, enjoying views into the countryside. The trail bends left and then veers right, with the occasional beer mug sign pointing you in the right direction. After crossing a field, you'll come to a major trail junction. Go right here, towards Staffelberg. This is a wide, very distinct trail as it is part of four major routes, including the Frankenweg and Jakobsweg.

When you come to the next junction, continue straight. Going right on the Gößnitzerweg would bring you back to Uetzing more quickly, but you have another area to investigate. At the next trail junction, you will see signs for the Keltenweg G trail and the Brauereienweg 2 again. Go right here to head towards the Alter Staffelberg. You'll see the rock formation up on the hill. You'll also be walking towards a crucifix on an unpaved farm road. Just past the crucifix, you will see a smaller trail to your right. Take that to follow the Keltenweg G and Brauereienweg 2 trails. You will have views to your right of Kloster Banz in the distance. In a small clearing, you will come to another junction sign. You can go left to remain on the Brauereienweg 2, it's an easier route, but if you're feeling adventurous at this point, you can continue on the Keltenweg G trail. Just ahead, you'll see a wooden post with its scallop symbol sign and below it, "nur für geübte Wanderer." This means "only for experienced hikers." Continue ahead to walk on a much narrower path that leads to a crevice in a large rock. This is the Alter Staffelberg and you are about to scramble up it. Once on top, you can enjoy the views into the valley below.

From there, you'll see a distinct but narrow path cutting through the forest. Follow it, with the occasional Keltenweg signs marking the way, to a clearing with a bench. This is a good spot to catch a breather, especially if scrambling isn't part of your normal routine. There are even better views of Kloster Banz from here. If you continue along this trail, you'll see a sign – beyond it is the Celtic ruin. It's not in the best shape, but check it out if you're so inclined. Your route continues from the bench. On the back of the bench, you will see the trail sign pointing down through the sloping hill. The narrow dirt path has an occasional Keltenweg sign on a tree and arrows pointing you in the right direction. Follow it down as the route goes right to a main trail junction. There's a log cabin shelter there and you'll see the Brauereienweg 2 sign pointing you to the right. You're also still on the Keltenweg G trail. You will now be heading towards Uetzing.

Follow this path through open farmland. After the trail bends left you'll come to another junction. There's a small parking area with a picnic table and crucifix. You will more or less go straight to stay on the Brauereienweg 2 towards Uetzing, just under two kilometers further. Follow this paved road, passing a small chapel on your right until you come to a T. There's no sign here and the natural inclination is to go left to stay on the paved road, which would also take you to Uetzing, but the true route is to go right onto an unpaved road. It will bend left at around the 7 kilometer mark, marked with both hiking signs. You will start to get views of the church in Uetzing as you make your way back to the village. It's all downhill now, and before you know it, you'll be at the original fork in the trail. Continue on Heugasse, which turns into Kirchweg. Follow it to the left at the stream, and then, when you get to Oberlangheimer Straße, go right. Take another quick right on Stublanger Straße and Metzgerbräu is just ahead on your right.

METZGERBRÄU

Metzgerbräu is one intriguing brewery. In 2004, Manfred Reichert decided his considerable butchering skills could be expanded into brewing beer. It might sound like an odd idea to non-Germans, but there is little that goes better with German beer than sausages. The idea caught on and he expanded the brewhouse in 2012. It's quite an operation and has become super popular with both hikers and cyclists. You can go up to the brewery area where there is some limited seating or linger around on the first level, with part of it covered and part out in the open. You go downstairs to the small butcher shop to get both beer and food. Aside from his tasty beer, ham smoked over beech wood is his specialty. The sausages are so good, it would be worth going there even if he hadn't opened a brewery!

Beers on tap: Lagerbier, Weißbier. Seasonal Maibock (Easter to end of May), Bock (November).

PRACTICAL INFORMATION

Metzgerbräu
Stublanger Straße 2
96231 Bad Staffelstein (Uetzing)
+49 9573 6304
www.metzgerbraeu.com

Open Monday to Saturday
6:30 am to 6:00 pm
(butcher sales, but beer served until 8:00 pm)
Closed on Sunday unless announced otherwise on their Facebook page.

Hours seem to be in flux. Sundays were previously only for events, so if going on a Sunday, it's advised to confirm if they will be open to the public before setting out.

SCHEßLITZ

A HILLTOP CASTLE AND MOUNTAIN CHURCH

UPPER FRANCONIA

▷⋯ STARTING POINT	⋯✕ DESTINATION
BRAUEREI DREI KRONEN, SCHEßLITZ	**BRAUEREI DREI KRONEN, SCHEßLITZ**
🍺 BEER	DIFFICULTY
SCHÄÄZER KRONABIER	**HIKE** 🚶
⌾ MAP	
ATK25-D09	🕐 DURATION OF THE HIKE
SCHEßLITZ	**9 KM** **2–2.5H**
🔎 HIGHLIGHTS	〰 ELEVATION GAIN
GIECHBURG, GÜGEL, ST. KILIAN'S CHURCH, HALF-TIMBER BUILDINGS ON MAIN STREET OF SCHEßLITZ	ASCENT: 460 M DESCENT: 460 M

5.1% ALCOHOL CONTENT

CLASSIC FRANCONIAN LAGER

DEEP GOLDEN

CEREAL, SLIGHT HOPS

DRY, FRUITY, BITTER FINISH

BITTERNESS   SWEETNESS

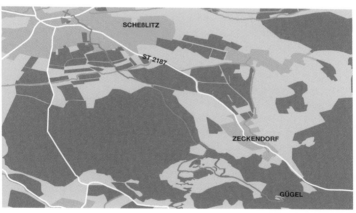

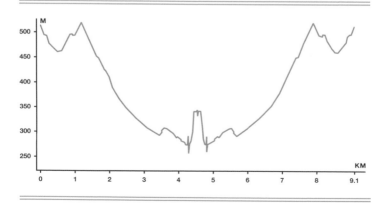

DESCRIPTION OF THE ROUTE

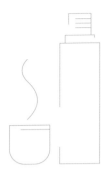

The Gügel is a church that sits atmospherically atop a rocky outcropping across a sloping valley from a hilltop castle called the Giechburg. Situated near the A70, it's visible from the highway running between Bamberg and Bayreuth. This route describes the in and out walk through a forest to the two sights. Scheßlitz is a picturesque small town along the highway – its main street is full of half-timbered buildings. It makes a good base if exploring the northern part of Franconian Switzerland.

Scheßlitz is serviced by limited regular buses from Bamberg. The trip takes about 20 minutes.

Coming out of the Drei Kronen, go left on Hauptstraße. Take the first right onto Wilhelm-Spengler-Straße and continue to Altenbach, where you will go left. There is a street sign for the Giechburg as well as numerous trail signs, including the Frankenweg and one with a shield and the letter "A." Follow this to the Gügelweg and take a right on it. When you come to an intersection, go left on Am Kreuzschleifer to remain on the Frankenweg, among a host of other trails. You will soon go right on Andechsweg and follow it out of town. You'll see a post with some trail signs. You're on the Frankenweg and Main-Donau-Weg (marked by a yellow horizontal stripe and a red horseshoe respectively). You'll be out in open farmland now, heading across the fields. You will start to see the Giechburg high on the horizon. There's a small stone shrine along the route to your left before you cross a stream, and soon you will veer left to join a brick farm road, marked for the Frankenweg and the "A" sign with the shield. Follow the farm road to a tall electrical tower on your right. Signs on it say to turn right, towards the forest.

Once at the forest, you will veer left to skirt it before ducking into it. The trail meanders through the forest and passes a couple of small junctions, where you keep going straight, following signs for the Giechburg. When it comes to a T, you'll go left towards a parking lot. Go up some steps and across the lot. On the other side of the lot are some signs for the restaurant at the castle. You'll go right here, and initially there's a pedestrian path that mirrors the road going up. Follow it until it meets the road and join it for the remainder of the way up to the castle. Explore the castle at your leisure. If you're hungry, the restaurant has great food and beer from the St. Georgen brewery in Buttenheim. When you're finished, return the way you came.

Continue on the trail you came up on. There's an information board at the junction and it says the Gügel is only a kilometer away on the Frankenweg. Follow the well-worn trail as it skirts and wraps around a forest before breaking into the open in the valley between the Giechburg and Gügel. The route between them is obvious and scenic. Head across the open expanse towards your destination. The route dips down and then back up, the last bit through a forest. After investigating the church, head back the way you came. When you get back to Hauptstraße, go left, and the Drei Kronen is on your right, just where you left it.

BRAUEREI-GASTHOF DREI KRONEN

Scheßlitz's main street is filled with one great old building after another. The Drei Kronen, a small, cozy pub founded in 1749, is a timeless wonder, and more than meets expectations. There were once three such places in Scheßlitz but the other two have since closed. What sets this place apart from the other two? The brewer. Joseph Lindner brews not only his traditional lager but also a host of other styles, even venturing into the craft beer realm with his FPA (Franconian Pale Ale). His Weizenbock has won a gold medal at the European Beer Championships. Though I didn't eat here, I noticed a few dishes outside the standard Franconian fare box. I guess that fits in with trying to mix the new in with the old.

I'd been to the Drei Kronen in its three-brewery heyday, and to be honest, I'd not have bet on any of them outlasting the other. I was surprised a few years ago to see the Drei Kronen at a beer festival in Munich, with a big selection of new brews. I tried a few and was impressed enough to vow to get back to the brewpub. After finding the hike to the Giechburg, I did just that. You know what I ordered? The Kronabier. It just felt right, to drink that old-style lager in this old-style tavern.

Beers on tap: Schääzer Kronabier plus one rotating beer.

PRACTICAL INFORMATION

Brauerei-Gasthof Drei Kronen
Hauptstraße 39
96110 Scheßlitz
+49 9542 15 64
www.kronabier.de

Open Thursday to Tuesday
9:30 am to 1:00 pm / from 5:00 pm
Closed Wednesday

BISCHBERG TO WEIHER

THE STEIGERWALD-PANORAMAWEG TO BEER NIRVANA

UPPER FRANCONIA

▷··· STARTING POINT	···✕ DESTINATION
BRAUEREI ZUR SONNE, BISCHBERG	**BRAUEREI KUNDMÜLLER, WEIHER**
🍺 BEER	▦ DIFFICULTY
WEIHERER / FAT HEAD'S HOPFERLA	**HIKE** 🚶
🗠 MAP	
ATK25 D08	⏱ DURATION OF THE HIKE
BAMBERG	**10 KM 2.5–3.5H (ONE-WAY)**
👁 HIGHLIGHTS	∿ ELEVATION GAIN
RURAL SCENERY, HALF-TIMBERED HOUSES, BAMBERG SKYLINE IN THE DISTANCE	ASCENT: 250 M DESCENT: 249 M

7.5% ALCOHOL CONTENT

IPA MADE WITH SEVEN VARIETIES OF HOPS: SIMCOE, WARRIOR, CENTENNIAL, MOSAIC, EQUINOX, CITRA, AND CHINOOK

LIGHTLY FILTERED AMBER, AMPLE ROCKY HEAD

CITRUS HOP

CITRUS HOP, SOFT, MALTY, LONG DRY BITTER FINISH

BITTERNESS

SWEETNESS

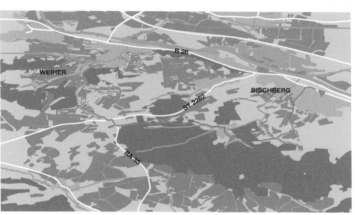

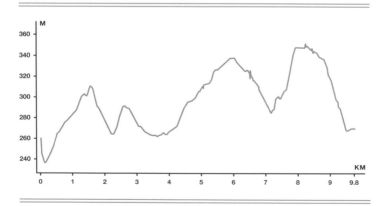

DESCRIPTION OF THE ROUTE

The Steigerwald-Panoramaweg is a wonderful 161 kilometer trail that runs from Bamberg to Bad Windsheim. Featuring a variety of terrains, it is popular with both hikers and cyclists. Many towns that are not even on the route have made it very accessible by putting up signs leading you to it from their centers. One such place is Bischberg, just outside of Bamberg. While not a tourist town, it is a pleasant place and home to Brauerei zur Sonne. Locals in Bamberg make the short trek out to enjoy fine meals and beer there, so it must be pretty good. It makes for a good access point if your destination is Brauerei Kundmüller in Weiher as it is a fair distance to walk even if traveling with an overnight backpack.

Buses to Bischberg from Bamberg ZOB are frequent and take about 20 minutes.

Depending on the time of year you do the hike, spending the evening at the Brauerei zur Sonne the previous day would make for a nice, relaxed start. Much of the hike is exposed, and if it's a hot, sunny day, getting an early start makes for a more pleasant hike. Exiting the brewpub, go left on Regnitzstraße and then a quick right on Haupts-traße. Follow this a short distance to your first available left, Schuls-traße. You'll see a sign with two walkers on it, heralding the "Zugang zum Steigerwald-Panoramaweg/Sieben-Flüsse-Wanderweg" (access point) being a mere 1.6 kilometers away. Much of the route follows both of these noted trails and is very well marked. You'll follow Schulstraße all the way out of Bischberg, with the occasional sign of the two hikers to let you know you're headed the right way. Before you know it, you'll be out in the countryside with views of Bischberg down below to your rear and Bamberg's more renowned towers soon visible to your left. When you come to a marked intersection, there will be a small, raised shady spot with a bench. If you don't need a break yet, go right towards Weipelsdorf, which is another 1.8 kilometers down the pleasant path. If it's a hot day, you'll be happy to duck into your first patch of forest about 3 kilometers into the walk. It's short-lived, and as soon as you pop out, you'll be in Weipelsdorf, a pleasant village with a cute little church. It's a straight shot down the Dorfsee-straße to Zieglerstraße, where you'll make a well-marked left. You can't miss it – it's the same corner the church is on. Follow it out of town, and when you come to a large crucifix at a fork in the road, take the left side. Soon after there's a building on your right at a less distinct fork. Go right this time – thankfully, it is very well marked.

You'll get a few longer stretches of forest now. Once in the clear, you'll go right on Walsdorfer Straße as you enter Tütschengereuth. At the intersection, go left on Tütschengereuther Hauptstraße. You'll see a pretty church on that corner. Not far up the street, take the first right on Zollnerhof, marked by two large chestnut trees. Not too far up this street, turn left onto Weiherer Straße. Steigerwald-Panoramaweg signs abound, even on these town street turns. Stay on Weiherer Straße until you come to gravel road on the left, which is marked only by trail signs. It's a steep but short climb and levels out a bit when you go right at the top. It meanders a bit before going left, and then at the end of the road, go right with open farmland all around you. When you reach a patch of forest, you will take the right side of the fork. At this point, leave the Steigerwald-Panoramaweg and Sieben-Flüsse-Wanderweg. This is a local trail called the V-T-6-Rundweg.

Follow this as it at first skirts the forest and then crosses a field. You finally get a bit of shady relief as you make your way downhill to your destination. You'll see signs for both the V-T 6 and V-T 4, as well as signs for Weiher. You're almost there. Once out of the forest, you'll see the small village of Weiher to your left. Follow the road as it goes left towards town. At the end of this road, but before the main road, go left to enjoy a quieter stroll through the village. When you soon run out of street (and village!), go right to the main road (Weiherer Straße), carefully cross it and approach the legendary Brauerei Kundmüller in front of you.

BRAUEREI-GASTHOF KUNDMÜLLER

Founded in 1874, Brauerei Kundmüller is a great example of a brewery that can remain traditional while keeping an eye on the future. Brewing one of the largest selections of beers of any small brewery in Bavaria, they make both typical Bavarian styles as well as more experimental brews, many of them certified organic. The remodeled restaurant is all dark wood and oozes old-world atmosphere but also has nice, modern touches. Again, it's a great mix of old and new. Hot meals are available at lunch and dinner, with daily specials as well as weekly specials noted on their informative website. Cakes are excellent as well. Out front is a nice self-service Biergarten with a huge chestnut tree providing shade. And as if all that weren't enough, they have their own distillery onsite, too. It's a good thing they have rooms.

As you might imagine, this is a very popular place. It's a destination in itself and people bike out here from Bamberg just to have a meal and beer. If the weather's good, and especially on the weekend, expect to have plenty of company. Book rooms well in advance.

Beers on tap: Weiherer Lager, Weiherer Pils, Weiherer Zwickerla, Weiherer Rauch, Weiherer Keller, Weiherer Weizen Hell, Weiherer Landbier, Weiherer Urstöffla, Weiherer Bock, Weiherer Keller-Märzen, Weiherer Rolator, Weiherer Weizenbock, Weiherer Schwärzla, Weiherer Sommerweizen and Weiherer / Fathead's Hopferla IPA.

In addition to this rather large tap line-up, they offer many bottles, including some large magnums of barrel-aged products.

This was by far the hardest place to pick one beer as the go-to, but since Weiher teamed with American craft beer legend Fat Head's to make the Hopferla, I felt it deserved the designation – though as a session beer, I'd probably drink the Schwärzla.

PRACTICAL INFORMATION

Brauerei-Gasthof Kundmüller
Weiher 13
96191 Viereth-Trunstadt
+49 9503 4338
www.brauerei-kundmueller.de

Open daily from 9:00 am
Closed Wednesday

Rooms can be reserved on their website
which is also available in English.

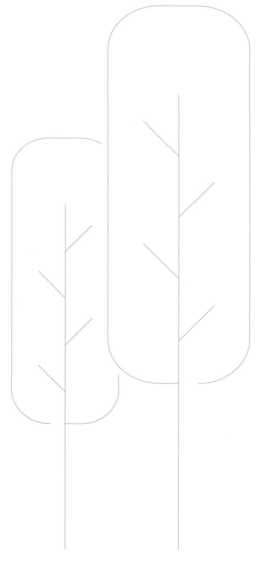

LOWER FRANCONIA

ZEIL

BEER AMONG THE VINEYARDS

LOWER FRANCONIA

▷··· STARTING POINT	···✗ DESTINATION
BRAUEREIGASTSTÄTTE GÖLLER "ZUR ALTEN FREYUNG," ZEIL	**BRAUEREIGASTSTÄTTE GÖLLER "ZUR ALTEN FREYUNG," ZEIL**

🍺 BEER	🎲 DIFFICULTY
GÖLLER PILSNER KELLERFRISCH	
🗺 **MAP**	**HIKE**
ATK25-D07	🕐 DURATION OF THE HIKE
HAßFURT	**15 KM 2.5–3.5H**

🔍 HIGHLIGHTS	〰 ELEVATION GAIN
ZEILER CHAPEL, STATIONS OF THE CROSS, VIEW OF ZEIL FROM ABOVE, VINEYARDS, RUINS OF SCHMACHTENBERG CASTLE	ASCENT: 495 M DESCENT: 500 M

LIGHTLY FILTERED
PILSNER

 HAZY YELLOW,
BREADY HEAD

 LIGHT HOP GRAIN

 DRY, FRUITY,
HINT OF GRAIN,
LONG DRY BITTER FINISH

BITTERNESS   SWEETNESS

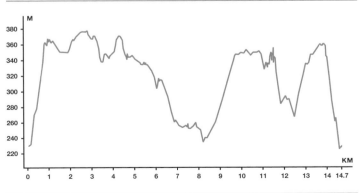

DESCRIPTION OF THE ROUTE

Though Bavaria is definitely more noted for its beer than its wine, parts of Lower Franconia, mostly clustered around Würzburg, make some lovely wines. Heading out that way from Bamberg is another smaller vineyard area along the rambling Main River. One charming town in this region is Zeil am Main. Set among rolling hills, often covered in grape vines, the cute little town is largely full of half-timbered buildings and makes a nice designation in itself, especially if you like beer. Despite being surrounded by vineyards, it is also home to Brauerei Göller, which makes many traditional beers as well as a seemingly expanding array of craft beer seasonals.

Zeil is easily reached by frequent trains from Bamberg which take about 15 minutes.

One of the things you will notice upon disembarking the train is a chapel set up high on the hill overlooking the town. This route will take you up there – just in case you were thinking of going anyway. You'll walk right through town, following signs for the town center but also many for "Zur Alten Freyung," the brewery's popular restaurant and tap. This hike begins from the brewery, and your only decision is whether to sample one of their many beers on tap before or after (or both).

Walking out the door of the brewpub, take a hard left, wrapping around the corner. You'll walk alongside an old city wall until you come to a doorway on your right. The Biergarten is to your left – in case you've changed your mind about that pre-hike beer. Go through the doorway and go right on Bachrahm, looking for a small stone bridge crossing a brook. You will get nice views of the brewpub from here; a marvelous old stone building.

Cross the stone bridge, and Kapellenbergstraße is straight on and bends to the left. You'll see some trail signs shaped like castle towers and also the distance to the Zeiler Kapelle, only 700 meters away. You're not on the street long before you see a sign for the Fußweg zur Kapelle (footpath to the chapel) on your right. It starts with a set of stairs but soon becomes a narrow path. It's pretty much all uphill, as you might have guessed from the chapel's location. You'll pass some Stations of the Cross markers and mossy stones along the way. It's an atmospheric route that brings you swiftly up. Occasional red and green castle tower trail signs adorn trees, but the path is obvious. At the top is the pretty chapel and an overlook, which affords nice views of Zeil down below, including the Church of St. Michael.

After checking out this area, follow the brick road around the church and you'll come to its parking lot at about 1 kilometer from the hike's start. Follow the road past the lot and continue straight, bypassing the right path that would bring you more quickly to the castle ruin. That will be closer to the end of the hike. Along with the castle tower trail signs, you start to see Zeil 1 markers. This is the hike you're doing today. Right before a large junction, go left onto another farm road. You'll be out in rural farmland now, with fields in all directions. At about 2 kilometers, you'll go right on a well-marked gravel road. Follow this to its end and turn left at the T, again marked. A relatively quick right comes up and this trail wraps you around the field at first, and then along the forest edge. Once back out in the open, you'll turn left, followed by a right, zigzagging the field. The next left brings you around another patch of forest.

Once around a big curve hugging the trees, you'll take the natural left and walk along an open field. These are all either well-marked or obvious turns. At the end of the field, you'll go left, briefly into some forest. You'll soon pop out on the other side on the curve of Am Pfaffenberg. Take the right side of it. This enters a forest, and just after 6 kilometers, it curves sharply to the right, bringing you back along the parallel path you just came from. This road goes pretty steeply downhill. You may have noticed some trail signs that look like the old rosé wine bottles. This is the "Bocksbeutel," the short, rounded bottle used in the Franconian wine world. You are now on a joined route that passes through some vineyards. In fact, at the bottom of Am Pfaffenberg, go right and it's a flat road doing just that, with vines descending to your left and rising to your right. You're still up high enough to look down on the valley and the cars passing quickly through it. I remember being in one of those cars and wishing I could walk among the vineyards, so it was nice to finally get to do it. You'll also see signs for the "Winzertreppe," a set of stone stairs heading up through the rows of grape vines. These are okay to go up, but the ones not marked as such are private, so you should stay off them. Also, if you go up the staircase, do not leave it as the surrounding area is fragile.

You'll pass the Pfaffenberg and there will be an information board. The road forks here and you want to head to the left. The right goes to a geological site. You'll pass more rows of grape vines as the road bends to the left. You'll go right at the junction, followed by a very quick left. These little turns are well marked too. You will still be walking through a vineyard and even pass a small wine tasting restaurant on your left. When you come to the fork of Neue Steig, go right. The trail heads back uphill again, but you'll still be surrounded by vineyard scenery. Once in the forest, the path veers left, then curves hard to the right before popping out into a more open area. Take a soft left there, followed by a hard left. This road skirts the forest on one side, but on the other is the open field area from much earlier in the hike. In fact, if you're tired at the next turn, you could continue straight on back to the chapel and Zeil, 2 and 3 kilometers away respectively. Of course, then you'd miss the castle ruins. So, at the junction, take a hard left following signs telling you the Ruine Schmachtenberg is only 700 meters away. The path first crosses an open field and then heads into the forest where the ruin is located. It's a few hundred meters off the main track but a worthwhile detour. There's a circle route around it that's easy to follow.

Back on the main trail, you will follow signs for the chapel and Zeil. According to the sign, it's only about 2 kilometers to town, but this route will show you that not all kilometers are created equal. First, you drop down a long set of stairs and more downhill path. Your reward is another vineyard with nice views over the valley, but as you come to the end of the road (and grapes), you turn right and head right back uphill. Keep an eye out for Schloss Schmachtenberg on your left, a private residence. This section is shady thankfully, and before you come back up to the main farm road junction from much earlier in the hike, go left on a marked, wide dirt path. You will pass an old stone ruin of an entrance of some kind and are soon at the original brick farm road you came from the chapel on. Take a left onto it and return the way you came, passing the chapel and heading back down the path with the Stations of the Cross. It's blessedly all downhill to that beer you've surely worked a sweat up for by now.

BRAUEREIGASTSTÄTTE GÖLLER "ZUR ALTEN FREYUNG"

Their labels state "since 1514," and indeed brewing was granted to the house where the current restaurant is located in the middle ages, but the Göller family founded the current operation in 1908. The actual brewery is located on the edge of town but is strictly a large production facility to accommodate their large regional distribution needs. "Zur Alten Freyung," in the old town center, is their brewery tap and a fine one it is, offering hot meals at great value all day and a large assortment of beers on tap. It's a fairly large place housed in a great old building and always seems to be bustling. The name comes from it having been a safe house in the middle ages. If a person made it inside, no worldly judge could apprehend them. As nice as it is inside, if it's good weather, the Biergarten out back is the place to be.

This is yet another traditional brewery making headway into the craft beer revolution that is finally taking some form in Bavaria. Along with their already expansive regular line-up and seasonals, they have a beer calendar with a different beer each month. Some have caught on and are regulars for that month but others pop up occasionally, too. This is well advertised on their informative website. I've only had two and they were both excellent. When I was there for the first day of their Frühlingsbier, the Biergarten was very busy, mostly with people drinking that beer. It's good to see more people open to change and with great specialty beers like these brewed by Brauerei Göller, I can see why. About the only thing they don't have is rooms. If they did, I'd be happy to spend the night in Zeil, working my way through through their impressive line-up.

Beers on tap: Göller Pilsner Kellerfrisch, Göller Premium Pilsner, Göller Dunkles, Göller Weizen, Göller Rauchbier, and Göller Kellerbier, along with whatever seasonal is on offer plus the beer calendar beer of the month. They also carry every beer they brew not on tap in bottles.

PRACTICAL INFORMATION

Brauereigaststätte Göller "Zur Alten Freyung"
Speiersgasse 21
97475 Zeil a. Main
+49 9524 9554
www.zur-alten-freyung.de

Open daily from 9:30 am June/July/August
(full hot meals until 9:30 pm)
Closed on Tuesdays from September to the end of May

EBELSBACH TO STETTFELD

THE FOX MEETS THE 7 RIVERS TO BRING YOU THE EAGLE

LOWER FRANCONIA

▷⋯ STARTING POINT	⋯✗ DESTINATION
EBELSBACH TRAIN STATION	**ADLER-BRÄU, STETTFELD**

🍺 BEER	🁢 DIFFICULTY
ADLER-BRÄU ALT FRÄNKISCHES LAGERBIER	**HIKE** 🚶

⛰ MAP	🕐 DURATION OF THE HIKE
ATK25 D08	**5 KM**
BAMBERG	**1H (ONE-WAY)**

🔍 HIGHLIGHTS	〰 ELEVATION GAIN
EBELSBACH CASTLE, STETTFELD TOWN HALL AND CHURCH, EBELSBERG	ASCENT: 134 M DESCENT: 136 M

OLD-STYLE
FRANCONIAN
LAGER

LIGHT AMBER,
DENSE HEAD

FAINT GRAIN

FRUITY,
DRY,
MALT, HOPPY

BITTERNESS

SWEETNESS

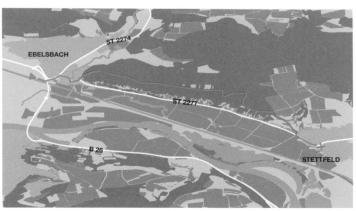

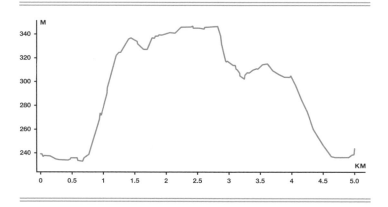

DESCRIPTION OF THE ROUTE

 Ebelsbach Castle was a nice excursion from Bamberg until it was nearly destroyed by a fire in 2009. The castle was built in the 1500s and modernized over time as it was a residence until 2000. It's planned restoration remains murky due to financial reasons and ownership. It remains an interesting site, even if in passing, on this largely forested route that brings you from the namesake town to nearby Stettfeld, home to Adler-Bräu.

Trains to Ebelsbach-Eltmann from Bamberg are frequent and take about 10 minutes. There are buses, as well, but they take much longer. The buses do pass through Stettfeld en route but please note that they do not run on weekends.

Exiting the Ebelsbach-Eltmann train station, you will notice an overpass to your right. Walk along the Bahnhofstraße under it to George-Schäfer-Straße and go right. This is a busy street but there is a bicycle/pedestrian path that runs parallel to it. As you walk along, you will get your first glimpse of the ruin of Ebelsbach Castle. Just beyond it is the Ebelsberg, the green hill you will soon be walking over. At the intersection, turn right onto Stettfelder Straße. As it winds to the right, you'll pass the castle, still photogenic even in ruins. Its half-timbered gate is still intact. It must have been grand in its day. Continue on this street until it comes to Schützenstraße. Go left there rather than following Stettfelder Straße, a quicker but far less scenic route to the brewery.

You'll start to see trail signs with a 7 and others with an M on them. These are for the Sieben-Flüsse-Wanderweg and Mainwanderweg respectively. Both are long distance routes but they will guide you to Stettfeld well. As you walk up Schützenstraße, keep an eye out on the right for signs to Ebelsberg and Stettfeld. Stettfeld is just under 5 kilometers away at this point. Turn right here and take note of the old kellers on your right as you start to climb the Ebelsberg. These are old storage areas dug into the hill to keep things cool before refrigeration was invented. This is a nice, narrow, forested path that is fairly steep and well marked. Follow signs with a 7 and M on them. You'll come to a fork and take the right side, the one going uphill of course! You'll pass some other paths and logging roads, but your path is marked so keep following the 7/M. Eventually, you'll exit the forest and enter an open area with fields to your left. Skirt the forest on your right until its end. The trail goes to the right here and joins the FU trail, marked with a depiction of a fox ("Fuchs" in German). You'll follow the three co-mingled trails through the forest for a short spell. It winds a bit, but as you come to the end of the forest, the FU trails goes left into a more open area. You will go right on the 7/M route through a forested route that thins out and offers you the first glimpse of Stettfeld in the form of its church tower, a pretty sight with hills in the background. Follow this road downhill to the Hauptstraße and go left. This is a busy street but again there is a small path along the opposite side. Be careful crossing the busy road and proceed into town on the bicycle/pedestrian path, still marked with the 7/M signs. As the main street starts to bend to the left, you'll see Adler-Bräu on your left, a fine, yellow building adorned with flowers in warmer months.

ADLER-BRÄU BRÄUSTÜBLA & BIERGARTEN

Adler-Bräu is a classic countryside pub with an old ceramic wood-burning oven in the cozy interior and a cute little Biergarten out back. It was founded in 1730 just up the road and has a bit of a cult following in the surrounding area. Oddly enough, it had escaped my radar for about 20 years until I ran across their beer at Bamberg's annual Sandkerwa, a formerly religious celebration turned beer festival held in late August. I imagine this was because it wasn't in Upper Franconia despite its proximity to it. Eventually I discovered their great beer and after doing this hike, a great brewpub.

The beers on tap are in great form and nicely poured. They also have a simple menu if you're feeling hungry. The friendly and talkative owner said if I couldn't find a place for their annual Bockbier festival, he'd put me up! There are two more circuit hikes emanating from town, so that's just another reason to spend more time here.

Beers on tap: Adler-Bräu Stettfelder Pils, Adler-Bräu Altfränkisches Lagerbier, and Adler-Bräu Weizen. Seasonal: Adler-Bräu Bärentrunk and Adler-Bräu Bock.

PRACTICAL INFORMATION

Adler-Bräu Bräustübla & Biergarten
Hauptstraße 19
96188 Stettfeld
+49 9522/369
www.adlerbraeu-stettfeld.de

Closed Tuesday and Saturday
Open Monday, Wednesday and Friday
from 3:30 pm
Sunday and public holidays
from 10:00 am

ACKNOWLEDGEMENTS & DEDICATION

As no man is an island, no man writes a book by himself. He might come up with the words and put them on paper, but who he is, is the book, and who he is, is a product of the people who have touched him over the course of his life. Thanking everyone who falls into this group individually would fill another book, but anyone reading this who knows me can feel this sentence is for you. I've always been lucky when it comes to family and friends, who have supported me and encouraged me to use what talents they saw within me. While the book took a lot of sacrifice on my part, they also gave up having me in their lives for the past few months.

The book would have never been possible without my loving, supportive and incredibly understanding wife. She talked me into taking the challenge, put up with my being away a good chunk of spring 2019, kept me from freaking out on more than one occasion, proofed my writing, accompanied me on as many hikes as she could, and calmly cajoled me to the finish line. She knows what makes me tick. She keeps me ticking.

Of course, she couldn't have talked me into accepting an offer if one hadn't been made. Thanks to Hadi Barkat for asking me to write *Beer Hiking Bavaria*. It's been an incredible experience and your team is truly top notch. Speaking of which, huge thanks to Laura Simon for not only her editing skills but for knowing how to get me going. I really had my doubts I could finish on time, but she managed to make it happen a lot more effortlessly than I'd imagined. Since the book is not just about words, many thanks to graphics man Florian Bellon for being another pillar to hang onto and giving me some early glimpses of what the book would look like. It made it more real and easier to aim for. Aaron Melick deserves thanks for cleaning up some untidy sentences and reeling me in when I went too far in an unnecessary direction. Previous authors from the Helvetiq beer hiking series Brandon Fralic and Rachel Wood *(Beer Hiking Pacific Northwest)* and Monika Saxer *(Beer Hiking Switzerland)* helped pave the way for the ground-breaking series. These are the people of Helvetiq I was in contact with, but I know there have been many more behind the scenes making the book a reality. Thank you all, too.

Many beer writers have influenced me but none more than Graham Lees of the Campaign for Real Ale (CAMRA). His *Good Beer Guide to Munich and Bavaria* lit a spark in me for the pursuit of getting to out-of-the-way Franconian breweries. When I met my wife, she called it my beer bible. Though out of print and with some outdated information, its weathered pages still remain an inspiration.

A couple of friends drove me to places not easily reached by public transportation. Thanks to former student and good friend Tibor for the lift to and company in Schönram and to my wife's cousin and good friend Ronny for taking us to Zwiesel and Böbrach to round out the last two hikes of the book.

Thanks also to some friends who joined me for hikes. Some of them made the book, some didn't, but your company was a pleasure nonetheless. David Simon of Dark History Tours, Franz D. Hofer of Tempest in a Tankard, Kevin Holsapple of Prime Passages and fellow teachers Todd Palazzolo and Brian Rivas.

A special thanks to my father, who graciously accepted and understood our not coming to visit him this year due to the time constraints of the book. You've always supported and encouraged me so it didn't come as a surprise and not seeing you was my biggest regret of doing the book. I wish my mother could be here to see her son doing something she always thought I should do. I'm sure she's still smiling knowingly. She always did.

To my mother, my father and especially to my wife, this book's for you. The beer's for me.

FROM THE SAME COLLECTION:

Beer Hiking Switzerland
The Most Refreshing Way to Discover Switzerland
ISBN 978-2-940481-13-2

Beer Hiking Bavaria
The Most Refreshing Way to Discover Bavaria
by Rich Carbonara

ISBN: 978-2-940481-82-8
Photos: Rich Carbonara
Graphic Design and Illustrations: Florian Bellon, Daniel Malak,
Elżbieta Kownacka
Editing and Proofreading: Aaron Melick, Karin Waldhauser
Printed in Czech Republic

© 2019 Helvetiq (RedCut Sàrl), Basel and Lausanne

All rights reserved.

www.helvetiq.com